Where was I again?

Geoff Hill's alternative A-Z of the world

Second edition

Geoff is a critically acclaimed author and award-winning journalist based in Belfast. In a previous life, he was Ireland's most capped volleyball player and a much younger man.

He writes a weekly motorbike column for the Daily Mirror which is a desperate attempt to disguise the fact that he knows bugger all about motorbikes.

He's also the editor of Microlight Flying magazine, in spite of the fact that he knows even less about aeroplanes than he does about motorbikes.

He's the author of 18 books, including three novels and bike adventure books about epic journeys from India to the UK, Chile to Alaska, around Australia and around the world recreating the journey of Carl Stearns Clancy, the first person to take a motorbike around the world 100 years ago – complete with the original boots Clancy wore on that trip.

He's either won or been shortlisted for a UK travel writer of the year award nine times. He's also a former Irish, European and world travel writer of the year.

He lives in Belfast with his wife Cate, a cat called Cat, a hammock and the ghost of a flatulent Great Dane. His hobbies are volleyball, flying, motorbikes, tennis, skiing and worrying about the price of fish.

What the critics said

Travel writing

Geoff Hill has travel writing genius in his very soul. The funniest travel writer in our business.
Julie Shmueli and David Rosenberg, organisers of Travelex UK travel writing awards

Geoff Hill has an outstanding writing talent with a wicked sense of fun. For all the hilarious observations and polished one-liners, there is also thoughtful, informative travelogue with lots of useful recommendations. Brilliant writing, genuinely and originally funny, and a supremely entertaining read.
Martyn Lewis CBE, broadcaster

Geoff is one of the most talented travel writers ever to cross my path.
Melissa Shales, Chairman, British Guild of Travel Writers

He has wonderful views on life, a great turn of phrase and a great sense of humour. His off-beat observations and zany outlook on life are laugh-out-loud funny.
John Mullin, The Independent

Remarkable, astonishing writing.
Jeremy Atiyah, Independent on Sunday

Way to Go

Shift your arse, Kerouac, Geoff Hill's on the road - faster, funnier and still alive.
Colin Bateman

The Road to Gobblers Knob

The most inspiring and laugh-out-loud funny travelogue of the last fifty years.
Garbhan Downey, Verbal Magazine

A brilliant read, a book I simply couldn't put down. Ted Simon meets Flann O'Brien, it's a cracker.
Dave Myers, BBC's Hairy Biker

Anyway, Where Was I? Geoff Hill's alternative A-Z of the world, first edition

Geoff Hill is a comic genius. I laughed until I cried, my nose bled and I lost control of my bowels. I may well have to kill him when I meet him.
Patrick Taylor, author of New York Times best seller An Irish Country Doctor

Incredibly funny. I loved it. I was laughing out loud on trains in a thoroughly embarrassing fashion and going to sleep with a smile on my face after the completely anarchic tales of killer dormice, Xavier Furtwangler and how not to get eaten by bears.
Melissa Shales

In Clancy's Boots

The funniest travel writer in print.
Tom Adair, The Scotsman

Brilliant. At times laugh-out-loud funny, and at others intensely moving, which is part of Geoff's genius. He's a writer for whom the words highly and recommended were invented.
Brian Page, Mensa magazine

This Way Up

Deserves to become a classic.
David Bremner, author of Scout 1264

This book bewitches, as Flann O'Brien also succeeded in doing, to the point where you wholly enter Geoff Hill's different, unique world.
Anthony Preston, author and pilot

Smith

Hill has a voice all his own - both lyrical and lunatic - which casts the world in a new light. Few first novels achieve as much.
Mark Sanderson, Independent on Sunday

Quietly hilarious. An offbeat and imaginative debut.
Lois Rathbone, The Times.

I found it fascinating, was bowled over by it, and read it at one sitting. It is pure writing.
Vincent Banville, Sunday Press.

Dialogue so real, it's frightening. Breathtakingly good.
Casey Evans, Irish Tatler.

Weeks later, you're still haunted by it...exerts a power that is quite astounding.
Anthony Jordan, Books Ireland.

Cover photo: Geoff on the road in Oman.
First edition of Anyway, Where was I? published by Blackstaff Press.

Contents

8

Starting out

On a bright September morning in 1975, a young man set out to see the world.

As he walked down the road from his parents' home with a disturbingly new rucksack over his shoulder, he was wearing a faded university rag T-shirt, matching jeans and a pair of Dunlop Green Flash which had seen better days, and would see worse yet.

He was, now that I think of it, me, and to this day I remember the moment when I fell in love with travel.

It was the moment the following afternoon, as I stood at Victoria Station watching the clickety-clack board unfold its dreams. I felt, at that moment, that life was full of infinite possibilities, and all I had to do was step on a train to find them.

Two mornings, later, I sat on the platform of a little station in the south of France, eating an orange. Across the road, a girl with a swing in her hips and a baguette in her wicker basket walked past a white wall bright with bougainvillaea. She looked over, and smiled, and I was besotted. Not with her, but with that same sense of infinite possibilities.

I finished the orange, and took the next train north, and for the next four weeks, roamed through France, Switzerland, Austria, Germany, Holland, Belgium, Denmark, Norway, Sweden and Finland. I had no guidebook; only a Thomas Cook international timetable and a map of Europe on which the name of every country, every town and every village sang with romance.

Every morning, I would haul out the map, decide where to go just because I liked the sound of it, and get on a train with no other aim than to find out what lay over the horizon. I came home, but my heart stayed away. After university, I worked as a fork-lift trucker in a Dutch bulb factory, then played volleyball in California before coming home and getting a proper job as a journalist.

Now, my travel was limited to holidays, but it was still the finest feeling in the world to close the front door, leave the everyday world behind for a while, and just go.

Then, in 1990, I had a stroke of luck: Geoff Martin, the editor of the daily paper I worked for, asked me if I fancied becoming features editor.

"I'll do it if you let me do travel as well," I said.

He thought for a moment.

"All right. You can have 25 days a year," he said with a calmness which belied the fact that my teeth were buried in his ankle at the time.

I added the same again from my own time, and for the next 14 years, every six weeks or so I had that feeling which the passage of time never diminished.

Of flying into a foreign city late at night, taking a taxi through the mysterious streets to a hotel and the next day flinging open the shutters then going walking through the rainwashed morning.

In my head was the knowledge of an adult, in my heart was the joy of a child seeing the world for the first time.

And in my soul, it was always Christmas morning.

These are some of the writings from those years, now updated with stories from later years, after one of Geoff's successors as editor took me off travel and I left the News Letter to write for other newspapers and magazines.

As an A-Z guide to the world, they are of no use whatsoever, but if they inspire you to close the front door, walk down the road with a rucksack over your shoulder and take a bus to the airport or the first train north, then you are the luckiest person alive, and I wish your soul a Happy Christmas Eve.

Geoff Hill
February 2020

A is for Azerbaijan

A short history

Fourth Century BC, just after breakfast
Country named Media Atropatene after ruler of area under Alexander the Great.

Fourth Century BC, teatime
Alexander dies. Persians rename country Aturpatakan as part of Caucasian Albania, not to be confused with Balkan Albania, home of Mother Teresa and King Zog.

Fifth Century AD
Arabs conquer and rename country Arran, not to be confused with Scottish island, home of damp sheep.
Treaty of Endless Peace signed.

Sixth Century AD
Endless Peace ends. Endless War begins between Romans, Arabs, Turks, Mongols and Tartars over control of country.

1828
When rest not looking, Russians grab northern half and rename it Азербайджан. Persians grab south, followed by much enraged carpet-thrashing after Russians discover huge quantities of oil in north.

1900
Country producing half the world's oil, and 95 per cent of Tsarist Russia's. Baku becomes Paris of Caucasus. As opposed to France. Or Texas.

1917
Tsars go out in Russia. In Baku, independence declared, women given vote, Latin alphabet adopted and country renamed Azerbaycan.

1920
Russians check national oil gauge, discover they're running on empty, invade country for refill and change language back to Cyrillic.

1980s
Good news: even huger huge oil and gas deposits discovered off coast. Coincidentally, Western governments suddenly become interested in country.
Bad news: war with Armenia over Nagorno-Karabakh creates refugee crisis.

1991
Country becomes independent and decided to call itself Azerbaijan just for a change. Natives, uncertain whether to celebrate in Albanian, Scottish, Persian, Arabic, Russian or Latin for fear of starting another war, hug each other in mute optimism.

1994
So-called Deal of the Century signed with international consortium for exploitation of oil and gas fields.

2003
Respected president Heydar Aliyev hands over power to son Ilham with dying breath.

CIA verdict on Ilham, notorious former playboy converted to family life, is: "Lacks his father's charisma, political skills, contacts, experience, stature, intelligence and authority. Aside from that, he will make a wonderful president." Azerbaijanis, used to waiting and seeing, wait and see.

15

Azerbaijan

At first Marco Polo came with bales of silk, his hands aromatic with saffron or shimmering with the shadow of jade. In the lilac evenings he walked by the Caspian Sea and cursed the black mud that ruined his golden slippers.

Then the Zoroastrians came, and lit an eternal flame that lasted longer than they did. Then the Rothschilds and the Nobels, here for the same oil that had ruined Marco Polo's slippers, their fantastical mansions rising from the gloop and suck of ruined forests.

Then Stalin came, and the mansions were divided into a thousand tiny apartments, each one still with fear.

Then the oilmen came again, breaking the stillness with loud voices and the rustle of dollars. A hundred years ago Azerbaijan had produced half the world's oil, and now the world was back looking for the other half.

And then, at last, the tourists came. In 1997 the first of them wrote to the Azerbaijani embassy in London, asking for a tourist visa, and the embassy wrote back asking why. Today, foreigners are still so rare that as you walk past the people blink in amazement. Then try to sell you a carpet.

I arrived in Baku, the capital, in the middle of the night, driving through streets where only the flower shops were open, selling lilies to romantic insomniacs.

The next morning, dawn broke over the medieval quarter to reveal a scene from the hotel window which, apart from

McDonald's, Mothercare and the mobile phone shop, had not changed in 400 years.

Along the shore stretched the gloriously lunatic mansions of the 19th Century oil barons, mostly farmers who woke up one morning to find themselves millionaires and immediately sent telegrams to Italy for the first available architect to come at once.

On the hill behind rose a vast Soviet edifice whose countless windows had been teased into Islamic arches, like a shot putter who had discovered eye shadow long after steroids.

I rose, ate a fig for breakfast and wandered through rain-damp streets with the feel of a Paris that had not been washed for half a century, until I came at last to the State Carpet Museum, a monolithic neoclassical pile which smelt of shoe polish. On the grey walls of its many rooms hung thousands of carpets, and in the corner of each room sat a dark, beautiful and utterly bored attendant.

You see, the thing about carpets is that one in a white room is breathtaking, but several thousand on peeling grey walls inevitably results in you being led away suffering from a rug overdose.

What has happened is that a singular Oriental skill has become the victim of the Soviet obsession with quantity, and the result is a fracture that cannot be healed.

But then Azerbaijan has been fractured so many times since it was a crossroads of the Silk Road: by the Persians, by the Mongols, by the Soviets, by war with the Armenians over Nagorno-Karabakh, by the war between the Russian desire for vodka and the Islamic disdain for it, by the gap between the oil-rich and the dirt-poor.

It has even been fractured by the very tool of communication, with two changes of language and three of alphabet - Arabic to Latin, to Cyrillic, and back to Latin - in 80 years.

It is no wonder that the past and the present sit uneasily side by side here, like the grandfather and child of estranged parents.

No wonder that, at any crossroads in Baku, you will see impeccably dressed men from among the one-eighth of the population who are refugees - or the one in two who are unemployed - standing looking in bafflement at a Mercedes taxi on its way to Crescent Beach, an exclusive coastal resort for expatriate oilmen.

Or me inside the Mercedes, looking equally baffled for the same reason: that Azerbaijan's share of Caspian Sea oil reserves is reckoned to be at least £50 billion, but none will find its way into the country until the companies pay off their development costs, and even then much of it may well end up lining the pockets of corrupt politicians, businessmen and their relatives.

At Crescent Beach, I ordered emu.

"I am sorry, sir, but the emu is only served at evening time," said the waiter carefully, conjuring up an image of a flock of emu sitting outside, waiting with fear and trembling for the gleam of a Sabatier at twilight.

When I returned to town in the afternoon, the rain was still falling. In crepuscular carpet shops, negotiations began, faltered and continued over endless cups of tea, until tourists emerged blinking into the drizzle, clutching rolls of wool and silk on which pearls of rain were already beginning to form.

Night fell. To the south of Baku it fell on the abandoned Soviet oilfields, a scene out of Mad Max by way of the Kremlin.

Amid the rusting oil derricks, baffled cows pottered about in pools of oil and ruined water, calling out softly to each other: "Here, Gertrude, am I unleaded or four-star?"

Further south, it fell on a barbed-wire encampment where for the price of a bottle of vodka the guards would let you in to gaze on row upon row of abandoned Soviet tanks glistening dourly in the moonlight.

It fell on Fisherman's Wharf, an expat restaurant where from a waiter with an accent halfway between Baku and Boston I inexplicably found myself ordering a chip butty.

And it fell, at last, on the Chechnyan nightclub where I found myself later. Inside, men who had arrived with unidentifiable bulges under their clothing bought Champagne for women with entirely identifiable bulges under theirs.

I slept in a vodka daze, and the next morning took a rattling minibus north with a guide called Lianna, who had sharp cheekbones and matching opinions.

"We are victims of the Chinese curse, 'May you live in times of change'," she said. "Something is being created, but we do not know what it is yet. The ugly part of all this is that a waiter earns more than a professor, and now you phone friends before you call around to see if they have food on the table. In the Soviet times, everyone was poor, but no one was starving."

She was right. Azerbaijan is fascinating because of the influences that have shaped it in the past, and because at the moment it is going through the turmoil that Marx called dialectic, when one political system becomes another. It is the drama of which epic narratives are made: great to write about, grim to live through.

In the northern suburbs, vast Soviet apartment blocks stood apparently derelict. Until you saw hanging from a balcony a row of white shirts, growing grey in the rain.

A few miles on, in the shadow of a rusting factory, a shepherd sat by a guillotine, waiting for someone who could afford a headless sheep for supper.

On all sides stretched an arid plain which had been forest until refugees chopped down the trees for winter fuel. From time to time there appeared crumbling villages and roadside cafés desperate with longing. Lianna looked out through the window and clutched her silent mobile phone, an icon of a brave new world that was always coming but never came.

It was 100 miles before the dun plain gave way at last to deciduous forest. The earth breathed again, and in the shade of the trees boys in astrakhan hats sold apples, peaches and walnuts.

At Quba, gay lights tinkled on the long road into town, and such had been the unremitting gloom of the landscape earlier that the sight made me quite absurdly happy.

We got lost, and commandeered the services of a local man with gold teeth. A construction engineer until the Soviets left, he had returned to his village to work as an allotment farmer and repair man.

He led us up the green and dripping lanes to a little Albanian fire temple and graveyard. Dating from the Third Century BC, and fabulously engraved, it lay utterly untended in a hilltop field, watched by two querulous ewes.

We climbed back on the bus and bounced through the village street as a man in an immaculate beige suit and white shoes came picking his way through the mud. Behind him, the little houses had tin roofs decorated with doves and deer, and the valley was heavy with peach orchards.

We found a restaurant in which the speciality was chicken curry, and a long time later, since the recipe had obviously involved first catching the chicken, we returned, burping politely, to Baku.

The day's catch of tourists had finished buying carpets and caviar, tut-tutting at the poverty and the corruption and salving their conscience with a generous tip at the little Italian restaurant around the corner, and were returning to hotel rooms which contained little bottles of corporate unguents and copies of the city's not one, but two, English language newspapers.

I threw a bottle of vodka and a toothbrush into a bag and drove to the airport, and an hour later my plane rose into the early evening sky, leaving behind the two lives of Baku.

The life of ambassador's cocktail parties, export beers and dinner with the Johnsons from Texas this Friday.

And the other life. A hundred years ago it was the life of the oil workers who came from all over Russia to live in canvas tents from which they peered out at the oil barons strolling in whispering silks to their fabulous mansions.

Today, the oil barons wear Armani chinos, but the refugees are still the same, looking out from under the rim of their dripping tent now as the plane to London turns west, and trying to imagine what kind of world it is going to.

The plane in which I sit, looking down for one last time at the gleaming curve of Crescent Beach, where twilight is already beginning to fall on the long dark night of the emu.

2001

...and Armenia

A short history

5000BC, give or take a millennium, but not long after the Ark.

Noah begats Japheth begats Gomer begats Togarmah begats Haik.

Haik builds Tower of Babel, has 300 children, makes it to 130 with curly hair and perfect eyesight and decides to celebrate by founding Armenia.

Tyrannical Assyrian ruler Nimrod, pissed off at not having thought of it first, invades new country, wearing state of the art impenetrable iron armour. Haik pierces armour with three-feathered arrow. Nimrod returns to Assyria in bad mood, dead. Haik patents three-feathered arrow and lives on to 400.

9th Century BC

Country absorbed by Urartu Empire, whose deities include Tushpa, God of War with insatiable appetite for beheadings of bulls and sheep. Armenians spend three centuries running around like headless chickens creating vast mounds of headless animals.

590BC

Armenia conquered by Persians, who ban bull and sheep sacrifices. Armenians sacrifice horses instead, then have to walk everywhere.

314 AD
Armenians, having run out of animals to kill, become Christians under Gregory the Illuminator. King Trdat IV, who quite enjoyed a good sacrifice, flings Gregory into snake-infested pit for 12 years.

1400
Eastern Armenia conquered by Turkmen dynasty called Black Sheep. West invaded by second dynasty called White Sheep. Armenians long for good old days of headless sheep.

1878
Britain promises to protect Armenia against Russian and Turkish threats.

1894-96
Britain looks the other way as Turks slaughter 300,000 Armenians.

1915
Turks, having developed a taste for slaughtering Armenians, kill 1.5 million more, then deny everything.

1921
What's left of country taken under caring arm of Lenin. Ever-optimistic Armenians start planning new utopia.

1923
Stalin steps in. Armenians sigh and put away utopia plans.

1930-1945

Over 100,000 Armenians die in purges, followed by 300,000 in Second World War. Last person left in country asked to turn out the light.

1991
Independence. Armenians dust off utopia plans.

1999
Prime Minister, Speaker and six others assassinated in Parliament, followed by endless series of corrupt elections. Armenians sigh, put away plans again, and open a bottle of brandy.

Armenia

The time: any morning for the past 1700 years. The scene: two old men sitting on a park bench, in a cobbled square.

First man: "Well, we've had invasions, massacres, occupations, genocides, wars, starvation, refugees, emigration and poverty. At least nothing worse can happen."

Second man: "What's that noise?"

If countries were people, Armenia would be a black nun living in Mississippi: one who's just been mugged by a bunch of skinheads who've run off with her Vatican Gold credit card.

Then, just as she's getting up and dusting off her wimple, she's run down by a truck driver delivering a load of burning crosses down the road.

After becoming the first Christian country in the world in 301AD, for a thousand years it was a vast empire taking in much of what is now Iran, Turkey, Georgia and Azerbaijan and leading the world in architecture, literature, music, mathematics and astronomy.

Then came the Mongols, the Safavids, the Ottomans and the Russians.

In 1915, the Young Turks of the Ottoman Empire slaughtered 1.5 million Armenians living in eastern Turkey, an act for which Turkey has, to its eternal shame, refused to apologise to this day.

A few short years later, the Russians arrived, killed all the priests and banned religion. In 1996, the war with Azerbaijan flooded the country with refugees. Two years later, an earthquake killed 50,000 and, just as Armenia turned to the Soviet Union for aid, it fell apart.

Today, half of the population is living below the poverty line, and another third are living on less than a dollar a day. Many have fled to the States, and send what money they can.

I arrived by plane in the middle of the night, sitting beside a man in a multicoloured jacket and an even more multicoloured shirt, in the open neck of which hung a large gold and crystal cross. He looked like the Pope on his way to a Saturday Night Fever audition.

Yerevan Airport, the shape of a giant sputnik, was populated entirely by statuesque women in military uniforms, and a small cat. Had I been James Bond, I would have felt obliged to seduce at least half the women before passport control, but as it was, my charms only worked on the cat, who wrapped itself around my ankle as I queued for a visa.

If the drive from the airport was anything to go by, the entire economy was based on casinos and flower shops, and at the hotel, the receptionist was telling a Japanese man that he could not have a room without confirmation of his arrival.

"You want confirmation?" said the man, spreading his arms as wide as they would go, which in truth was not very far. "Here I am! I confirm that I have arrived!"

He got his room, and celebrated by going immediately to the bar and ordering a brandy.

It, and religion, are, of course, the country's two most famous exports.

The brandy is famous because Churchill was introduced to it by Stalin at the Yalta conference and when asked years later for the secret of his long life, said: "Never be late for dinner, smoke only the best cigars and drink Armenian brandy."

And the religion is famous because of buildings like the fabulously frescoed cathedral of Echmiadzin, home to services once more since the departure of the Russians.

Since the Bishop of Armenia was paying a visit, we arrived to a flurry of genuflections and were forced to decamp temporarily to the nearby chapel of St Cayenne, a persecuted virgin who is buried in the 7th Century crypt, below a portrait of her looking glum, although whether from persecution or virginity is unclear.

Outside, a small boy was selling Orthodox crosses emblazoned with the pagan evil eye, as a sort of two for one insurance policy which was entirely appropriate in a country where they still regularly slaughter sheep before Mass.

Anyway, that was quite enough culture for one day. It was time for dinner, at a traditional restaurant in Yerevan where I had a vast feast for about 5p, while in the comer a stern triumvirate of elderly men played joyful airs on violin, flute and qiyamancha, which looks like the offspring of a guitar and a short-sighted giraffe.

We left the city the next day, bouncing south on a rutted road across the fertile plain past vast, deserted Soviet factories and crumbling blocks, with cows grazing in their courtyards as the former workers attempted to make a desultory return to subsistence farming.

"You know," said Nouneh, the guide, "under the Soviets, everything was planned. You knew what you were doing every day for the rest of your life, so we had food, but no tomorrow. Now we have all our tomorrows, but no food."

And no roads: it took us to noon to bounce our way to the spot where Gregory the Illuminator brought Christianity to Armenia in 314, then got thrown down a well by King Trdat for his trouble.

When he wasn't persecuting virgins, Trdat would pop by from time to time and take a look down the well to make sure the saint was suitably miserable.

Of course, Gregory had the last laugh, and Khor Virap, the 13th Century monastery built on the spot, celebrates his success in converting the country.

Today, it is the holiest spot in Armenia, and the most poignant, for only a few miles south is the divine mountain of Ararat, supposed home of the Ark.

Armenians can see its mighty peak from everywhere in the south of the country, and yearn for it, but they can never go there - for it is just across the closed border with detested, unforgiven Turkey.

Nouneh gazed at it for long minutes, then turned away.

"Come. Lunch." she said. Lunch, at a nearby farmhouse, was a table groaning with breads, sweetmeats, sorrel, lamb, beans, soup, fruit and yoghurt, served by Seda, the 68-year-old grandmother of the house. Three years before, her sister had invited her out to Los Angeles to live. She had lasted six months before declaring the place an uncivilized madhouse and returning to the farm.

"When she came back, she complained that we'd got an inside toilet," said her grand-daughter Meline. "'That filthy thing inside the house? How disgusting!'" she said.

On the balcony, a geranium sprouted from an American Blending Corporation powdered milk tin, the sole reminder of Seda's visit to the Babylon of the West.

For a gentle post-prandial walk, we staggered to our feet and climbed the 7,500ft to the mountaintop fortress of Smbataberd, which was built in the 5th Century and sacked by the Mongols 800 years later.

More power to the Mongols, I thought as I collapsed onto the ruined walls. After a climb like that, they deserved all they could lay their hands on.

Still, at least the way down was easier, stumbling through the golden evening into a flock of sheep who surrounded us with the mutter of a thousand tiny feet.

At one stage we were joined by a man and his horse, whose foal walked along behind, occasionally investigating my pocket shyly with her nose.

We regained our car and came at last by moonlight to a monolithic grey building by a river. Two large dogs sat drooling gently on the doorstep, and in an upstairs building, a single light burned.

"Nouneh, what is this building?" I said, as one of the dogs politely nibbled my knee.

"It is the bishop's summer orphanage. But all the orphans have gone," she said.

At length, a small dark man opened the door. It was the bishop, who led us upstairs to dine on reluctant mutton while he drank tea from a large mug emblazoned with the words: "Earl Grey, named after a British Nobleman renowned in International Circles".

I slept on a small bed, in a large dormitory, while somewhere deep in the bowels of the building, our driver played Bach long into the night.

The next morning, I was feeding apples to a horse when a man came up, gave me a fish and drove off in a chocolate-coloured Lada.

Milk, that is, not plain.

I put the fish in my pocket and we drove north to Yeghegnadzvar, where an increasingly insistent drumming from the rear announced the imminent disintegration of a tyre under the incessant battering of Armenian roads.

While the driver went off to get it fixed, I wandered through the derelict streets, past old men sitting on benches waiting for money from America, until I came to the town museum. The entire staff came out, visibly stunned to see a tourist, then gave me a personal tour of several ancient artefacts above labels describing them as A Stick, A Bear Pot of Rituals and A Spindle from Unanimous Cave.

The driver appeared, announced that the tyre was as well as could be expected in the circumstances, and we set off for the mountains, up a road which had mercifully been repaired with money from Kerk Kerkorian, the Armenian-born MGM film magnate, who had recently poured $200 million into renovations in old Yerevan.

I made a note to write to him, saying: "Dear Kerk, you don't know me, but I am in fact your long-lost son", as Nouneh announced for the third time that morning that the roads were worse in Georgia, then launched into a medley of old Armenian folk songs and finished with an encore of Jingle Bells as we arrived at Selim, the best preserved of all the caravanserai on the old Silk Road.

A sort of medieval trucker's stop, this was a long basalt hall, inside which the camels slept down the centre and the merchants in arched naves along either side.

It is all splendidly atmospheric, and as you stand at the ornately-carved entrance and look out, you can almost smell the damp heat of the beasts, incense and cooking behind you, and see before you a distant caravan toiling its way up the mountain, laden with silks and spices from Persia and Samarkand.

With, behind it, of course, a queue of horsemen honking their horns and muttering: "Get a bloody move on, lads, or we'll miss the happy hour!"

It began to rain, and in a flourish of rainbows we came by evening time to Lake Sevan, the victim of an ill-fated Soviet scheme to create more arable land by lowering the water level 60ft, then an even-more ill-fated scheme to introduce whitefish, crayfish and goldfish, which promptly ate virtually all the indigenous trout.

We stopped by a bleached road sign, in front of a derelict railway station. All the way along the shore were abandoned Soviet projects: hotels, apartment blocks, concert halls and miles of pipeline.

One enterprising chap had requisitioned one section, sprayed it red, decorated it with Coca-Cola logos and turned it into a lakeside diner. Other bits had been transformed into makeshift houses for families left homeless by the 1988 earthquake.

I wandered down through the oak groves, planted on the newly naked shore in the Fifties, and stood at the edge of the lake, looking at two fishermen in a boat trying to catch the last trout in Sevan.

It suddenly occurred to me that if I'd been standing here 50 years ago, I would have been underwater, and dead. If I'd been alive then, that is.

We climbed back into the car and bounced along the lakeside road for another hour, until all my teeth had fallen out and my innards turned to strawberry jam.

But it was worth it, for, at the end of the road was a hotel built by carpet magnate James Tufenkian which was as stunning as the orphanage the previous night had been basic. I wandered around my room in a sort of sumptuous-minimalist trance, pressing feather and down pillows, admiring muted earth tones, drooling over the bleached wood, stroking the copper Do Not Disturb sign and climbing the minstrel gallery stairs to stand on the little balcony in the rain, dazed with gratitude.

And, if you think I'm going on a bit, you've obviously never stayed in an Armenian orphanage. Even better, there was a restaurant in the same idiom.

I had pear and tahine, tiny dolmades, lamb wrapped in spinach and cosseted by several herbs and spices, then staggered to my room and slept deeply, troubled only a dream that I was the last trout in Lake Sevan, being pursued by a giant goldfish.

In the morning, the roads, impossibly, got worse. We climbed into the mountains at a speed so slow that the speedometer could not even be bothered to register it. An eagle, pausing briefly from feasting on a dead dog, soared alongside, mocking us with its effortless freedom.

In the town of Dilijan, cradled by mists and mountains, four cows sat in the middle of the main street and a pig watched us gravely from an ornate balcony. Several of the old houses had been bought by the town's ethnographic museum, restored to how they would have been in the 19th Century and turned into little shops. They looked infinitely preferable to the way most Armenians, a proud and intelligent people struggling against a series of disasters, lived today.

I emerged, unaccountably clutching a Russian Charlie Parker LP, to find Nouneh.

"We are going to the House of the Composers," she said, then grinned. "And remember; the roads are worse in Georgia."

This, along with the House of the Cinematographers and the House of Creativity of Writers, was one of the Soviet artists' retreats in the wooded hills nearby where the likes of Shostakovich and Khachaturian would come to listen to the wind in the leaves and ostensibly compose music which would inspire the proletariat to even greater beetroot production.

Today, they are home only to the occasional passing tourist and, from the cottages in the grounds, the notes of unwritten symphonies rise into the trees to become the songs of birds.

"Come," said Nouneh, "we are going to a unique monastery."

"Nouneh, you've said that about all of them."

"Ah, but this one is absolutely unique."

Funnily enough, she was right. Built in the 12th Century on a mountain high above Yerevan, Geghard combines the lofty arches of Romanesque architecture, the hulking solidity of Medieval and the soaring grace of Renaissance into a synergy which is, well, er, unique.

As we arrived, the national choir was practising in the mausoleum, outside which were carved, rather serendipitously, two Homeric sirens.

The music they were singing, which still makes my spine tingle when I think of it, was from a 4th Century manuscript, kept with 17,000 others in the remarkable Matenadaran museum in Yerevan. For, when the Armenians were not building, they were writing, storing up words and music against the uncertain future.

We returned to the city that night, and the next morning, I walked up the hill, past the teenagers queuing outside the American visa office, and stopped in front of the statue of Kara Bala.

A rich rose-grower in the Thirties, with a beautiful wife and son, he was jailed after murdering a love rival and ended his days alone, selling flowers on the street.

It is a very Armenian story, made even more poignant by the fact that behind him you can see, as you can see from everywhere in Yerevan, the holy mountain of Ararat, across the uncrossable Turkish border.

The snowy peaks of paradise, so real and so unattainable, so near and yet so far away.

2003

B is for Bangkok, in search of sex on flying motorcycles

A short history

1769
King Taksin establishes Siamese capital in nearby Thonburi,
then goes mad and declares himself to be the next Buddha.
Ministers beat him politely to death in a velvet blanket so
that no royal blood touches the ground.

1785
New King Rama moves capital down the road to Bangkok
and decides to rename it Krungthep mahanakhon amon
ratanakosin mahintara ayuthaya mahadilok popnopparat
ratchathani burirom udomratchaniwet mahasasathan
amonpiman avatansathit sakkathattiya witsanukamprasit,
which I don't need to tell you means Great city of angels,
the repository of divine gems, the great land unconquerable,
the grand and prominent realm, the royal and capital city full
of nine noble gems, the highest royal dwelling and grand

palace, the divine shelter and living place of reincarnated spirits.

Everyone ignores him, decides life's too short, and continues to call it Bangkok.

Any of you who prefer the old name should rush out and buy Fak Thong, the 1989 album by Thai rock duo Asanee & Wasan, an epic funk rave which consists of the old city name chanted over a hypnotic rhythm.

1964-73

City gains reputation as so-called Rest and Recreation bolthole for US soldiers in Vietnam. Sex being more fun than politics or finance, reputation endures through dictatorships, democracies and economic boom and bust.

Bangkok

It was a Friday evening, and I was sitting in a hotel bar in Bangkok with several men from Dublin, as you do.

It was Shane who started talking about sex on a flying motorcycle, and at first we thought it was sunstroke.

He had fallen asleep the day before on a junk going to the islands, and had arrived scarlet on the front and snow-white on the back.

When he was awakened by a sudden tropical downpour, his chest steamed gently, and when he sat up, his back was so blinding in the late afternoon sunlight that the junk owner's Filipino wife was rushed to hospital with snowblindness.

Now, he was sitting bolt upright in the hotel bar, drinking beer and holding my guidebook very carefully.

"Look," he said. "It says here, in your book, that there's a club called Supergirls which has sex on a flying motorcycle. As featured in Rolling Stone," it says.

"What sort of motorcycle is it?" I said, sipping a cold beer with those lovely beads of moisture on the outside of the glass.

"It doesn't say."

"You're the motorcycling correspondent for your paper, aren't you?" said Shane.

"I am," I said, knowing what was coming.

"Well, you should really go and find out. Shouldn't you?"

I sighed, and put down my beer.

We set off in a taxi, six of us, into the hot and humid night. The rest were all under 30, except for myself and Charlie, a bald photographer who the day before, while carefully helping Shane ashore from the junk, had dropped his glasses into 35ft of water.

"Where you going?" said the taxi driver as we sped off. It was midnight, which is about the only time you can speed off anywhere in Bangkok traffic.

"We want to see sex on motorbikes," said Shane from the back, where he was doing his best to sit carefully between four other people. "Flying motorbikes."

"He means the Supergirls club," I said to the driver, who like most Thai men could have been anywhere between 30 and 60.

"Superwha?"

"Supergirls. Motorbikes. Sex."

"Ah, sex! Patpong!" he said, brightly.

Patpong was originally four acres of banana plantation owned by the bank of Indochina, which sold it to the Patpongphanit family just before the Second World War.

After the war, massage parlours and bars grew to satisfy the needs of airline staff and soldiers, and today it is a hive of markets, bars, clubs and sex shows from which the Patpongphanit family collects £200,000 a month in rent.

Anyway, where was I? Ah yes, in a taxi. Twenty minutes later we pulled up outside Patpong, which I recognised from my extensive local knowledge, and also because it said Patpong in large letters above the entrance.

On all sides stretched market stalls selling T-shirts and CDs, still doing a roaring trade at a quarter past midnight.

Shane walked carefully up to a beautiful Thai girl standing outside the bar on the comer, wearing a dark business suit.

She smiled sweetly at him, politely overlooking the fact that in the neon from the bar sign, his skin looked as if it had recently come into contact with weapons-grade plutonium.

"Can you tell me where the flying motorcycles are?" he said.

"Motorcycles?" she said in perfect English. "Have you tried a garage?"

I felt a tug at my elbow. It was Neil, another of the group.

"Here, help me bargain for this. I'm so crap at haggling I always end up paying more than they asked for in the first place," he said.

I looked at what he was holding. It was a red string vest. With sequins.

"Is it for yourself?" I said.

"It's for a friend. It's a long story."

Suddenly, we were interrupted by Charlie.

"Listen, this isn't Patpong. Patpong is miles away," he said.

Before I had a chance to point out to him that not only was he not wearing his glasses, but that he had never been to Thailand before, he had leaped into a taxi with two of the others.

"Bloody hell. Bloody hell," I said, flagging down a passing tuk-tuk, the rickshaws named for the sound of their two-stroke engines and driven by men like Michael Schumacher; only faster

"Follow that taxi," I said to the driver. Neil got in beside me, and Shane got in carefully beside him.

Twenty minutes later, we pulled up at a derelict building in a deserted part of Bangkok. In front of it, three men in vests lounged on plastic chairs, and in front of them, the owner was talking to Charlie.

"Ping pong balls. Bananas," he was saying. "Only 500 baht."

"That's very expensive for bananas," said Neil.

"You haven't seen what they do with them yet," I said.

"We don't want ping pong balls or bananas. We want flying motorbikes," said Shane.

We got back into our respective vehicles and hurtled off into the damp darkness. Half an hour later we pulled up in a battered alleyway, outside an even more derelict building.

An elegant Thai woman came out, in a black dress.

"Well, it looks like a garage," said Shane. "So they might have motorbikes."

He walked carefully inside, followed by the others.

"Do you have motorcycles?" I said to the woman.

"I'm afraid not. Just girls and beer"

I sighed, and got back into the tuk-tuk.

It was two in the morning by the time I got back to the hotel, paid Vilam the driver 240 baht, or about £4, for his night's efforts, and stepped out, smelling faintly of oil.

I was hot and tired, and as I looked up at the stars, I thought it would be an ideal time for a swim. To my surprise, someone else had had the same idea: Ahmed, the marketing manager of the airline I had flown out with, was sitting in the shallow end of the hotel pool with a glass of red wine.

Above our heads, the Milky Way wheeled through the heavens as carefully as Shane getting out of a tuk-tuk.

"You know," said Ahmed, "every time I look up at the stars and think of all the worlds that must be out there, I think of my dead brother.

"I was 40 days old when he died. He was four, and my grandfather had sent him out to get some soup from the store. He reached up to lift the pot down off the stove, and spilt the boiling soup all over himself. He died a few hours later, not because of the burns, but because of the shock.

"My grandfather always blamed himself, and he was never the same man again.

"Then, when I was 11, I was lying sleeping one night when I suddenly woke to see a boy standing beside my bed.

"He looked at me for a little while, then turned and went into my grandfather's room.

"My grandfather died that night, and when I described the boy to my parents, they said I had described my brother, who I never knew.

"I like to think that he had come to take my grandfather, and to tell him not to blame himself.

"And I like to think, when I look up at the stars, that they are up there waiting for me in another world, when at last it is my turn to pass out of this one."

The next day, I met Shane at noon.

"Well, did you find the flying motorcycles?" I said.

"No, they just had girls and beer. So we sang to the girls, and drank the beer," he said, walking on, carefully and optimistically, towards a breakfast room which had long since closed.

2003

Brazil

'Driving standards in Brazil hover between abysmal and appalling, with one of the highest road death tolls in the world'

The Rough Guide to Brazil

We had two Triumphs fresh from the new factory in Manaus deep in the Amazon jungle, full tanks of gas, half a packet of Werther's, it was dawn and we were wearing sunglasses.

We were all set to hit the road for the 2,600 miles to Rio, except for one small problem.

There was no road to hit. Five hundred miles of it had been washed away by torrential rain.

"Here, what idiot organised this in the middle of the rainy season?" I muttered plaintively to my mate Peter Murtagh.

"You did."

I sighed deeply, for what I suspected was not going to be the last time.

You see, no matter how many adventures I organised, I was still crap at organising them. So far I had managed to arrive in India on the hottest day of the year, leave Ireland in three feet of snow, turn up in the Netherlands in the coldest spring since 1922 and arrive in Sri Lanka in the middle of the monsoon.

I sighed again, and phoned Ed, the man from Triumph.

"Tell you what," said Ed. "Fly to Rio, pick up two bikes from the dealer, and I'll work out a nice route from there."

And so, finally, we were off, our plan not only to discover an undiscovered biking destination, but to see if the locals were looking forward to the first World Cup to be held there since 1950, when a 2-1 defeat to Uruguay plunged the nation into a depression from which it took years to recover.

We arrived in Rio, and went walking on the beach, realising immediately that this is impossible to do without humming *The Girl from Ipanema*.

Behind the endless energy of beach volleyball and soccer, the buildings were down at heel apart from the glittering neoclassical glory of the Copacabana Palace Hotel, built in 1923 and the first to bring what was then the turboprop set flying down to Rio.

The Metropolitan Cathedral, dreary on the outside, was an epiphany of soaring stained glass inside, like a postmodern Chartres, and in the Maracanã Stadium, Sao Paulo were playing Flamengo, the atmosphere inside one of such supercharged testosterone that I fear if Brazil reach the World Cup final in the same stadium, the resulting critical mass of patriotic passion will destroy the city, leaving the statue of Christ the Redeemer looking down on the devastation with weary serenity.

Talking of whom, the view of the sprawling metropolis and Sugar Loaf Mountain beyond was one of the events in my life, like riding Route 66 or the Orient Express, that was every bit as good as I hoped it would be.

"Are you looking forward to the World Cup?" I said to Matthias the guide as we admired it.

"Sure am. I've got six tickets for the final. If Brazil's in it, I'll take my girlfriend, sell four and make a small fortune. If not, I'll sell all six and make a bigger fortune," he grinned.

The next morning, we walked through the door of Rio's Triumph dealership to be greeted by the cheery figure of salesman Nicolay Figueroa.

"You looking forward to the World Cup, Nicolay?" I said, as he handed us the keys to two Triumphs.

"Not so much," he shrugged. "A month's happiness for £10 billion which would be better spent on education."

We shook his hand, rode nervously into the traffic, and tilted southwest along the Costa Verde, or green coast, rendered slightly less idyllic by the Petrobras oil terminal and two nuclear power stations which the military rather cleverly built in an earthquake zone.

Looking at the jungle, it was impossible to imagine the struggle the first explorers must have had hacking their way through it in cuirasses, helmets and splendid pantaloons in the hunt for El Dorado.

At the roadside diner where we stopped for chicken and rice, the TV showed a freak hailstorm in Sao Paulo, just down the road, and on the other wall hung a painting of a thatched Tudor cottage and an English rose garden.

We rode on, glorying all the afternoon in a glorious symphony of sweeping curves between the mountainous jungle and the glittering ocean, and we were two happy men who rode at dusk into Paraty, an ancient colonial town of whitewashed houses, terracotta tiled roofs, a rainbow of pastel woodwork, and huge irregular cobbles which mean that everyone staggers about drunkenly, so no one notices how much you drink.

We took full advantage, dining to the strains of the resident jazz quartet at a small restaurant in the square while the local kids played basketball in front of the town's venerable church.

The cobbles are aligned to allow rainwater to run down to the sea, and that night as we slept, the high tide returned the favour, creeping through the streets by the light of the full moon and leaving in the morning a briny tang and the body of a small, disappointed sardine whose attempt to short cut evolution had not, after all, succeeded.

We returned his body to the sea and went to say a small prayer for him in the church. In the vast cool space sat a young woman, her head bowed. As I tiptoed past, I saw the band of pale flesh where her wedding ring had been.

Subdued, we retreated into lunacy and went looking for a steam train so we could make up ludicrous puns involving Paraty of a steam, but finding none, left town as disappointed as a sardine and rode north to Sao Paulo, through a landscape of wooded hills and lakes.

Once, a girl sitting proud on a horse waved from a meadow.

It was a more idyllic scene than Sao Paulo, which contains 20 million people, all of whom had for some reason decided to go out for a drive that day. It also contains 70 museums, 120 theatres, 50 parks and 15,000 pubs, but after laboriously filtering through traffic for two hours in baking heat, and at one stage finding a family of grazing capybara looking at us quaintly from a city centre verge, we turned tail and fled to the village of Santa Isabel an hour outside the city.

There, in the kindness typical of strangers, a local man got into his car and led us to the Pousada Lua, where a friend of the owner let us park the bikes in his garage.

Even better, it was my birthday, so Peter popped out and returned with a bottle of bubbly, a vuvuzela and a World Cup deely bopper, and then in the village restaurant, and I use the term loosely, I ordered pizza in Portuguese so bad we were served two chicken and bacon rolls.

The next day, the road north to Brasilia turned from arrow-straight motorway to fast dual carriageway then two-lane blacktop, mostly immaculate and snaking its way through a landscape that was once coffee bushes and is now maize, soya bean and finally savannah so redolent of Africa that I was only mildly surprised to see a family of giraffes on the horizon.

Sadly, they turned out to be plastic ones on top of a filling station.

In Brasilia, we found an expensive hotel with cheap soap and ate dinner at a Greek restaurant in a shopping mall owned by a slovenly German and run by Abdelteef Adman Achmed, an enthusiastic Sudanese civil engineer who was paying his way through his Masters degree, and who looked and sounded exactly like Eddie Murphy in Trading Places.

"World Cup?" he said. "I'm working too hard to watch it."

Brasilia is the Ottawa or Canberra of Brazil; a purpose-built political capital conceived by President Juscelino Kubitschek in 1956 and designed by modernist architect Oscar Niemeyer.

Ultra-modern for about 10 seconds, it's been stuck in a time warp ever since, as we found the next morning when we went looking for its beating heart.

It was not in the empty weekend boulevards, or the faceless glass façades of the towering government buildings, which could be in Anywhere, USA.

Neither was it in Niemeyer's Metropolitan Cathedral, with its exterior a glittering white crown of thorns and its interior, with a glass ceiling of blue and green swirls. It was like being underwater and looking up to heaven like an aspirational sardine.

No, it was in the lake, bright with the sailing dinghies of people who had stopped being politicians or civil servants and were just happy children at play again.

"Perfect day for a spot of gentlemanly motorcycling," I said as we set off for Belo Horizonte the next morning in glorious sunshine.

I should have kept my mouth shut.

It started well. Once I stopped just to enjoy the sound of silence, and as I sat looking out over the endless fields of maize, I noticed a hummingbird watching me with a quizzical expression from a bougainvillea branch.

Then we came across a family lazing by a river. Dad was fishing for catfish, mum was breastfeeding a baby, the kids were splashing about, a macaw flapped overhead and a giant butterfly with cobalt blue wings settled briefly on Peter's shoulder, then fluttered off.

After that, things went from bad to worse. My bike kept cutting out on a diet of dodgy fuel, which made progress so slow that by dusk we were still an hour from Belo Horizonte.

Then the torrential rain started. Two hours later, soaked and knackered, we spotted the lights of a hotel on the outskirts of Belo Horizonte, and climbed wearily off the bikes for a hot shower, a warm meal and a very cold beer.

The next day was even worse, with more torrential rain and spray from passing lorries covering us in a layer of red mud. But it was worth it for two things.

The town of Ouro Preto, cradled in mist and mountains, with its whitewashed buildings, ornate wrought iron balconies, pastel woodwork with the patina of age, cobbled streets and mansions and churches worthy of its status as the former state capital.

It is also the birthplace of Aleijadhinho, the 18th Century womanizer, bon vivant and sculptor, but his finest creation lies down the road at the Basilica of Bom Jesus in Congonhas: a series of statues representing the Passion of Christ and the prophets.

What is remarkable about them is not just the exquisite skill of the carving, or the infinitely gentle, infinitely suffering humanity of their faces, but the fact that by the time he carved them, Aleijadinho had been struck down by leprosy.

Crippled with pain, unable to walk or use his hands, he was carried up the hill to the Basilica every day to create his masterpiece with chisels strapped to his wrists.

Compared with that, dodgy fuel and a liberal coating of mud is a very small problem indeed.

2014

... and Bulgaria

D awn was rising over Belfast as we took off some hours later than we had intended. As we passed over Germany, the stewardess mistook my look of hunger for one of deep inner contentment, passed me by with the breakfast trolley and had to be cajoled into returning with a piece of excitable chicken, a languid tomato and an exhausted gherkin.

Several hours later, Plovdiv appeared under the starboard wing. Heavens, I could see the very road that Paddy Minne and I had ridden down on our way from Delhi two years before, being soaked by torrential rain, almost killed by forked lightning and, in my particular case, stung in the neck by a reversing bee.

The plane landed and drew to a halt. The Bulgarian businessman sitting in front of me stood up, smoothed his brown corduroy suit, and carefully took a brown corduroy coat from the overhead locker.

Outside, Plovdiv was warm and sunny, which was a little worrying, since we were there to ski. Still, not to worry. We climbed into a bus and set off for the mountains, passing after 10 minutes a red Lada saloon from the back of which two small, brown cows gazed placidly out.

Things had obviously picked up in Bulgaria; the last time I had been there, the cows had been walking. Indeed, two minutes later, we passed a gypsy encampment with a satellite dish sprouting from the roof of every shack, and in Borovets, our hotel rooms had been renovated recently to Ikea standard.

Sadly, the upgrade had also included the temperature, for it was like a warm summer day outside, and of snow there was no sign. Now, call me a traditionalist, but I do like snow on a skiing holiday.

"Don't worry," said Nikolai, the man from the tour company, "there is snow at the top of the mountain. Tomorrow we will ski."

In the meantime, there was nothing to do but go for a drink in the nearby Shark Club, whose sign outside described it rather quaintly as an energy bar. Inside was the world's most powerful ultraviolet lighting, turning everyone instantly tanned, sparkly and glamorous.

With teeth flashing and shirts gleaming, we got slowly, sparklingly drunk.

Several bars and hours later, I staggered back to the hotel, having consumed by my estimation 427 schnapps and 536 beers.

"You've been drinking, haven't you?" I said to myself in the bathroom mirror.

"Afraid so," said my reflection, shamefacedly.

The next morning I rose, breakfasted heartily and presented myself on top of the mountain to a skiing instructor called Alex.

Since it was two years since I had been skiing, I was splendidly appalling, although I did find several new ways of hurtling down the mountain, some of them even with my head above my feet, which had other skiers looking on with what I like to think of in retrospect was open-mouthed admiration.

There was only one thing for it, and that was to stop for lunch at a little mountaintop hut, where Alex and I enjoyed what according to the menu was a Big Make, accompanied by the refreshing tinkle of hailstones on our foreheads and the cheery sound of sea shanties from the resident piano-accordionist.

In the afternoon, a dodgy cartilage in my left knee which made turning right almost impossible forced me to develop a technique of descending the mountain in a series of left-handed loops. It was not entirely successful.

There was only one thing for it, and that was to go back to the hotel for a dinner of pork and potatoes, accompanied by the very same peripatetic piano-accordionist from the top of the mountain.

"Clap! You must clap!" he demanded cheerily, giving his performance the martial jollity of a pre-war Luftwaffe officers' ball, before launching into a little ditty called Kalinka, whose lyrics interpreted more or less as: "The Russians are taking over the world."

"Stop, stop!" said our hosts, who were tucking into huge steaks which were not on the menu, but which had mysteriously materialised from the kitchens. "Play something Bulgarian!"

"You know," said Jordan, the extremely pleasant chap sitting beside me as the accordionist launched into the fourth verse of a traditional air, "there are always three crucial elements in every Bulgarian folk song."

"What three?" I said.

"Women," he said. "And love."

The next morning, I met Alex in a little café for coffee, to the sound of a splendidly obscene American rap song.

Above our heads, a poster for the Bonkers nightclub impelled us to Come and Feel the Beet.

We finished our coffees, walked out into fresh spring sunshine under a bleached cotton and indigo sky, and took the gondola up the mountain.

As we ascended heavenward, my heart sank at an equal rate.

For yesterday I had been the worst skier in the world, and if Alex had turned to me this morning and said: "Hey, let's give it a miss today," I would have been in the bar and had the beers set up before he'd got his boots off.

All the more remarkable, then, that today I turned out to be a Master of the Universe, laughing gaily at red runs and grinning inanely in the face of moguls.

"Amazing," said Alex, as I sailed past him in a perfect parallel turn, stopped, and promptly fell over.

It was, I agreed at a brief meeting with myself in the bar afterwards, the best I had ever skied.

Tragically, our hosts had decided that we were going that night to Pamporovo, Bulgaria's other ski resort, in spite of the fact that we had been told there was barely any snow there.

"Why don't we stay here?" we asked as one.

"No, no, we must go. It is in the programme," we were told peremptorily.

Even more of a shame, on the way to Pamporovo, I could detect the faint but definite signs of flu.

We arrived to a beautifully renovated hotel, but even the sight of deep armchairs and a crackling log fire in the lobby failed to make me feel any better. I had two paracetamol and a brandy and went to bed, where I dreamt of fish.

And although I had fallen asleep convinced I was dying and would never walk again, never mind ski, much to my surprise I found myself yet again at the top of the mountain the next morning, stuffed with every form of flu drug known to mankind.

Sadly, as we had been told, there was little snow, and the only runs open were a nursery slope and a half-bald red run.

There was only one thing for it, and that was to use the nursery slope to learn snowboarding. As far as I could see, there was only problem with this: I was not a dude.

I thought about this for a moment, then approached a Belfast chap called Arthur, who was obviously a dude from the fact that his hair was like an explosion in a mattress factory.

"Here, Arthur, I need to become a dude so I can go snowboarding," I said.

"No worries. I've got some Dr Zog's Hot Hair Wax, and if that fails we can stick your fingers in the shaver socket," he said.

"And do you have any death thrash ambient techno hip-hop garage funk CDs I can listen to?"

"It's the only type of music I have."

Splendid. Now all I needed to do was actually learn to snowboard. I presented myself immediately to the snowboard depot, only to find that size 13 snowboarding boots were a thing that had not yet been invented.

As a result, I became possibly the only person ever to go snowboarding in a pair of docker's shoes bought for $17 at a discount store in Philadelphia.

Learning to snowboard is, in some ways, a similar process to learning to ski. You fall down a lot, then eventually surprise yourself by getting it right.

Towards the end of the afternoon I executed a turn without the usual look of blind panic followed by an exit into the trees at speed, and swished to a spot beside a young chap wearing baggy cargo trousers, a Tin Tin in the Congo T-shirt, Killer Loop shades and a baseball cap firmly on backwards.

"Looking good, dude," he said, giving me the Nanu Nanu sign from Mork and Mindy.

It was official. I had been elevated to dudedom.

My day entirely made, I went off to borrow an ambient techno CD from Arthur, stick my fingers in the shaver socket, and have a sparkly beer in an ultraviolet nightclub.

2000

C is for Cruising with the Colonel

Air hell-air thaih. One has been on a cruise, don't you know, and quite a splendid one at that.

Now, one knows only too well that cruising in the Caribbean can be simply dreadful, what with all those ghastly Americans with their leathery tans and their gold lame catsuits. The women are even worse.

However, cruising in the Atlantic is quite a different kettle of ball games altogether. After all, if it was good enough for our chaps in the war, it should be good enough for one, what! However, before one tackled the mighty swell, one flew down to Malaga to join one's ship.

Thankfully, one got upgraded to cashmere rather than plain old goat class, and arrived at the other end thoroughly refreshed after a few glasses of champers with breakfast - not the whole bottle, mind, just enough to give one a spring in one's step as one strode out into the sunshine ignoring the pleas of those foreign johnnies to carry one's bags, and found a splendidly agreeable taxi driver, name of Jesus – can't understand why these foreign chappies are allowed to take the name of our Lord in vain.   :

Anyhow, what with one's smattering of idiomatic Spanish and Jesus' surprising command of the mother tongue, one agreed a fare - crucial in these parts, or one will be taken to the proverbial cleaners - and set off in the direction of the jolly old ship.

Not that one needed much local knowledge in finding it, since the bloody thing was bigger than Malaga and was right there in front of us, looming over the town like the dear old white cliffs of Dover. Can't understand why they didn't just land the plane on the ship and save one the taxi fare.

Anyhow, decamped from the taxi, gave Jesus a couple of extra potatoes, or whatever they're called, for his trouble, and got one of the ship chappies to haul one's bags on board after he assured one that one wouldn't have to tip him the moon and the stars for the privilege.

And then, rather splendidly, arrived on board to find that one had a stateroom complete with balcony, bottle of champers chilling on table, and butler.

Rather strangely, though, one's butler turned out to be a gel, name of Zyta, Polish by origin. Still, since Polish chaps spent much of the last war on horses charging German tanks, can't imagine that a spot of butling would be much of a bother to their gels.

Even better, one was given a gold card to charge all one's drinkies to, which seemed like a splendid idea until the end of the week, when one only discovered after running up a bar bill for squillions of spondulicks that one was actually expected to pay for it. Resolved on future cruises to make one's own card with the help of old video rental card and tiny pot of Humbrol gold paint left over from Airfix modelling days.

Anyhow, that was all in the future. At this moment, one's back, which one had put out a couple of years earlier after giving one of the servants a damn good thrashing for riding his bicycle around the grounds without a light - fortunately it was in the middle of the day - was troubling one after the journey, so one resolved immediately to put one's new gold card to good use and book a hearty pummeling in the ship spa with one of those splendidly healthy gels that one sees in these places, all crisp white cotton and matching teeth.

Tragically, when one emerged from the spa office and looked at one's appointment slip, one discovered that one had been booked in at five pip emma with a gel called Tore, who sounded suspiciously like a chap.

Even worse, he sounded Swedish, and we all know that the only thing Sweden ever produced, apart from the damned fine Bofors anti-aircraft gun, was those dreadful Ingmar Bergman films in which one sits and watches a broken chair in an empty room for three hours then leaves the cinema and kills oneself by driving one's Volvo into an elk.

In any case, one wasn't too keen on the thought of a chap pummeling one's buttocks. One has been to public school, after all, and knows only too well where that sort of thing can lead.

All in all, one's only resort was to return to one's room and phone the spa making up some excuse about a business appointment at 5pm and asking if one could make an appointment for the same time tomorrow.

"Indeed, I can fit you in with Tore again," said the very pleasant gel on the other end.

"Em, no, one seems to have an appointment then too. What about the day after?" one spluttered.

"Ah yes, Melissa can fit you in then."

Splendid. Melissa sounded neither Swedish, nor a chap.

To celebrate, one went out and drank rather too much at dinner. Thankfully, that night the clocks went back, so by the time one went to bed one was an hour more sober than one would otherwise have been.

And the next morning one found oneself in Tangier, the only part of Morocco ruled by an international conglomerate when the French and the Spanish divided up the country in 1912.

Lucky old Tangier, one cannot help but think: the Spanish, following the tradition they had begun with the Americas, took much and gave little, whereas the French followed General Hubert Lyautey's colonial dictum: "Do not offend a single tradition, do not change a single habit."

Silly old Spanish, silly old French. One was nasty to the Berbers, who got angry and threw them out, and the other educated the Berbers, who got smart and threw them out.

Bloody difficult business keeping empires. As one knows.

However, one did long for the days of the gunboat as one trundled down the gangplank to be met by the entire population, all of whom claimed to be qualified guides and have a brother who owned the best little tea/carpet/silver/leather/glassware etc etc shop in town.

Fobbing them off man and boy, one proceeded west with guidebook in hand through the tumbledown streets to the Sunday morning market.

All splendidly seedy, what with air of ever-present danger mingling with smell of over-ripe aubergines.

Presently found oneself outside quaint little white St Andrew's Church, built in authentic Sussex Moorish style.

Outside, beside a plaque in memory of Hervey Tucker Lloyd Bruce, 4th Baronet of Downhill in Co Derry - splendid chap, my grandfather fought with his at the relief of Khartoum - was the caretaker, name of Mustapha Chergui, clad in a magnificent tweed robe in spite of temperature in the eighties.

Hoisting a finger to his lips, he tiptoed to the church door and eased it open. Inside, the Sunday morning sermon was droning on splendidly to a congregation of two women and a chap, their thinning hair wafting slightly in the breeze from the open door.

The rest were all outside, six feet under, with Mustapha's dog sniffing at their graves and snatching a quick tiddle against the headstone of General Sir Harry Maclean, turn of the century adviser to Sultan Moulay Abd El Aziz. Splendid chap. Used to go shooting with his cousin. Harry, that is.

Grabbed a quick cup of tea - refreshing stuff, tasted of mint – at the Café Paris. Devilish place: once could just imagine all the deals which were struck there during the last war between our chaps and the rest.

And so, mightily refreshed, on one plodded up hill and down dale - and Tangier has plenty of both - through the Kasbah, a warren of white tunnels in which the voices of the little boys on which homosexuals notoriously came to Tangier to prey rang like bells in the cool spaces.

Among the coterie of homosexuals who lived in the town was the late American publishing tycoon Malcolm Forbes, whose white palace on the coast road was the venue for a 70th birthday party which cost the old fruitcake $2.5 million chartering a 747, a DC 8 and Concorde to fly in 800 of his chums, paying Elizabeth Taylor to hand around the canapés and rounding up 600 swordsmen and 300 horsemen for a Berber cavalry charge.

How unlike the home life of our own dear Queen, what! Tragically, Forbes' home, now a museum, was closed, so one was unable to peruse his vast collection of toy soldiers, motorcycles, hot air balloons etc.

Returning through the town, one was accosted by a particularly persistent fellow who seemed somewhat taken aback that one was not overcome with enthusiasm at the prospect of accompanying him to his father's carpet shop.

"We don't need people like you here. Go back to Europe," he finally declared from behind a pair of what one believes are called fake designer sunglasses.

One took his advice and left, accompanied all the way to the ship by three remarkably annoying little children demanding dirhams.

One went to dinner, slept, and woke the next morning to find that one was in Lisbon, which is the rather splendid thing about cruising, that one can travel simply by going to bed.

Rather foolishly, one had arrived in Lisbon on a Monday, when all the museums
were closed, including the rather remarkable Gulbenkian, founded by that Armenian oil baron chap who took British citizenship then went off in a huff because we called him a spy in the last war. Bit of a cock-up by us, one must say.

Museumless, one wandered the streets. The Lisboetas have had the quaint custom since the 19th Century of making their pavements of multicoloured stones called dragon's teeth, set in flowing patterns of pink, ochre and terracotta which seem to weave to and fro as one toddles along.

Tragically, since one had rather over-indulged in Nuit St Georges and Laphroaig the night before, the effect of this was to make one feel somewhat queasy, an effect not helped by arriving at the National Theatre, which stands on the site of an auto-da-fé was held during the Inquisition.

The starving, vermin-ridden prisoners were dragged out and asked three times if they would repent their faith. If they refused, their thumbs were crushed, their nails pulled out and their scalps removed.

If they refused a third time, they were chained to an iron chair over a fire and roasted.

Charming. You wouldn't catch the British treating people like that. Well, except in the Tower, of course, and one imagines anyone who was stupid enough to get themselves in there deserved it.

Still, at least we never had that sort of religious conflict in dear old Blighty, thank God. Well apart from Ireland, and that doesn't count.

Bless, me, look at the time – must be off for a swim and my rubadubdub with Melissa. Pip pip!

Splendid gel, Melissa turned out to be. South African, don't you know. Gave me the most remarkable pummeling since I chased a dog fox over the moor for three hours on Boxing Day 1957 atop old Thunderer. Splendid horse, but then he died, and was never the same after that.

Anyhow, one was lounging on one's balcony in one's bathrobe afterwards when there came a knock upon the door and one found this sultry chap standing outside in white gloves, dark suit, name of Carl. The chap, that is, not the suit.

"Afternoon tea, sir?" he said, indicating a tray on which were placed various delicacies of the pastry variety.

"And who might you be?" one said.

"I am your butler, sir," he replied imperiously.

"What? Thought young Zyta was the butler!"

"Indeed not. Zyta is the cabin steward."

Oh well, can never have too many staff these days, so had several ham sandwiches and a pot of English Breakfast, even though it was the middle of the afternoon.

Afterwards, went for a constitutional by the pool, beside which several German captains of industry lay beached, and returned to one's cabin to find an invitation from the captain to an ouzo party.

Dreadful stuff. Had to drink several to find out quite how dreadful. Captain a very jolly Greek chap, name of Papanikolaou. Can't understand why these Greek chappies can't have simple names, as I remember saying to old Bunny 'Wet Towels' Fetherington-Blythe-Giblet-Hastings when we toured the Acropolis some years ago.

Anyhow, told the captain the old joke about the Greek method of abandoning ship: captain and crew first. Didn't appreciate it, though. Some people have no sense of humour, what! After dinner and a whisky and cigar in the club, toddled off to bed and a series of disturbing dreams involving Melissa galloping across the fields on old Thunderer in '57 wearing jodhpurs and little else.

Hardly surprising, then, to wake up and find that one had gone blind. However, closer inspection revealed that ship had docked in Spain in heavy mist.

Pottered off into narrow streets of Vigo past ancient widows selling oysters. However, after night dreaming of Melissa had no need of same, and eventually found little café where proprietor, seeing me yawning volubly, brought tiny white cup of coffee which exploded like caffeine bomb in region of central nervous system.

Returned to ship and walked around deck several hundred times in mist to ward off effects.

Tragically, when the sun came out at noon, one became mysteriously afflicted with the conviction that one was Italian or some such and spent the afternoon sunbathing, with the result that one woke the next morning a rather fetching shade of cerise.

As a result, one decided to stay out of the sun for the morning and go instead on a tour of the kitchens, which was possibly unwise in retrospect, since at any moment a passing sous-chef could have mistaken one for a lobster and flung one into a vat of boiling water.

Accompanied on tour by chief food-wallah Marco Goetz. Splendid chap, Swiss by origin and as happy as a cuckoo clock in spite of having to come up with 9,000 meals a day. Made a mental note to point this out to the dear lady wife the next time she gets a little tetchy at organising dinner for Bunny and Mrs Bunny.

Anyhow, woke the next day to find oneself in Le Havre. Of course, there was nothing there to see, since the entire city had been bombed to a pancake by our chaps during the last war then rebuilt rather appallingly in concrete by that chap Auguste Perret.

Instead, hailed a cab, pottered down the coast to Honfleur and had a delightful lunch by the harbour, spoiled only by accidentally telling the waitress that her French was terrible, when one meant to say one's own. Lucky one's old French mistress wasn't in earshot, or one would have been given a damn good thrashing and sent off to the dorm with a dog-eared copy of *Salut Danger*.

And so to Belgium, famous for... er, yes, quite.

Could have gone to Brussels for the day, but since one had been before, and one's seeing of the only sights - the little boy having a tiddle and the Grand Place – had taken precisely 47 minutes, there seemed little point in going back.

Can't see the point of Brussels, come to that: bunch of fat pen-pushers with even fatter salaries paid for out of one's bloody taxes. I mean, what was the point of fighting the bloody war if we were all going to become Europeans?

Still, tried to enter into the spirit of things by going ashore and having several tons of mussels and chips washed down with gallons of beer while enormous women trundled past with small, yappy dogs.

After meal, got to feet with difficulty, staggered back to ship and was met by one's butler with afternoon tea, which one took on one's balcony as one admired a sunset exactly the colour of old Bunny's nose after one pink gin too many.

And then the strangest happened as one sat there in the powdery twilight looking back on one's rather splendid week of cruising.

One cannot think of how to describe it, except to say that one felt quite at peace with one.

1999

...and Copenhagen on the trail of Kierkegaard's outside toilet

Tragically, I had arrived just in time to miss the World Santa Convention, in which more than 100 Clauses dance around a Christmas tree in the town hall square before adjourning to a nearby hostelry to get red-nosed on Yule Ale, compare beards, complain that you just can't get the reindeer these days and discuss whether or not little Jimmy at 3 Edgbaston Close really deserves a new Power Ranger set after that little incident with the neighbour's cat. However, all was not lost.

I had to my possession a copy of *A Necessary Warning to Everyone Who Visits Copenhagen From A Man Who Knows The Town*, Julius Strandberg's 1861 guide which contains timeless advice from the very first sentence: "One has the Pavement Rights when one has the Road-way on one's right Side, and one need not then move to the Side for those Ladies to whom one would show good Tact. If one has the Road on one's left Side, then one does not have the

Pavement Rights, i.e. when walking on the Flagstones, one is obliged to give way to on-coming Pedestrians not voluntarily giving Relinguishment to that Right."

Well, thank heavens to get that cleared up.

Strangely, I had also brought with me seven ancient LPs which I had bought the day before in a shop six miles from Scotland.

They included cello concertos by Vivaldi and Boccerini, overtures by Rossini, Beethoven's fifth and ninth symphonies and one called Lola Tsakiri sings with The Trio Manitaras, for which the only excuse I can offer is that was just 50p. It later turned out, when I got it home and played the entire collection of scratchy monophonic recordings on my hugely expensive stereophonic apparatus, to be Greek table dancing and plate smashing music.

But then, if God had meant us to be sensible, he would never have invented the Citroën 2CV.

Anyway, where was I? Ah yes, in Copenhagen. In 1881, according to Strandberg, the Danish were noted for their kindness, and today they still are, even when they are not Danish.

Our taxi driver, for example, a Serbian called Goran, kept our bill as low as possible by driving most of the way from the airport to the hotel at 75mph, helpfully pointing out on the way the university buildings dotted around the city where his brothers and sisters were studying. The languages department, naturally, was near the airport.

We had a pint of Murphy's in the hotel's traditional Red Lion English bar, tipped the barman well, bearing in mind Strandberg's advice: "Gratuities are an unpleasant Evil, but...I would advise you not to forget a little Token for the

Waiters; they have nothing else to live on, and if you forget them, then next time they'll forget you, and let you sit until the very last", and went to bed.

Strangely, there seemed to be no Danish bars in Copenhagen, for the next morning, the first sight that greeted us around the corner as we set off with Susanne the guide was an Irish pub called Rosie McGee's, whose attractions, according to the sign outside, included ceilidh dancing, theatre, Mexican haciendas, a log cabin, Scottish and American lounges and that well-known Irish tradition, a mermaid bar.

"Copenhagen has been an important port ever since we sold fish to the Catholics," said Susanne. "For Fridays, I mean."

Today, more profitable activities include buying tax-free Mercedes, running them as a taxi for three years, then selling them to private citizens, who have to pay the tax, at the same price you bought them for.

Less financially rewarding but more socially aware pursuits in the city include running one of several community newspapers such as the one named after the former red light district known as Pisserenden, literally the street of...well, work it out for yourself.

Indeed, the subject of going to the toilet crops up more than once on a walking tour of Copenhagen.

Five minutes' walk away from Pisserenden is Magstrade, or Street of Calm, the setting for the former public toilets where the populace gathered for a bit of peace and quiet, perched on planks above the canal reading the Ekstra Bladet, having a smoke and contemplating the price of herring and the meaning of life, which for many years in Scandinavia were the same thing.

Indeed, it is not unlikely that Søren Kierkegaard, the father of existentialism, first came up with his theories about the meaning of life while sitting there wondering why his fiancée Regine Olsen had failed to understand his deeply significant epistle to her called Either/Or.

Mind you, few other people understood it either, and if you've read any Kierkegaard you'll understand why Regine ran away and married someone else, since he was possibly one of the gloomiest philosophers ever, whose championing of individual will over social convention and rejection of materialism found him few friends among his stolid fellow Danes.

Still, it could have been worse. If he'd been born a few centuries earlier, he would have been one of the friars who pottered about the city in wooden sandals and grey habits, denied the right to own property and deeply respected for their piety until the Protestants arrived, accused them of being a bunch of lazy good-tor-nothings and threw them out.

Very spiritual folk, Protestants.

As a result, you never see a friar on the streets of Copenhagen these days. Or a dog, come to that. I pointed this out to Susanne over a lunch of chanterelles, those well-known singing mushrooms, and was rewarded with the information that there is in fact half a dog for every household in the city.

Unfortunately, she never clarified whether households got a choice over which half they got, or whether you had to spend your time buying cans of Pedigree Chum for the front half of a Rottweiler while your next-door neighbour wandered around propping up a back half which fell over every time it tried to lift a leg.

I was still trying to work it out as we set off for a splendid boat tour of the city, which included such intriguing moments as chugging down a channel between on one side the carefully tended torpedo boat sheds of what was until recently the Danish Navy headquarters and, on the other side, the rambling wilderness of Christiana, since 1971 a commune of 1,000 alternative souls who are to bourgeois Danish life what George Best was to synchronised swimming.

The tour also includes the Little Mermaid, which is the same colour as the Statue of Liberty, but smaller.

Do not expect the Little Mermaid to be spectacular, or you will be disappointed. Approach it rather with the attitude of Buddha when he said that when you expect nothing, everything is a gift, and you will be quietly pleased with it, in a Danish sort of way.

For the rest of the afternoon I wandered through the streets, watching people playing chess on corners - Copenhagen is one of the few countries in the world where chess is a spectator sport - and in the evening I ended up in a fine old harbourside restaurant at Nyhavn, where the wine bottle was graduated from 0-70 up the side. At first I thought this was to indicate my decreasing chances of getting home safely the more I drank, but it turned out to be just to show the waitress how much to charge me.

And then I went for a walk by the canal at the twilight time of day when for some reason colours seem to glow more brightly than in the day: the ochre and rust of the buildings, the lilac and red of window box hydrangeas and geraniums.

And above them the arched windows which seemed to tilt as the minutes crept by, reaching for the last light of the dying sky.

I went to bed, and as I slept the jet trails which had been left in the evening sky froze in the night and fell to rest between the telegraph poles of the city, so that children who woke early enough could telephone all their friends before the trails melted and their parents picked up the phone to pay bills or call their offices on the ordinary telephone lines used for ordinary things.

Having spent the evening drinking Carlsberg at a furious pace to keep up with the Danes around me, I woke up with probably the finest hangover in the world.

It served me right for having ignored Strandberg's advice: "Let yourself not, in the dry Summer Time, be lured by Thirst into stowing one Lager after another under your Waistcoat, for the Copenhagen Lagers are of the very highest Quality."

In any case, the best course seemed to be to return to the scene of the crime - the Carlsberg Brewery - accompanied by a guide called Henrik who leaned confidentially closer as we entered the main gates and said: "You know, Carlsberg Elephant Beer is the strongest in the world - apart from the stronger ones, of course."

Above our heads, carved into the sides of the four stone elephants which hold the arched gateway upon their backs, was the original symbol of the brewery, a swastika. It is, however, the 3,000-year-old Indian symbol of good and happiness, rather than an indication that after drinking Carlsberg all night your liver win feel as if it's been dive-bombed by Stukas.

Today, the brewery produces a billion beers a year, welcomes 136,000 visitors and contains in its cellars the world's biggest beer collection - 12,049 bottles bought over 25 years by a Danish engineer called Leif Sonne who's still at it - three days earlier he'd popped in with another couple of bottles he'd picked up in Greenland.

The brewery even has its own electricity generating plant. It's powered by natural gas, the inevitable result of the workers drinking beer all day. Actually, it's not; I just made that up.

In fact, like most modem breweries, it seems to be operated entirely by one man who presses the On button first thing in the morning, and the Off one when he goes home at night.

However; in spite of, or perhaps because of, the minimalist operation, Carlsberg seems to be so successful that if its promotional video is anything to go by, the company has taken over every other firm in Denmark, including the Royal Copenhagen Pottery.

Now, I'm afraid that my feelings about this are the same as about Belleek: that I can appreciate the skill that goes into making it more than the end result. Too overblown to love, too expensive to use, it fails to stir anything in me.

Thankfully, by the time the tour of the pottery was over it was time for lunch, which was three different types of herring, including a red herring which wasn't there. I think it had an effect on me, for in the afternoon I went to a design museum which wasn't open.

There was only one thing to do, and that was to go to the Tivoli Gardens for dinner.

The gardens are exactly the kind of place that when you are a child you hope being grown up will be like. Bands play, birds sing, people stroll under trees hung with lanterns and couples dine by candlelight.

What could be more perfect, especially if you dine at the Balkonen carvery in the middle of the gardens. Since it's self-service, just make sure you're the perfect host, give

yourself a 100 per cent tip, and get a free meal.
.

With the money I'd saved on dinner, I bought a pair of shoes in a sale the next morning and left for the airport at the same time as a convocation of men in grey suits arrived at the hotel and tried to get into their rooms through the keyholes.
They were, it transpired, the world's leading gynaecologists, who have a convention there at the same time every year.
So if you're ever planning to have a baby in the first week of August, just make sure you do it in Copenhagen.

1997

D is for dormouse hunting in Slovenia

A short history of Slovenia

6th Century
Slaveni arrive from Carpathian Basin and create Slav Duchy, which lasts about 10 seconds before arrival of Franks, Magyars and Hapsburgs.

16th Century
Reformation leads to publication of first Slovene book and grammar. Counter-reformation leads to both books being burnt before the ink is dry.

18th Century
The Enlightenment. Art and culture flourishes. Baroque buildings spring up all over Ljubljana with surprised looks on their façades.

1809-1813
Four years of rule by Napoleon gives Slovenes a taste for liberté, egalité and fraternité with their fellow Slavs.

1914-1918
Four years of First World War gives Austrian Slavs a taste of fighting Serbian and Russian Slavs, resulting in mutiny and the formation of the Kingdom of Serbs, Croats and Slovenes, including Bosnia, Montenegro and Macedonia just to be on the safe side.

1929
Locals, fed up taking all day describing where they're from, rebrand kingdom under snappier title of Yugoslavia.

1945
Yugoslavia becomes Communist Lite nation under Tito. Citizens, for example, allowed to travel abroad freely.

1980
Tito dies. Anarchy. In Slovenia, revolution led by artists, journalists and a punk band called Laibach.

1992
After a 10-day war in which 21 die, independence declared. In careful leaps and bounds, Slovenia transforms itself from communist satellite to democracy, joining Nato and EU and finally adopting euro.

Slovenia

In Slovenia, dormice were once hunted all year round, until they became so scarce that the dormouse hunting season was cut back to a single week every autumn.

A short but intensive period of activity which marks the beginning of a long, dark winter, especially for the dormice, this culminates in Dormouse Night, an evening of carousing, dancing and boasting about the one that got away.

To recreate the effect in the privacy of your own home, simply drink several bottles of wine, hold your finger and thumb a few inches apart, and repeat after me: *"Bil je talo relic."* ("It was this big").

As the plane descended towards Ljubljana in the afternoon light, the mountains all around were draped seductively in snow, forest and cloud, as if they couldn't decide what to wear that morning and had simply put on everything in their wardrobe.

Somewhere down there, dormice huddled in the shelter of trees, communicating with tiny walkie-talkies.

At the airport, Manja the guide was waiting. Like most Slovenians, she was tall, finely sculpted and fluent in 486 languages, plus dialects.

"You know," she said as we drove away, "when I was younger I couldn't wait to get away, but the more I travelled, the more I loved Slovenia."

I could see what she meant: as Slovenians will always point out to anyone who cares to listen, they're part of bright, modern efficient Central Europe, not the down-at-heel East or, God forbid, the turbulent Balkans.

If you ever see George Bush, who regularly confuses it with Slovakia, do have a word. And, while you're at it, tell all the tourists who've been avoiding it for the same reason that it only ever had a 10-day skirmish, while splitting up from Yugoslavia in 1991.

"Anyway, Manja, tell me about the dormouse hunting," I said, as we passed a string of shiny new Volkswagens and Audis.

"You know about dormouse hunting?" she said, her eyes widening. "Well, we hunt them at night and, when we catch them, there is much singing and dancing and, of course, drinking."

"Of course. What do you hunt them with?" I said, imagining tiny rifles exquisitely hand made by Italian mountain dwarfs.

"With nets. We cannot damage the fur or we would not be able to make coats with it."

"Good grief. How many dormouse furs does it take to make a coat?"

"Oh, lots," she said, which will hopefully teach me to stop asking stupid questions.

"And are we going to get a chance to go dormouse hunting?"

She gave me a strange look, but I gave it back, since I have enough of my own.

"Maybe tomorrow. Anyway, here we are at the ski factory," she said.

When the Slovenians are not stalking dormice, they are skiing. Forty per cent of the population can ski, and 60 per cent of the country is covered in forest. Since that leaves nothing much for dormice, they have gone underground, nibbling out vast bunkers lined with little Kalashnikovs for their Day of Revenge.

The first man to ski down Everest in one fell swoop, for example, was local hero Davo Karnica, and, of course, he did it on Elan skis, which, along with wine, bee keepers and dormouse coats, have been the country's most famous exports since the factory opened in 1945.

Inside, in a room lined with symphonies in poplar and ash, fibreglass and titanium, the firm's Matjaz Sarabon, a former downhill racer, was talking about the future of skiing.

"Today's skiers are more interested in fun than technique. They are less fit than before and just want an easier time," he said, with a palpable air of regret for the days when only men of steel could hurtle down mountains.

The future is even stranger: Elan has already patented a fusion ski in which the bindings are part of the ski so that the whole construction curves together, making turning easier.

"By 2005, separate skis and bindings will be history," said Matjaz confidently.

The factory is also experimenting with fabric-based materials to make skis. So, the next time you see a farmer hurtling down the Sperrins with a pair of Aran pullovers strapped to his wellies, do not mock, for he is at the cutting edge of ski technology.

On the way back to the car, laden with ski brochures, Manja dropped her keys in a snowdrift.

"Tri sto kosmatih medvedov," she cried.

"What does that mean?" I said, bending to dig them out from the snow.

"Three hundred hairy bears. It's the worst curse in Slovene. Apart maybe from 'Duck on the lake' and 'You are the mother of a chicken'. We don't really have any swear words in the language, to be honest."

And so, the next morning, to the slopes of Kranjska Gora, with the added excitement of wearing my very own ski boots, finally bought the week before after several years of dithering.

Sadly, I was admiring them so much in the queue for the ski tow that it found me first, with a whack on the side of the head which bled all morning.

"Good grief. What happened to you?" said Manja when we met for lunch.

"I was attacked by a rabid dormouse in the woods," I said, ordering the soup.

"Yes, they get very annoyed at this time of year because all their friends are coats,"
she said.

"When are we going hunting them so I can get my revenge?"

"Maybe tomorrow."

We were in the sort of traditional inn which features lots of meat, potatoes and strudel served by high-cheeked waitresses in low-cut dresses. It was like being an extra in a Hammer horror movie, except that Christopher Lee didn't stride in and sink his teeth into your neck after the pudding, which I find always takes the edge off a meal.

After lunch, I waddled back to the slopes to continue admiring my new boots, which were enabling me to crash so much faster and more comfortably than before that, by the end of the day, I was able to bury myself in snowdrifts with only the skis protruding.

Satisfied, I went back to the hotel, bled all over the bathroom and went out for a dinner of goulash with extra dumplings.

Afterwards, my stomach lapping over my belt like a high tide, I found myself in a pub called Papa Joe Razor. Inside, several people were dancing to a Slovenian pop song.

"What do the lyrics mean?" I asked Manja, who had appeared with two beers.

"They mean more or less: 'Let's drink until we feel like partying, then party till we feel like drinking some more'," she said.

At the bar, a girl with bright red locks was talking to a boy whose hair looked like a series of wheat sheaves springing from scorched stubble, below a ceiling from which hung a variety of agricultural implements.

I tried to think of this for a while as a metaphor of Slovenia's postmodern exodus from its rural past, then I stopped thinking and had another beer.

The next morning was Sunday. Church bells rang out in the clear, still air, and on the mountains, waterfalls froze like witches' hair.

Considering what my head had done all the day before, it was rather appropriate that we were on our way to Bled. Now in an ideal world, Bled would be twinned with Transylvania, but it is, in fact, a stunning lakeside town where the former Yugoslavian royal family, then Tito, spent their summer holidays in the monolithic pile which is now the Vila Bled Hotel.

My suite was so big that it came with its own boardroom. I had a bath, then got a taxi back to the bedroom and fell asleep.

The next day, realising by now that I was never actually going to get dormouse hunting, I took a cable car up Mount Vogel and spent the day hurtling down from the mountaintop, proving yet again the Micawber principle applied to skiing, that 100 per cent speed and 99 per cent ability equals disaster.

By the time I finished, the setting sun was painting the peaks rose pink, and the mirrored flat of Lake Bohinj far below was the colour of midnight.

The evening came, as cold as ether, and I walked up the hill in Bled to the baroque church of St Martin for an organ recital.

All the way up the path, candles flickered in the snow, and underneath the blue and golden arches as I stepped in, soprano Janja Hvala was singing *Sveta noc*, the Slovenian translation of that most memorable of Christmas hymns.

Outside, after the concert, all was still in the cold, dear air, and it was, indeed, a silent and holy night: in the stars above my head, in the candles at my feet and, most of all, in the sight out there in the dark of the moonlit spire of the church on the island in the middle of the lake which is to Slovenians more than anything else a symbol of their country.

It is to this church that they row out, to break the holy silence with its bell, and wish for the appearance of children, the health of grandparents or the love of strangers.

Manja's own mother had come here, after childless years of marriage, wished for a daughter and been pregnant within a month.

They come and make their wishes and then walk back down the ancient steps, their hearts full of hope.

And, as they do, they pass the little chapel of St Maria, in which a statue of the saint sits between two adoring cherubs, her hands a few inches apart, in exactly the manner of a dormouse hunter describing the one that got away.

2003

...and Donegal

A short history

Beginning of the universe to 1980
Sheep and poverty, occasionally interspersed by poverty and sheep.

1980 – present
Bungalows in hacienda styles I-IV with PVC windows, occupied by weekending lawyers. Sheep flee to Mayo in protest at both lawyers and windows.

We had a Harley, a full tank of gas, shades, leather jackets, faded Levi's and the open road in front of us, stretching all the way over the horizon to...Donegal.
Well, you have to start somewhere.
And when you're setting off next month to ride Route 66 from Chicago to Los Angeles, what better preparation than leaving Belfast on a cold and rainy Friday morning for Ardara?
You see, unlike what you might think, there are more than a few similarities between the two routes.
Chicago and Belfast, for example, have the same number of letters.
So do Ardara and Los Angeles, give or take a few.

And both Route 66 and the road to Ardara are black, with white lines down the middle.

In fact, the only difference I can think of is that Los Angeles doesn't have a mad Frenchman who owns a bed and breakfast exactly in the middle of nowhere.

Born in Morocco, Paul Chatenoud studied philosophy at the Sorbonne, then in the Seventies opened Librairie Musicale, a unique bookshop containing just about every book ever written in French on music.

On its dusty shelves, John Cage nestled up to Schubert and Pete Seeger jostled for space with Pau Casals.

Then, 10 years ago, Paul came to Donegal, fell in love with a hilltop cottage on a Wednesday, bought it on the Thursday and flew back to Paris on the Friday knowing somehow that life would never be the same again.

He sold the bookshop and the beautiful flat in Paris, moved into the cottage and sat down to write the definitive book on life, love, music, the universe and everything.

He finished the book, but like most great books, it remained unpublished, and Paul woke up one morning and realised that being an unpublished author is one of life's less lucrative vocations, only just worse in financial terms than being a published author.

"When I sold up in Paris I had plenty of money. I bought a Jaguar, gambled on the stock market and lived expensively. Now I was broke," he had told me on the phone.

However, all was not lost: he had become so used to hosting friends who came to stay that the obvious step was to turn the cottage into a bed and breakfast, slowly transforming the outhouses into extra bedrooms.

It helped that he is one of the world's most remarkably organised publicists. His pack of press clippings, photographs on CD-rom and comments from the visitors' book would have done credit to the marketing department of Disney, and the praise therein enough to make you think that the only difference between The Green Gate and heaven was that you didn't have to die to enjoy the former.

There was, in short, only one thing for it, and that was to see for ourselves. Which was why late that afternoon, frozen to our bones after the long ride from Belfast, I and Cate, my new girlfriend of three months, found ourselves in Ardara, and after asking a local man for directions and getting four different answers, finally rode up the steep, winding lane to The Green Gate.

Which was where things started to go what I believe is referred to in the trade as pear-shaped.

You see, Harley-Davidsons are built for going from New York to San Francisco in a straight line at 55mph.

They are not built for negotiating hairpin bends on steep, winding Donegal lanes at 0.5mph. Especially when the man in charge of gear selection has unaccountably picked second instead of first.

That was me, and as a result I quickly found myself in the rarely used horizontal motorcycling position, while behind me Cate was sailing through the air with the greatest of ease to land on the part of her body normally used for attaching her to sofas rather than Donegal lanes.

"Oh dear," she said when she had landed. "I don't seem to able to get up. It's either because I am paralysed, or because this lane is so steep that my head is below my feet."

"I do apologise, dear," I said politely, "but even worse, there seems to be petrol leaking out of the fuel cap over the hot engine, so we may well shortly be immolated."

She struggled to her feet and grabbed the bike, and we set to the task of hauling it upright, at which point we discovered that the problem with making a motorcycle with an engine the size of a car's is that you create a motorcycle which weighs the same as a car.

"You know," said Cate, "they really should build these things with sensors so that when they start to fall over, little stabiliser wheels pop out and stop them."

"And a stout rope with a block and tackle so you can haul them up steep Donegal lanes," I said.

Eventually we got it back on its wheels, only to find that the carbs had flooded and the engine wouldn't start.

"Never mind," said Cate, "we can just push it to the top of the hill."

Sadly, that proved easier said than done, and after 10 minutes we had covered, oh, a good six inches.

"I think we're going to be here for the weekend, dear," I said.

Thankfully, at this stage the engine coughed into life, and it was a weary duo who finally presented themselves at the door of The Green Gate five minutes later.

Paul, on crutches as the legacy of a recent knee operation, brought us in, led us to a bedroom with a window beside the bed so that we could lie in it and look at the sea, then sat us down in a living room and fed us tea, toast and jam from a wooden tray which contained 15 different preserves. I counted them.

A turf fire chuckled in the hearth, books on philosophy and music snoozed on each other's shoulders on the shelves, the humming chorus from Madam Butterfly drifted through the warm air, and outside the window a robin and a bluetit hopped among the daffodils.

Paul poured another coffee, and looked at his ancient watch. "What we need is dinner," he said, picking up the phone and calling Kevin, the local taxi driver.

An hour later, Kevin dropped us at Castle Murray House Hotel, where Claire and Thierry Delcros run the rather splendid restaurant. I could be wrong, but I don't think they're from around these parts.

"How much do I owe you?" I asked Kevin as we got out.

"Ah sure, I'll be picking you up later," he said.

We made our way inside, collapsed in front of the fire, and had a feast of grilled oysters, warm scallops, duck, ham, smoked chicken, walnut and goat cheese and salad.

Then we moved on to the main course.

Several hours later, we staggered out, fell into Kevin's taxi and were transported back to Ardara.

"Do you want some money yet, Kevin?" I said as we decamped outside the smallest of the village's 13 pubs.

"Not at all. I'll get you later," said Kevin.

Actually, when I say pub, I exaggerate. It was more of a large cupboard into which nine people, including a man from Anchorage, Alaska, had managed to squeeze.

At least I think it was nine: it was hard to tell, because the smoke was so thick that you could have cut it up and sold the slices as cakes to people who were pretending to give up smoking.

The barmaid, a handsome woman in a green anorak, was wearing a flying helmet, sunglasses and an oxygen mask.

"Is it because of the smoke?" I asked an elderly man sitting in the comer, dropping cigarette ash onto a two-bar electric fire, where it flared into a brief resurrection then settled dully onto the chrome.

"No, she thinks she's Amelia Earhart," he said in a voice all hills and dales.

His name, it transpired, was Patrick. He was wearing a pair of unlaced training shoes which had last been white when Elvis was thin, a pair of tracksuit bottoms from which the concept of shape had departed around the same time, a pullover of uncertain provenance and colour and a black plastic jacket which looked as if it had already begun to melt in the wavering heat from the fire.

His face, nevertheless, had the look of a sponge which had soaked up all the optimism in his life yet been rendered waterproof against cynicism.

What was left of his hair, finally, resembled a series of abandoned sketches for Hokusai's tsunami.

"Are you looking after yourself, Patrick?" said Paul from the other side of the room, or about three feet as the crow flies.

"Aye, although I still have the flu from Christmas," said Patrick, as if the illness had been a present from an unpleasant cousin.

"Do you have a turf fire?" said Paul.

"I have plenty of turf, but no fire," said Patrick.

Satisfied with this answer, Paul turned to the bar and ordered two bottles of stout and a whiskey from Amelia Earhart, and Patrick lit another cigarette from the embers of the previous one.

"You know," he said, "in 1970 there was a woman sitting where you're standing. Her name was Bolin Andersen, and she was from Copenhagen.

"When she left we kept in touch, and then she moved to Stockholm, and from there she wrote to me one October to say she was going to Kiruna, the last junction on the rail line north, because she had heard of a tiny blue flower which grew there.

 "I wrote back to tell her not to go in October, but the letter was delayed, and by the time it got there, she'd gone.

"Of course, when she got there she found nothing but snow, and I think she blamed me, for she never wrote back."

"Did you ever see her again?' I said, taking a sip of my stout.

"Three years ago another Danish woman walked through that same door. Her name was Kirsten Klein, and she was taking photographs for a book.

"I got talking to her, and when I mentioned Bolin her eyes lit up. 'Do you know Bolin?" I said to her.

"'Well, I did,' she said. 'I'm afraid she died of cancer two years ago.'"

"What a sad story," I said.

"It's a strange one, all right."

"What does Patrick do?" I said as we walked down the damp street later, thinking he was a slightly derelict character upon whom the owner had taken pity.

"He's the owner," said Paul. "His family have had that pub for 150 years, except for two years ago."

 "What happened then?"

 "Patrick bought his first TV and closed the pub for six months so he could watch it for 24 hours a day. Then he got fed up with it and opened the pub again."

Some time later, we found ourselves in Nancy's bar. Naturally, it was owned by a woman called Margaret, an elegant matriarch who we found holding court in a side room. At her feet, a dog called Guinness slept with his bum so close to the fire that it could only be a matter of time before it went up in flames and Margaret was arrested for arson.

"Is this your living room or part of the pub?" I said.

"I sometimes wonder," she said. Inside, the bar was crammed with everyone in Ardara and most of its hinterland, but as always happens in Donegal, stools were found for us and within five minutes we felt as if we had lived there all our lives.

Several pints later, Kevin appeared outside the door in his taxi.

"Kevin, for God's sake let me give you some money," I said as we finally fell out at The Green Gate.

"Aye, all right then," he said with a sigh. We shook hands with him, said goodnight to Paul, tumbled into a feather bed and slept the sleep of the gods.

- Sadly, Paul Chatenoud has died since this piece was written. A great loss.

2000

E is for Egypt

A short history

3000BC
Ancient Egyptians arrive, build pyramids, worship cats,
sleep with their cousins and die out, leaving cats sitting
around with smug expressions waiting for the next bunch of
mugs to worship them.

E gypt uses three calendars: the Islamic, the Coptic and
the Western. The Coptic dates from 284, the
accession of Diocletian, and is not much needed.
   To convert an Islamic date to a Western one, then, you
divide the Islamic year by 33, subtract the result from the
number you started with, and add 622.
   I added my granny's shoe size and divided by the average
number of goldfish in a posse just to be on the safe side, and
as a result left Belfast in the winter of 2002 and arrived in
Egypt in the middle of a medieval summer.
   The air was as warm and aromatic as buttered toast, and
from nowhere a flock of hawkers descended, as they would
every day for the next week, trying to sell postcards, camels
(one hump or two), goats, donkeys, the Pyramids, their
granny, Tutankhamun's coffin, mummified ibis, genuine

fake temple carvings, alabaster scarabs, papyrus and the Sahara.

Telling them all I would see them later, which was fatal, since Egyptian traders have a photographic memory for every victim they have ever met, I made my way down to the shores of the moonlit Nile.

All around, fishermen were furling the sails of their *feluccas*, the boats which have graced the river since before the Queen Mother was born, as I stepped aboard a floating Victorian palace called the Nile Legend. All dark wood and hanging lamps, it resembled a Mississippi riverboat from which a hawker had sold the paddle wheels to a passing American tourist.

The staff, all moustaches and smiles, ushered me up carpeted stairs to a dining room and handed me a drinks list which offered new French wine at a tenner a bottle, and the old stuff at a lot more. The whiskies were listed as Regular, Special and Extra Special.

I ordered a local beer, the cheapest thing on the menu, dined on a slightly reluctant chicken and went to bed.

The next day, I rose at dawn and went to see an empty graveyard: the Valley of the Kings, which is the most exclusive suburb in the world for dead people, and still being uncovered in spite of centuries of grave robbing.

The largest tomb of all, that of Ramses II and his 98 sons, is so big that excavations will not finish in our lifetime, but even that of Ramses IX, a tenth of the size, is breathtaking.

It is astonishing to stand there gazing on the images of kings and queens, of golden barges and burnished thrones, and to think of the armies of men who stood here and created, over three millennia ago, an edifice monumental yet graceful, vast yet infinitely detailed.

At first, in a mad frenzy, you rush around them all: Amenophis II, with its colours as bright as dawn, or Ramses IV, with its monstrous sarcophagus.

But then you realize that they are all astonishing, and that they have all another thing in common: they were all robbed, by everyone from disgruntled tomb workers to corrupt officials, from the pharaohs themselves, desperate for gold to pay for iron weapons, to 19th Century gentleman thieves looting the graves for drawing room souvenirs.

All robbed, except the one I left until last, that of Tutankhamun. Even the name sent a shiver down my bones, as it had for Howard Carter when he opened it in November 1922, with his bankrupt sponsor, Lord Caernarvon, breathing down his neck.

At first, he could see nothing, then everywhere, the glint of gold.

I made my way down the steps and gazed on the golden face of the boy king, and found it hard to believe that this was one of the smallest tombs in the Valley, built in haste after Tutankhamun died at 19.

And yet it yielded 1,700 treasures which take up an eighth of the national museum in Cairo.

As I walked away, I tried to imagine the scale of the other riches which had vanished from this desolate valley into the hands of fools.

And failed, utterly.

In the shimmering heat, we visited briefly the vast temple of Hatshepsut, the Thatcher of ancient Egypt who ruled as a man for 20 years, complete with false beard. When she finally fell, like Maggie she fell hard, and all her images have been obliterated throughout the temple.

Even a history set in stone can be rewritten: sometime, as in the Colossi of Memnon in the verdant valley below, by an earthquake.

These 70ft seated statues were knocked up by Amenophis III, who loved his wife, his mistress and the 317 damsels he kept for cold winter nights so much that he called his palace The House of Joy.

Still, that was enough sex and culture for one morning, and it was time for lunch back on the boat. We weighed anchor - it was about half a ton, dripping weight, since you ask - and headed south.

Sailing down the Nile Valley in the limpid afternoon, it was immediately obvious how much it is the artery that feeds this dry and barren land.

It was as if God, clearing out the cupboards on the sixth day of creation, had suddenly discovered a ribbon of lush greenery he'd forgotten about, and only a desert left to put it in.

The truth, of course, is more prosaic: 10,000 years ago, Egypt was the Ireland of Africa, until disastrous climatic changes. Today, 96 per cent of the country is uninhabitable because it is desert, and the rest is uninhabitable because there are too many people in it, most of them trying to sell you something.

This was not so much of a problem in 1882, when the population was seven million, the same as it was in Cleopatra's day. But today it is 68 million, and rising at a million every nine months. In Cairo, three million alone live in the Necropolis among the dead.

Nasser's plan of education and jobs for all, which looked so possible during the Seventies, when the country was £15 billion in the black, now struggles under the weight of a national debt of £18 billion.

It was all Amenophis' fault. All that sex has become the national pastime, and the House of Joy has become a house of cards.

Good heavens, I didn't mean to get quite so serious there. One minute I was sailing peacefully down the Nile, the next I was in the middle of a political crisis.

Here, let me have a beer and calm down. Ah, that's better.

I went to bed, dreamt of the price of fish, and woke next morning refreshed and ready to go on the trail of Flaubert, who when he arrived in Esna, was propositioned by a courtesan who came aboard his boat with her pet sheep, its fleece polka-dotted with yellow henna.

This fabulous creature – the woman, not the sheep - sent the novelist into raptures by blindfolding the musicians, performing a languid striptease then ravishing him senseless several times over.

"Watching that beautiful creature asleep (she snored), my night was one long, infinitely intense reverie," he wrote at the time.

However, there being no courtesans or spotted sheep in sight when I arrived at Esna, I had afternoon tea instead. With two biscuits.

By nightfall we came to Edfu. In the lilac and marmalade dusk, a pair of white egrets, that most elegant of birds, rose and flapped across the mirrored Nile, as perfect as their reflections, each to each.

Then, as we turned to dock and the ship's lights flickered on, a row of children came to stand by the water and watch, as pale as ghosts in their loose, flowing *djellabas.*

To them, we must have seemed as incomprehensible as if the Starship Enterprise had come to visit. Perhaps Erich von Däniken was right, and the aliens who had come to show the Egyptians how to build the pyramids were actually a group of German structural engineers on holiday.

But no: Howard Carter would surely have found buried in the sand small but unmistakable fragments of beach towel.

We dined on several hundred courses, mostly starters, and in the absence of any entertainment, I went to bed with a large book.

At dawn I rose and walked to the Temple of Horus, 180 years in the building and the best preserved of its kind in Egypt.

You stand looking at its vast carved façade, and can only imagine what it was like painted, with flags fluttering down over the 100ft high cedar doors, which only opened for the chosen few.

Inside in the shadows, an endless hall of columns leads to the granite shrine to Horus, whose golden statue was clothed and perfumed daily.

The Egyptologist Michael Haag had written of a ceiling painting in an antechamber of the sky goddess Nut, "with unusually fine breasts and profile, pale green with a blue skirt of stars". But try as I might to find her, I left Nutless.

On south we sailed, and the band of greenery on either side grew narrower as the desert crept close. The air felt breathless, as if the life had been burned out of it, and along the shore, Arab boys could be seen at their favourite occupations:
a) Standing in the river
b) Fishing
c) Fishing while standing in the river

Nearby, watched by a sanguine pelican, a breakaway group in a rowing boat were towing a bullock across the river, much to its disapproval.

A mile down the river, I could still hear its anguished bellows as I stood up, staggered, and felt the unmistakable symptoms of heat exhaustion: headache, giddiness, nausea and a sudden desire to move to Iceland.

Fortunately, it was just coming up to teatime, and there are few things in life, except perhaps having your head chopped off by a mad axeman, that cannot be cured by a nice cup of tea.

All around me, the passengers, all Irish or English, were queuing for tea and buns. Most of them were white or fat, and several were both, which was worrying: we are used to Americans being bundles of lard, but this was the first time I had noticed the trend creeping east of Mullingar.

Now, I'm afraid I'm a bit of a fascist about fat, and put it down to sheer laziness clothed in a veil of excuses about slow metabolisms or sedentary lifestyles, whereas in fact the so-called secret of losing weight and staying healthy is blindingly simple: eat less, exercise more.

I was just about to suggest to them all that they might like to consider 30 press-ups or 200 sit-ups before they were allowed their dinner, but at this moment I noticed Salah, the guide, and went over to ask him if the tap water was safe, since I'd been drinking it for three days and the thought had just occurred to me that this was why I was feeling close to death.

"Well, I wouldn't touch it myself, but it's perfectly safe," he said.

That night, the boat had an Egyptian fancy dress party, and although dressed like Muslims, they still drank like

Christians, so it was a liverish party which set off the next morning for the great dams at Aswan.

The first of these was built by the British in 1898, and the second, finished in 1971, ended floods and famine, created three harvests a year and provided 70 per cent of the country's electricity.

Unfortunately, the Egyptians were so excited by all this that they immediately went to bed and started making more children, thus creating such a population explosion that the country is now back where it started.

The feeling here, at the southern tip of Egypt, is of being in Africa. The heat is more oppressive, the flies more persistent and the people Nubian: gentle, black as night and valued since long ago as slaves and dancers.

Eight hundred thousand of them were displaced by the building of the second great dam, and one of the few left drove us before lunch to a papyrus shop. Papyrus was the e-mail of its day, since before then letters were written on stone, weighed half a ton and had to be delivered by two Nubian slaves, or three for first class.

High on a wall in the shop was a copy of the most famous papyrus painting of all: The Judgement, the original of which is in the British Museum. In it, a dead man's heart is weighed against a feather. If it is lighter, he goes to heaven.

We could all hope for that, a heart as light as a feather. Or indeed, that we should smell as sweetly as we did after our next stop, a perfume emporium.

In a mirrored hall, veiled Nubian beauties brought attar of roses, frankincense, myrrh and black narcissus.

I emerged aromatic and blinking into the noon sunlight, and took a boat trip in the lake, passing in a languid daze the scenes of colonial life: the botanical gardens of Kitchener's

Island, the Old Cataract Hotel where Agatha Christie set part of Death on the Nile, and the mausoleum of the Aga Khan, for which his widow had fresh roses flown from Paris when none were available locally. As we returned to the shore, the boatmen burst into that traditional Nubian refrain She'll be coming round the mountain (when she comes).

After nightfall, the same boat took several of us under the full moon to a melodramatic but effective *son et lumiere* spectacular at the island Temple of Isis.

Isis was the It Girl of her day, a fascinating and vibrant goddess who rather tragically lost out as a female icon to the relatively boring Virgin Mary, who, having had the pain of childbirth without the fun of conception, started a love of suffering which is continued in Christianity to this day, particularly in Irish mothers.

Our boatman, meanwhile, was a Nubian who had only just got married.

"My mother picked her, so I only met her the day before. She is very nice, but not as good a cook as my mother, so I am only sad at dinner time," he said, his smile flashing white and gold in the moonlight.

In the morning, before the heat, I walked to the old bazaar, accompanied for most of the way by an insistent *caléche* driver whose motto, rather than the traditional Arabic greeting *Asalaam aleikum,* should have been *Hassle'em aleikum.*

Egyptian men, it seems, just don't understand the word no, which may be the real reason behind the population explosion.

I was the only white person in sight, and the warming air was thick with the smells of a thousand spices which lay in rainbows on either side for a mile, interspersed with gum, ebony, cotton, silk and, quaintly, Titanic baseball caps.

There was saffron, worth its weight in gold, and in one hessian sack a blue powder as vivid as lapis.

"Da ay?" I asked the shopkeeper, an old man with some teeth, but failed completely to understand his reply. He rolled the cloth of his *djellabah* between finger and thumb, and I understood. It was the dye used by the Tuareg, called the blue men of the desert because it rubbed off on their skin.

I thanked him, and looked away, above the heads of the Egyptians, the Nubians, the Sudanese and the Ethiopians.

And almost saw, in the dust clouds to the south, turbaned men with great scimitars, walking out of the burning sands with many head of camel, each of them laden with treasures as immeasurable as the lost gold of the Pharaohs.

2002

F is for Flanders

The numbers are the third worst.

Six hundred thousand dead at Passchendaele. Seven hundred thousand at Verdun. A million at the Somme.

The names are the second worst; row upon row on the Menin Gate, row upon row on the white Portland headstones of the graveyards, as tidy in death as this battlefield never was in life.

Names like the Australian twins Ina and Clement Moore, who enlisted together in their home town of Ballarat in July 1915, and were blown to bits together exactly a year later.

Names like Joe Valentine Strudwick, the youngest soldier to die a month before his 16th birthday, or Lt Col John McCrae, the Canadian surgeon who wrote In Flanders Fields in 1915 and died three years.

Or names like my Great Uncle John, who came home with lungs ruined by gas and spent the rest of his short life coughing through the long, lonely nights, his only reward the medals which sit on my desk as I write this.

At least he came home. Over a million did not, half of them lying in Flanders fields in named graves, and the other half either buried under headstones bearing the words chosen by Kipling, Known unto God, or not buried at all.

Just out there somewhere, under the poppies and the wind, leaving behind them a lost life, an empty chair by the fire, a ticking clock in a silent home.

But the faces are worst of all, in the photographs at the new exhibition in the Belfry in Bruges.

The lost, haunted faces of young men who thought they were marching out to honour and glory, but found themselves in a hell of mud, gas, machineguns and barbed wire.

And for what? Four long years of yards gained then lost, thanks to generals devoted more to a strategy rooted in the days of swords and cavalry charges than to the lives of those in their care.

As I stood and looked at the photographs, the bell in the belfry above began to toll with a deep, sonorous timbre; a sound not heard during the war, when the Germans melted down all the bells in the land to make guns, leaving behind a still, sad silence broken only the thunder of those guns.

I looked at my watch. It was 11 in the morning on the 11th of November; a century to the hour and day after the war to end all wars.

And then the bell stopped, and a few moments later there came from the street below the sound of a military band, marching along to the pomp and bluster of a jaunty air.

We will, it seems, never learn; as I found the next day when I drove to the battlefields of the Western Front through farmland so flat it was so easy to see the few meagre mounds both sides had fought so bitterly to have and to hold, their names now stains on the pages of history: Messines, Passchendaele, Hill 60 and Tyn Cot.

The last, named because the Northumbrian soldiers thought the German pillbox on top of the hill looked like one of the

Tyneside cottages of their home, was then a maelstrom of machine guns and mud.

Today, with 12,000 graves, it is the biggest Commonwealth war cemetery in the world, its headstones lined up with such military precision that you can almost imagine a ghostly sergeant major bellowing: "Jones, you horrible little man! Get your bleeding corpse back in line double quick, or your life won't be worth living!"

At the top of the hill, that pillbox still stands, looking down on the graves of all the men who finally captured it in October 1917, and it is the easiest thing in the world to simply walk up to it and read, among the wreaths, a handwritten copy by schoolboy Taff Jones of Dulce et Decorum Est, Wilfred Owen's bitter poem about how it is not so sweet and honourable, after all, to die for your country.

Unlike the 160 pristine Commonwealth cemeteries, the German ones, by contrast, are sombre places, their dark granite slabs shadowed by lonely oaks.

Strangely, many of them contained wreaths left by the British, perhaps as a faint echo of that famous Christmas Day in 1914 when both sides exchanged food and souvenirs and took part in an impromptu football match between the trenches.

The introduction of poison gas and sawtooth bayonets in 1915 led to such hatred that it was never repeated, and the British retaliated by using gas as well; and when the wind changed, managing to poison 16,000 of their own troops.

It was one of Field Marshall Douglas Haig's trinity of disastrous decisions, along with the Somme and Passchendaele.

In October 1914, his senior staff had based themselves in the beautiful old chateau at Hooge, giving the Germans a good reason to pound it to smithereens.

By 1915, it was called Hellfire Corner, where at one stage a German shell was landing every five seconds, and today it is a roundabout beside which a little shop was offering 40% off teacups.

On Hill 60, another strategic mound, sheep grazed on the grassy drumlins. Underneath lay tens of thousands killed by the massive synchronised mine explosions of June 1917, and a few yards away, a plaque marked the spot where the SS shot two Resistance members three days before the end of the Second World War. As I said, we never learn.

A total of 1.5 billion shells were fired during the war. A third of them are still there, killing people who find them, and a farmer near here found 800 mustard gas shells in one field alone. The Army took them away and dumped them in the North Sea, before the practice was banned in 1973.

In the golden light of late afternoon we came at last to Ypres, the lovely old medieval city almost completely flattened and so painstakingly rebuilt it was not finished until 1967.

It is, of course, the site of the Menin Gate, and if the headstones in the graveyards of Flanders are divided into known and unknown soldiers, on this 1927 arch are inscribed the 55,000 names of the really unknown who have no grave at all.

At 8pm the buglers of the city fire brigade would come here to play the Last Post, as they have done every evening since the arch was built apart from during the Second World War.

But in the meantime I wandered down to the market square and sat on a bench to enjoy the last of the late afternoon sun.

After a while I was joined by a small black cat taking the same pleasure.

He had that smugly contented look that cats have, as if they know more than we do, but aren't telling.

But then he had good reason. Across the square stood the magnificent Cloth Hall, the medieval base of the fabulously wealthy clothing merchants.

And until 1817, it was their custom to keep cats upstairs in the winter to chase mice away from the precious wool, then in the spring throw them to a hostile crowd below, their slaughter symbolising the death of evil spirits.

The tradition was restarted in 1938, but with cloth cats rather than real ones, so my furry friend had every right to look smug, not just because he was safe from slaughter, but because he knew that man's inhumanity to cats pales into insignificance compared to man's inhumanity to man.

I said farewell to him and escaped from the shadows of the past, going walking the next day through the cobbled streets of Bruges, the once fabulously wealthy medieval clothing centre which then fell into decline for centuries and returned to life as a tourist destination thanks to the British on their way to the nearby battlefield of Waterloo and the French visiting after reading about the city in Georges Rodenbach's novel *Bruges-la-Morte*.

I bought chocolate and lace, and took a canal tour, under 13th Century bridges, past bobbing swans and a dog looking out of a window, in the bittersweet blessing of an autumn sun, both a ghost of summer and a herald of winter.

Life. Ordinary, glorious, everyday, happy life. Denied to so many who lost it, enjoyed by too few who have it.

2014

...and Finland

A short history

3000 BC
Early Finns arrive from Siberia, having abandoned the Hungarians and the Estonians for not drinking enough.

1155
Country torn between home-grown paganism, Swedish Catholicism and Russian Orthodoxy. English Bishop Henry arrives on Crusade, and tells Finns that from now on, only drinking will be communion wine on Sundays. Finns think about it, then kill him.

1374
Swedish noble called Grip decides to live up to his name by taking grasp of entire country.

1495
Russians invade, and are miraculously driven back by tiny Finnish army. Finns celebrate with much drinking, only to wake up next morning to discover that they're not only hungover, but still Swedish.

1711

Peter the Great has another go, starting years of Russian occupation so bad they became known as The Great Wrath.

19th Century
Student leader and future statesman Johan Vilhelm Snellman begins wave of nationalism with the cry: "Swedes we are no longer, Russians we cannot become, Finns we must be."
Swollen by plays of Aleksis Kivi and Elias Lönnrot's publication of collection of folk tales as The Kalevala, wave becomes a tsunami.

1899
Russians ban Sibelius' Finlandia for being too patriotic. Rather than renaming it Russiaia, Sibelius calls it Opus 26 No 7. Russians then introduce conscription and install draconian governor-general Nikolai Bobrikov. Finns have a think about it, then shoot him.

1917
Independence. Civil war, which traumatises Finns so much they stop drinking for first time ever.

1932
Prohibition ends, followed by mother of all parties.

1939
Finns wake to hangover and war, in which vastly outnumbered Finns fight off Germans once and Russians twice. Russians, slightly miffed, seize lucrative east of country and impose huge reparations, which Finns pay off to the last rouble on time. Then decide to celebrate with a

sauna followed by a party which in spite of recession, unemployment and having an angry Russian bear permanently on your doorstep, continues to this day.

Finland

I was halfway to Helsinki before I realised that I only knew two phrases in Finnish.

But then, *Kaksi olut, olkaa hyvä* (Two beers, please) and *Anteeksi, missä on WC paperi* (Excuse me, where is the toilet paper?) should cover most eventualities.

And I need not have worried. By the time I got to the bar of the airport hotel, the owner had already doubled my vocabulary.

"Here, have a *glögi* before drunch," he said.

The first was a glass of spiced wine with almonds and raisins, and the second he'd just made up because it was too late for lunch but too early for dinner.

Suitably glögified and drunched, I found myself on a plane to Kajaani in the frozen north, where the national elf display team, clad in red outfits and floppy hats, had laid on an impressive display of synchronised scampering and carol singing.

Just down the road was Katinkulta, a collection of 158 holiday cottages dotted around a clubhouse.

The cottages were delightful, with the sort of sumptuous minimalism typical of Finnish design, the sort of cosy warmth typical of triple glazing and the sort of heroic sticking plasters in the bathroom cabinet typical of a nation which traditionally expects the best yet prepares for the worst. Comes from living next to Russia.

The clubhouse was even more impressive. Driving around the comer and seeing it in winter was like opening the fridge door to find the spaceship from Close Encounters.

Inside was a tropical forest, swimming pools, tennis courts, squash courts, a bowling alley, saunas and steam rooms, gyms, shops, bars and a restaurant where that night we had what looked like finely chopped elf but turned out to be lamb stew.

"That's funny. I was in Albania last week and we had reindeer steak," said the man beside me.

That explained it. In the mix-up after the French lorry drivers' strike, the Albanians got our reindeer and we got their lamb.

Roger, the man on the other side of me, meanwhile, was battering the chap opposite to death with travel statistics.

"Been to 77 countries – bam! Record's 10 in one day driving from Scotland to Italy - biff! Not to mention 22 American states - bop! Every province in the Netherlands – wham! And, of course, every district in Germany – kapow!"

"Roger, listen," said the chap opposite, gamely trying to change the subject, "I was just thinking this afternoon what a good idea it would be to compile a book of elves."

"What, like how they use the National Elf Service, listen to Elvis Presley on the BBC Gnome Service, go to Philadelphia or Belfast for their holidays, put themselves first, hang little plaques above the mantelpiece saying Gnome Sweet Gnome or Helf, Welf and Happiness, and say 'I think it's going to reindeer' every time they look out the window?" said Roger.

As the other chap collapsed under the table with a limpid groan, I thought for no obvious reason of what my three New Year resolutions would be.

1. Learn to play the piano.
2. Improve my memory.
3. Learn to play the piano.

I wrote them down in a little book I keep for just that purpose, then forget to take it with me and went to bed.

The next morning, I woke to the stillness which means that it has snowed heavily overnight. Outside, it was 15 below and felt like the middle of the night, but in the clubhouse, several early risers were swimming about in the tropical waters. From behind the nearest bougainvillea wafted Bing Crosby singing White Christmas, and outside the door the chief transport elf was waiting with a bus to the elf training grounds nearby, dozens of red-clad elves were busily engaged in reindeer patting, snowmobiling, falling into snowdrifts, sledging and general scampering duties.

"Are you cold?" said one.

"Not too bad," I said as I climbed into the 6ft 7ins romper suit he handed me. "And you?"

"Freezing," he said.

He turned out to be the chief snowmobile elf, in charge of instructions. Snowmobile instructions go something like: "That's the throttle. That's the brake. Off you go."

Off I went, zooming halfway up the nearest mountain and returning to find all the elves rolling around with laughter because an English tourist had just asked if he could have a go on a toboggan.

There were two reasons for this. Firstly, Finns think toboggan is the silliest word they've ever heard, and secondly, they are filled with joy that there is an English word longer than the Finnish equivalent – *pulka*.

In fact, the word toboggan has the same effect on many Finns as marijuana has on other people. They laugh a lot at first when they try it, then they're quiet for a while until one of them tries it again and starts everyone giggling.

I was just about to set off for a second snowmobile assault on the mountain when I heard the faint wailing of a siren in the distance. It was the Finnish drugs squad, and it was time to get out of here. Not just because I was about to be busted for possession of a toboggan, but because it was time to see Santa.

Santa lived a 40-minute bus ride away, through a landscape which had been reduced to its most fundamental elements – white snow, black forest, silver birch bark, the pale gold of the twilight sun creeping along the horizon followed by a ghostly rainbow, and in the vast deep blue above, a single star and a crescent moon.

It was such a magical sight that it seemed entirely appropriate to pull up after a while in front of a rambling log cabin, knock on the door three times and be shown by two elves down a flight of steps and along a corridor into a cosy room.

And there was the man himself, surrounded by knitting elves finishing off woolly pullovers, origami elves folding Christmas cards, catering elves making gingerbread men to a secret recipe then killing themselves because they knew too much, musical elves playing Rudolph the Red-Nosed Reindeer and off-duty elves playing Patience.

Santa, who was sitting in a rocking chair beside a leather-topped desk, looked exactly like Santa should. With masses of white hair, grandfather glasses perched on a round nose above a flowing beard and a merry twinkle in his blue eyes, he looked remarkably well for a 420-year-old.

Well, he thought he was 420. He'd lost his reindeer driving licence with his date of birth on it about 250 years ago, he was just telling us when the cynical chap from the Guardian broke in.

"Tell me, Santa," he drawled, "just how do you manage to get around all the houses in the world on Christmas Eve?"

"Magic, of course," said Santa. "And you know, I'm sure, that I only go to the houses where they believe in me."

Santa 1, Guardian 0.

Thousands of children, of course, come here to see Santa in the weeks before Christmas. Some of them, ridiculous as it may seem, don't believe in him when they arrive. But they always do when they leave. And quite right, too. A world with no magic is no world at all. And don't forget, children, every time you say you don't believe in Santa, an elf dies somewhere in Lapland.

Shaking Santa's hand and wishing him and Mrs Claus a merry Christmas, I got back on the bus and went to dinner at Karolinenburg, a wonderful old manor house built in 1836 and run today as a family hotel.

Father wandered around smiling amiably at everyone, mother did all the work, eldest daughter welcomed everyone in an Australian accent and daughters two and three entertained the guests with after-dinner elf dancing.

Much later, I found myself back in one of the cottages at Katinkulta discussing with two women the problems of love. Sadly, by the time we'd found the answer, we were so drunk we'd forgotten the question.

Somewhat confused, I staggered out into the biting cold intending to go back to my own cottage, only to find that a blizzard had sprung up.

After half an hour of wandering around, stopping briefly to give two Finns who were even more lost than I was a push to get their car started, I found myself back at the cottage where I had started.

By the time I finally made it back to my own, it was five in the morning and I couldn't find any of the light switches.

Few people know this, but the reason the Finns held out for so long against the vastly superior Russian forces during the Winter War of 1939-40 was not just because they were better fighters. It was because they hid all the light switches.

After quite some time I found a bed that I wasn't in, worked that it must therefore be mine and fell into it, waking what seemed like five minutes later to realise with a clang of horror that I was due to go on a snowmobile safari into the forest.

Crawling into my snowsuit and staggering out into the blizzard, I found the familiar figure of the chief snowmobile elf.

"Let's go. If I raise my left hand, it means stop," he said.

"OK. If I raise both hands, it means I've fallen off," I said queasily as we climbed on matching snowmobiles and bounced off into the forest.

It was all exciting boyish fun, really, like Biggles in the Fridge, I thought as I roared along, struggling to keep down the breakfast I hadn't eaten.

After an hour, we stopped at an isolated farmhouse to be welcomed by the farmer's wife with hot glasses of glögi and toasted cheese covered with cloudberry jam.

It was the sort of food that made you glad to be half alive, and by the time we got to the next stop, a primitive log cabin with a roaring fire, I was ready for lunch.

Lunch was salmon which had been cooked by the simple expedient of nailing it to the wall behind the fire for three hours, and something which the chef described, worryingly, as elf soup.

Oh dear. I'd assumed when I got off the snowmobile and looked around to find no elves in sight that they were still in the local clink from yesterday's big toboggan bust.

But all was well. He'd actually meant elk, and as I wandered back to the snowmobile later through the snowy forest, several familiar red-clad figures appeared in the gathering twilight.

It was like being in the middle of every Christmas postcard ever made.

Soon it was dark, but there was still plenty of time before dinner for a spot of floodlit skiing, at which I proved yet again the Micawber principle as applied to skiing, that 100 per cent speed and 99 per cent ability equals disaster.

At the top of the first slope I met a Helsinki man called Sauli. Like most Finns, he wore the latest designer spectacles, through which he peered at me briefly before announcing significantly: "Telemark is fun", then steering himself down the hill in a series of graceful turns while standing on one leg.

"Very impressive, Sauli," I said after I had got to the bottom with a series of barely controlled disasters.

"If you need any advice, just ask," he said cheerily.

Thankfully, I didn't take up his offer, for on his next two runs he managed to gracefully demolish a marker pole, his Armani spectacles and the right shoulder of a middle-aged Englishman.

The Englishman's companion, an attractive blonde woman in her late forties, meanwhile, had lost a 500 *markka* note worth about £66 in the snow and given up any hope of ever seeing it again, only to find later that a teenage snowboarder had handed it in to reception.

Very honest people, these Finns.

And courageous, too. On the way home from Kajaani, I spent a few days in the south of Finland with Seija Väyrynen, my oldest friend, with whom I had been a penpal since I was 13 and she was 11, and her husband Jarmo.

On the Saturday, we got home from playing in the park to find the feet of their two-year-old daughter so frozen that we had to soak them in hot water for half an hour. Yet she had not uttered a single word of complaint, and neither did their four-year-old son that night when he managed to hammer a nail into his foot.

Now, in another country, four-year-olds would be given a plastic hammer and nails, but in Finland they get the real thing.

The hole in his foot was washed and dressed by his mother, and he went back to hammering nails into blocks of firewood with slightly more careful gusto.

The Finns have a word, for that silent, tenacious courage. They call it *sisu*, a word which also sums up the sort of inner strength needed to live in a country which is both beautiful and fatal, as several Swedish, Russian and German armies have found to their cost.

They have an even more legendary quality than *sisu*, though, and that is their legendary drinking ability.

Only the Finns, for example, could think of throwing vodka onto the coals of the sauna so that you can get sozzled without even having to open your mouth.

So it is hardly surprising that my enduring memory of that week was not meeting Santa, eating elf soup or even smoking illicit toboggans.

It was not even the memory of the monumental feast that Seija cooked us that night, of ham with prunes, codfish, carrot and swede casseroles, beet-pickled herring salad with sour cream, salmon, cheese, cloudberry jam and smoked reindeer.

No, it was running out of the sauna at five in the morning and diving naked into a snowdrift at 20 degrees below freezing.

Some men leave their hearts in San Francisco, but I went to bed at dawn fearing I had left something even more important in a snowdrift in Finland.

We rose at noon, dressed up warm and had a lunatic breakfast at a wooden table in the snow-draped courtyard outside their home, as the neighbours looked over their balconies and came down to say hello. Polish sculptors, Australian actors, French painters came and went, over coffee and cheese, ham and pickled cucumber, dark bread and honey.

And then we walked down by the river in the winter sun, buying lilac cups and slender glasses, and drinking beer in a converted chemist's shop, its dark interior aromatic with old wood and hops.

We drove to Naantali, a village on the coast, where the sudden rain drove us into the Café Antolius, run by Aatos Tapala, a former opera singer who fell in love with a local beauty and became an innkeeper so he could be close to her.

There, we drank coffee and ate apple pie, toasting our toes in front of a log fire.

The tick of the grandfather clock and the slow ticking of the candle marked the passage of the afternoon as the rain washed the windows and the streets outside. I ordered more coffee and apple pie, and thought that there was nowhere on earth I would rather be.

The days stretched by, sharp and golden, aching for the grail of Christmas.

One afternoon we bought birch baskets and wooden brushes, and by accident tickets for a Sibelius concert, which is regarded by Finns the way more southern people regard chapel.

That evening we hurried by the river as the evening sky grew dark and the cathedral bell rang six, and as we walked across the bridge and up the hill the last pale light of the day caught and frayed on the wrought iron of the city's highest towers.

As we rushed into the foyer, almost late, we passed a flurry of friends in all the washed colours of the rainbow, somehow managing to agree with waves and handshakes to meet in the old chemist's shop afterwards.

In that moment, it seemed as if life was possible, after all. And the moment stretched on through the evening, as I sat at a rough wooden table in the old chemist's shop drinking beer and listening to the Finns laughing and joking in their utterly impossible language, as beautiful and incomprehensible as pebbles in a fast stream, or someone hunting through a cutlery drawer. Time and again I closed my eyes and dreamed that I was in heaven, then opened them and found that I was.

The day after, we drove to a little wooden house in the forest, to have a sauna and dinner with friends.

A wonderful place for baring your soul, the sauna. It's difficult to be pretentious when you're stark naked and dripping with sweat. It's also a great place for sorting out the world's problems, especially after a couple of bottles of beer.

For dinner we had the old stew from Karelia, *Karjalanpaisti*, and the little parcels of spiced rice called *Karjalanpiirakat*, washed down with wine and followed by liquer made from the cloudberries which glow like tiny suns in the darkness of the forests of Lapland.

In Helsinki, we had coffee in the Kappeli, the café down by the waterfront where Sibelius used to come when he was in town to gaze gloomily out across the bay to where I imagine he imagined happiness lay.

He should have known that happiness was where he was, sitting at a table in one of the bay windows, as cool and green as an aquarium in summer, and in the winter as warm and welcoming as the womb.

Or in the Finnish Forum of Design, full of objects far more beautiful than words.

Or sitting at teatime in the vaulted waiting room at Helsinki railway station, filled with Finns sitting on the sofas or leaning into conversations across the marble tables, contentedly slurping beer of coffee as they wait for the trains that will take them out of the city to where a rectangle of light marks the welcome of their wooden home in the dark and whispering frost.

Or even standing watching the work of art that is a birch tree, with its silver trunk, its gold and iron leaves.

Seija and Jarmo drove me to the airport, and I hugged them goodbye and took the last plane home to Christmas, feeling sure that I was going the wrong way.

1996

G is for the Great Wall (of China, that is)

Mandarin is one of the easiest languages in the world, with a mere 56,000 characters and four different tones to each syllable which completely change the meaning.

For example, the word *ma* with a high tone means mother, with a rising tone hemp or numb, with a falling then rising tone horse and with a falling tone to scold or swear.

So if you wish to swear at your mother for making your horse numb by feeding it hemp, you simply say: "*Mamamamama*".

In fact, Chinese is so simple that everyone in China speaks it, even small children, and by the end of a large gin and tonic on the flight to Beijing, I had completely mastered it.

Tragically, I then completely ignored the advice of Dorothy Parker when she said that one cocktail is never enough and two is always too many, and had another, by which stage I had completely forgotten everything again.

Oh, well. I sighed, and as the plane began to descend into Beijing, I took out my ticket and searched it in vain for the missing day.

You see, we had left Belfast on Saturday morning, travelled for a day and would arrive in Beijing on Sunday night, which meant I had lost a day somewhere.

Now, I've often wondered where yesterdays go when we're done with them, but this was the first time I'd lost a today. Even worse, it was a Sunday.

Stall, there's no point worrying about todays, since they're just the tomorrows you worried about yesterday, so I put away the tickets, settled back in my seat, and looked around at my travelling companions: 71 people who had raised half a million pounds for the mental health charity Mencap, and were now going to earn it by trekking the Great Wall of China, armed only with legs of steel, wills of iron and unlimited supplies of that gastronomic icon of the Ulster traveller, Tayto cheese and onion crisps.

At Beijing Airport, a large sign said: "Warning - no zygotes, embryos or genetically modified organisms may be brought into the country."

I checked my pockets carefully, found none, and entered China.

There are 1.2 billion people in the country, and most of them were in the arrivals lounge talking at the top of their voices.

The rest were outside. Once, all of them would have been riding bicycles with a finger permanently on the bell, but now half of them were driving cars with a hand permanently on the horn.

For the amazing thing about China, as Mao found, is that there are so many people in it that you can remove millions of them without anyone noticing.

In The Great Leap Forward of the Fifties, for example, the fat lunatic decided that everyone should build a blast furnace in their back yard in a bid to transform China from an agricultural to an industrial nation.

Using up scarce wood, taking farmers off the land and producing steel that no one wanted, the scheme starved up to 60 million people to death. That's the entire population of the UK, give or take Bernard Manning and a few stray cats.

It is no wonder that the Mandarin for "Hello" translates literally as "Have you eaten?"

As for the Cultural Revolution, along with the People's Liberation Army that other great oxymoron of 20th Century Chinese history, no one knows how many millions died.

It is, in retrospect, remarkable how one unhinged fanatic can rule a country through fear for so long, until you realise how many others have been at it: Hitler, Stalin, Ceausescu, Maggie on a bad day.

Anyway, where was I? Ah yes, on the bus from Beijing sitting behind a girl who, combined with 30 hours without sleep, jet lag, and the constant jangling of bicycle bells and honking of horns, was driving everyone within earshot close to justifiable homicide.

"It's very flat, isn't it? What are those trees for? What a lot of bicycles. Some of them have motorcycles, don't they? It's very dry, isn't it? The old women seem to sit around and talk a lot, don't they? Is that a mountain?"

Outside, the scene was unprepossessing: dun flatlands broken only by the occasional bright ribbon in the hair of a girl. In front of simple brick houses with a bicycle leaning by the door, chickens scratched in the dust. It was like Tyrone in a Fifties drought.

After several hours we climbed into the mountains and were decanted into a courtyard in front of an office whose various signs announced it to be the Center of Reception, Consulting, Lawsuit and Tourist.

This was the lodge which was to be our billet for the night.

I collected a key from the Center for Tourist and let myself into a frozen room in which 10 minutes of gurgling, coughing and moaning from the shower finally produced a rivulet of lukewarm water onto the brown tiles.

I washed, shivered, and arrived in the dining room, which was even colder, just in time for the briefing by Lucy, one of the expedition doctors. She looked about 14.

"Do take care of your drinking," she said. "I'd recommend at least four litres a day."

I went up to the bar immediately and bought 12 cans of beer, only to find out, tragically, that it was water she was talking about.

With a sigh I left 11 back, opened the other one and had dinner, which was so delicious that it can only be a matter of time before the Chinese start opening restaurants in other countries.

It was 9pm, and I had been awake for 33 hours. Back in the room, I crawled into bed with my feet dangling over the end, opened The Chronicles of Narnia, and fell asleep after two words.

At dawn the next day, I flung back the curtains to reveal the rugged mountains stretching all the way to the horizon and a queue stretching all the way to breakfast.

Just ahead of me when I got there were Avril and Janice, who by the look of their carefully coordinated trekking outfits were from Bangor or thereabouts, and who had brought not only unlimited supplies of tinned spaghetti bolognese, but a hot water bottle.

"My feet were still freezing. It's been ages since I did my Duke of Edinburgh. More tea, anyone?" said Janice as we took our seats beside Noel Thompson, the man from the BBC who was recording a radio documentary on the trek.

And so, spag bol and hot water bottles packed away, to the Great Wall.

At the top of the mountain we reached one of the guard towers which punctuate the wall every few hundred yards, straightened our backs and took in the vista for the first time.

As far as we could see, along each of the highest and most inaccessible peaks all the way to the edge of the world, snaked the wall, made of bricks cemented by rice flour, a substance so binding that later in the week I was to understand for the first time why so many characters in Chinese novels suffer from permanent constipation.

A signal made by fires of burning wolf dung could be flashed from tower to tower the hundred miles to Beijing in 12 minutes, although all it would say would be: "Cold. Bored. About to be overrun by Mongol hordes. Send help in three weeks to collect corpses."

The wall itself was an astonishing sight for which no amount of photographs or reading could prepare you, and my heart lifted as much as those of the slaves and soldiers, widows and children, peasants and convicts who built it over a period of 2,000 years must have sank as they looked at these same peaks and realised the task ahead of them.

Particularly if they knew, as we do, that one of them would die for every yard of its 35,000 miles.

On some sections, such as those built by the fastidious Lord Cai, each inch of the wall took a day to build. His lordship was later beheaded for such extravagance, although when his section was judged the finest part of the wall, he was posthumously rehabilitated, which must have been a great relief to him.

It was almost impossible to imagine such things, so instead I imagined something easier.

A million soldiers had guarded this wall, and one of them had stood at this arched window where I stood now. I knew because he had carved his name in the rock, along with some graffiti which presumably said: "Mongols out" or "Genghis go home."

He had stood here day after day, far from his family, frozen in winter, windblown in spring, roasted in summer and soaked in autumn, looking down at the slope up which at this moment a goatherd was bringing his flock to graze, the morning sun warm on his red smock.

He stopped for breath, looked up and saw me standing at the window a hundred feet above.

"Ni hao," he called up. *"Ni hao, ni hao,"* I called back, and for a moment the world was one.

But then, it was impossible to know where the ancient world ended and the modem one began here: in the afternoon, as we climbed down a valley of woods and terraced fields, we came upon an abandoned thatched cottage.

Inside was all the detritus of a medieval lifestyle; a wood and wicker yoke, a ladder bound with rope, a wooden bucket.

The family had moved a few miles down the valley and built a larger house which was guarded by twin gold and red dragons and an imperiously ruffled rooster.

In a dusty field beyond, two small donkeys with helicoptering ears chewed corn stalks, and a smattering of baffled cows discussed the weather. The family's number one son had just finished milking them, and was walking back to the house with two brimming wooden buckets swinging from a wooden yoke.

We downed our packs and slumped against a hedge for lunch, joined by Jason, who had set up the trek.

Helicopter pilot turned expedition organiser, Jason was the sort of chap who would have been shooting down Messerschmitts over the Channel two generations ago.

"Been doing much recently, Jason? I said as I shelled a boiled egg.

"Oh, not really. Just a dog sled race 30 miles north of the Arctic Circle in 35 below. The Norwegians said I'd take five days, if I finished at all."

"And did you?"

"Absolutely. Two days and a bit. Fifteenth out of 44."

"And the Norwegian teams?"

"Five dropped out. Three got lost."

Splendid. So if you're ever organising a war, give me a ring and I'll just make sure Jason is on our side.

As the afternoon slid down towards evening, we climbed back down the rest of the mountain to our lodging for the night to be met by a cadre of souvenir hawkers.

"Hey wa, you buy book, look, beautiful, this photo my brother, T-shirt, look, big size, postcard, look many photo, dragon carving very old, look handmade, necklace, look, for your wife girlfriend, wa."

"No, no thank you very much."

"No please thank you very much, look!"

In the room, the bed was harder than the Great Wall had been. Below the window, a white box produced noise, but no heat.

In the dining room, which was marginally warmer, I found Linda, who looked like a smaller version of Bjork.

"Here," she said as I sat down beside her with a plate of beef and noodles, "how many yuan are there to the pound?"

I told her.

"Oh dear," she said. "I've just paid 15 quid for a postcard."

I went to bed, and was reading through my Guide to the Great Wall when I came across the following disturbing sentence: "Warning: the ancient path along the Wall to Simatal is only for the brave and fit."

It wasn't joking: the next morning we rounded a corner and fell silent as we were confronted by almost vertical climb of several hundred steps.

"Eek," said Linda, who at a shade over 5ft, was about the same height as two steps.

"Boys and girls," said Gillian the guide, "welcome to the step class from hell."

Kevin, a veteran of previous treks in the Sahara and Namibia, produced a hip flask of Jameson's.

"Alcoholics Unanimous," he said. "Fancy a nip?"

"Bit early for me, Smedley, old bean. I'll have a pink gin when the sun's past the yardarm," I said.

"You'll be doing rightly if you find a yardarm around here," he said, taking a handsome swig as we set off.

Half an hour of assorted screaming, fainting and heart attacks later, it was a weary bunch who slumped against the wall of the tower at the top.

By now it was lunchtime, and we were glad of it. You are glad of many small things when you are trekking that you do not appreciate in normal life. Like the way your water bottle gets lighter as the day goes on, or the way your daysack weighs less after you have taken your lunch out and eaten it. Of course, you are still carrying the same weight in your stomach, but it is literally a weight off your back.

And we were just about to need it: after crossing a giddy suspension bridge high above a wide green river, we faced a climb which made the step class from hell seem like a Debenham's escalator.

Several of the girls in the group collapsed halfway up and were relieved of their daysacks by some of the more gentlemanly chaps.

After several hundred more steps, though, even the most gentlemanly among us were beginning to think it might have been easier to fling the bags over the cliff, particularly since some of them seemed to contain a year's supply of make-up and chocolate bars.

It's amazing how quickly adversity can turn you from Gandhi to Goebbels.

Fortunately for the future of chivalry, at this stage we came to the cable car which swayed us, steaming and panting gently, down the mountain under a rising moon.

And after that, it was just a gentle dander through a wood by a lazy river to our five-star hotel, a hot shower and a feather bed.

Only joking. It was a campsite on a grassy plateau, Wet Wipes all round and a sleeping bag. Well, except for Jason, who faced a two-hour trek back up the mountain to retrieve a camera and passport that two of the group had managed to leave behind.

The rest of us sat outside our tents as the sun sank and the full moon rose high above the mountains, rubbing aching muscles and examining painful blisters. Except for the trekking veterans, who had taped up all their toes in advance.

At last, when all were clean and healed, there came from a rise above the campsite the sound of a beer can being popped and chicken sizzling on a barbeque.

Fed and watered, we took to our beds and the campsite settled down for the night. The moon sailed on over the ragged peaks across which marched the silhouette of that most admirable and terrible of man's feats, the Great Wall of China.

We slept, silent in the arms of history. Until the entire campsite was awakened an hour later by John returning from the beer tent singing at the top of his voice: "I wish I was back home in Derry."

A sentiment which, at just that moment, we all profoundly shared with him.

In the morning, the sun rose beyond the mountains to reveal a scene of almost unworldly beauty. And Noel Thompson shaving.

"Noel, you don't need to shave for a radio documentary," I said.

"One must look one's best for a waiting nation," he replied splendidly as from all around came the sounds of the waiting nation waking.

"Bloody hell I've never been so cold in all my life! Did you sleep?"

"Not a wink. God, it's FREEZING!"

Indeed, they were not far wrong. I had forgotten unique trekking feeling of washing in sub-zero temperatures with a frozen Wet Wipe, dressing in clothes which crackled with the cold and staggering with hands deep in pockets to be more grateful than I thought possible for a hot breakfast of that traditional Chinese delicacy, fried egg butties and beef noodles washed down with warm peach juice.

Believe me, if you'd been as cold as we were, you would have wolfed down warm cardboard and asked for more.

There were other small pleasures, too, in the frozen dawn, like the heat of the sun on your face as it clears the mountains. Pleasures we forget, in our centrally heated and double glazed world.

And out of adversity comes great reward, like climbing late that morning with Elaine, who had struggled with fatigue and vertigo the day before, and who today had climbed an almost vertical cliff face with a pack on her back.

"You know," she said, "I lost my mother and father when I was three and six, and I've never had anyone to help me or guide me. When Gillian the guide held my hand for the last hundred yards, it meant more to me than anything that's ever happened in my life."

She was crying, and it was all I could do not to burst into tears myself. At the end of the trek, Elaine would say to me in the hotel in Beijing: "That was the best week of my life. It was worth being born for."

We stopped for a lunch of cheese and lettuce sandwiches which had been made by the intriguing method of placing the cheese at one end of the bread and the lettuce at the other, then set off for the scariest bit: the last climb up a crumbling wall to the highest tower of all, walking along a ledge a foot wide with the valley floor several thousand feet straight down.

The guardians of this lofty eyrie, as they looked down upon the four horizons of their vast land, must truly have felt the mandate of heaven upon them.

In the afternoon we made our way slowly down the terraced slopes of the valley, past a goatherd calling: "Wo ka ka ka ka" to his flock.

"What does 'Wo ka ka ka ka' mean?'' I asked Nikita, the translator.

"It means 'Wo ka ka ka ka', she said sweetly.

Silence fell. Through the dry grass, our boots made silvery whispers, like secret cocktail party conversations, as we approached the village where we were to spend the night.

When Jason came here two years ago, hiking in over the mountains, the village children screamed and ran away, because he was the first westerner they had ever seen.

Today, the strange foreigners are almost normal, and trekkers raise much of the £30 a year it costs to send these children to school.

It means so much to them that one girl stays during the week, sleeping in the classroom, and others walk four hours a day to school and back.

Some of them were coming towards us now, skipping and hopping along the dusty path. And although the land was as dry as a priest, they were as bright as Christmas decorations as they passed us, practising their English with a blossoming of bright hallos.   .

We camped in the village playground and ate goat and noodles under a full moon, while in the classroom behind us, her books under her pillow, slept a little girl who had been given the most precious gift of learning.

It rained in the night, bringing forth from the woods beyond the village the tender scents of jasmine and pine, myrtle and apple blossom.

And bringing forth the children, who had walked down the long mountain trails in daisv chains of two or four for the start of their school day.

At ten to eight, as they pottered about their desks putting out their books and pencils, the words of the Ode to Chairman Mao crackled forth from the loudspeakers above No 2 Classroom.

"He is the sun that rises in the east. And brings light to all the land.

He is the father of us all. And we will love him forever."

"Of course," said the translator with a nervous smile, "we do not necessarily believe this any more."

Then, with a whistle from the headmaster, the children ran out for morning assembly in the playground where, to the breezy air of the national anthem, they saluted the raising of the national flag.

At the top of the pole it fluttered gamely, a symbol of a land which is no longer quite communist, but not yet quite capitalist.

Of course, to a child with the mountains all around, the sun rising and the day of their lives just beginning, all that does not matter, and as they trotted and skipped back to their classrooms, laughing and smiling, several of us were close to sniffling as we remembered for a moment what it was like to be alive when the world was brand new every day.

Not me, of course. I'm a tough bloke. Hanky, anyone?

With a last wave, we shouldered our packs and set off reluctantly into adulthood.

Even grown up, though, it was a fine thing to step out into the day, strolling between the river and the trees in the warming sun.

Someone among us was whistling the theme tune to The Great Escape, and that was exactly what days like this were: a great escape from mortgages and bills, dry rot, rising damp and all the other shoddy cares with which we drag ourselves down from the peaks of youthful ambition.

Ahead of me, Mark was telling Janet that his father taught physiology at East Antrim Institute.

"Here, I think he teaches me," said Janet. "What do you call him?"

"Dad," said Mark.

Just then there came a soft puttering up ahead, and around the comer rode a farmer on an ancient Chang Jiang 750, four baffled chickens in one of his panniers and two white ducks sniffing the air from the other.

Half a mile further on, a dozen other ducks were splashing about in the river, saying to each other: "Here, isn't it exciting that Hei-San and Li-Jing got a ride on a motorcycle! What time do you think the farmer will bring them back from the market?"

I tiptoed past, looking the other way and humming pointedly to myself.

Compared to the rigorous climbs of the day before, today was a bit of a dander, through little villages where at the sight of us geese stopped splashing, hens paused in mid-cluck, dogs barked up all the wrong trees and the entire population of seven came out to see what the fuss was about.

As you would if 20 Chinese people arrived in your village.

At one house, the 75-year-old grandmother invited all of us into the courtyard so she could admire the whiteness of our skin, tell us that our breasts were enormous, especially the women, and introduce us to her grand-daughters, who were feeding their respective babies from rice bowls.

As we left, Bridget gave the grandmother a bar of expensively luxurious chocolate.

"No, please," said the old woman, handing it back. "You are walking all day and you are far from home, so you need it more."

An hour before dusk we arrived at our lodgings for the night, only to find every shower freezing, so that everyone stomped around in a bad mood for an hour until we were greeted by the sight of Noel Thompson, that most respected representative of Her Majesty's British Broadcasting Corporation, appearing freshly groomed and anointed with expensive unguents.

"Good heavens," he said, "the water in my room was so hot it was almost steam."

He was immediately set upon and lovingly beaten to death with many chopsticks.

The next morning, after much gurgling and wheezing, the reluctant pipes were finally coaxed into giving up their burden of hot water, and we set off, washed and dried, only for the heavens to empty as we made our way down the mountain for the last time.

With the downpour worsening and the temperature plummeting, it was like a summer's day in Donegal as we wound our way down through the little villages of thatched cottages. Hewn out of the same stone as the mountains all around, they seemed to have grown organically out of their surroundings.

It seemed as if man and nature, past and present, had melded into one seamless whole.

I mentioned this to Dr Paul, one of the trek medics, and the conversation got onto future trips. He had taken six months off work and was off to Malawi and Cape Town after this, and I was trying to find a sponsor for riding a vintage motorbike from Siberia back to Belfast.

And that was how we crossed the line under a dripping Mencap banner in pouring rain, talking of the great adventure that life should be.

In Beijing the next day, the cherry blossoms were blooming in the steel and glass canyons of the new city.

I left it behind almost immediately, hiring a rickshaw and plunging into the heart of the old town, where barbers' poles spun, chickens sat in cages awaiting a spicy fate and toothless herbalists sold snake gall bladder.

On the pavements, repairmen attended to punctures or broken chains on some of the 50 million bicycles which throng the city, tinkling their way down the narrow alleyways and out into the wide boulevards.

There, over the past decade, they have been joined by what seems like the same number of cars, whose surly *nouveau riche* drivers rush everywhere slowly with their hands on the horn, going nowhere fast except a heart attack. In the back of limos here and there, through tinted glass, can be glimpsed that newest and most unwelcome arrival in China, the fat person.

Suddenly my thoughts were interrupted as the rickshaw plunged from an alley out into the bright sunlight of one of the boulevards Mao had built during the Cultural Revolution, tearing down ancient and revered buildings with the callous disregard that every dynasty in China has shown for its predecessors.

The lights at the crossing were green for us, but it was of no consequence to the phalanx of advancing cars. We hurtled across them in a cacophony of brakes, pleas, accusations and horns, somehow emerging alive on the other side with several other rickshaw drivers, whose drivers all took to slapping each other on the backs at their good fortune. For in Beijing, the green man at a crossing just means you may not be killed crossing, the red that you certainly will.

I suddenly realised that I was near the old silk market, so I paid the driver, stepped out and fell immediately into a medieval world of bartering, haggling and hawking which, apart from the fake North face jackets, Gucci bags, Rolex watches and Levi jeans, has not changed in six centuries.

Ten minutes of polite exchanges with a toothless grandmother produced an exquisite silk Mandarin jacket for Cate. Sadly, a short walk to the Friendship Store nearby then produced an even more exquisite one.

I could do nothing but buy it too, this time by a Byzantine process which involved choosing the jacket, taking the chit to a cashier behind a Dickensian desk, paying the required amount then returning with another chit to the salesman, who by this stage had wrapped the purchase beautifully in several layers of crepe paper.

Clutching my two paper packages, I tiptoed by the old lakes of Houhai and Shishai.

In rowing boats, lovers were loving, and on the shore, under the shadow of the Drum Tower from which imperial timekeepers once beat out the hours, old men whose age had not tarnished their optimism slept by their fishing rods.

By now I was at the gates of the Forbidden City where, as the guidebook elegantly put it, 200 years ago the admission price was instant death, but today it is a more reasonable Y30.

Unfortunately, I had given the last of my money to the rickshaw driver and a beggar, and was left to gaze up at the bejewelled gates with as little hope of gaining admission as the peasants who stood here for five centuries and wondered at the fabulous life their emperors lived inside.

I went off to find the beggar to see if he gave change for deserving causes, but he had disappeared into the alleys of the city's past, so instead I set off to walk around the moated walls of the Forbidden City.

It took me almost an hour to arrive at the other end and the vast opening of Tiananmen Square, where Mao would review parades of a million people.

Today, of course, it is better known for the massacre of 1989, an event conveniently forgotten by western democracies in their undignified stampede to get into the country and make several billion fast bucks.

In the centre of the square, amid the kite fliers and the strollers, a soldier stood guarding precisely nothing. There are, it seems, a lot of occupations in China whose job description reads: Must like uniforms and standing still for long periods.

As I retraced my steps past the lakes to the hotel to pack for the flight home, the late afternoon sun was playing through the cherry blossoms and dancing in flakes of gold on the water.

I closed my eyes and listened for one last time to the sounds of old Beijing: the splish and splash of lazy oars, the rickshaw drivers calling to all and sundry to clear the way, the click of *mah jong* counters, the tinkle of bicycle bells calling the city back to yesterday and the honk of car horns calling it forward to a more urgent future.

When I opened them, a small girl with a lilac bow in her hair was standing in front of me.

"Please," she said, "I am an artist at Beijing University and we are having our exhibition. I would be very honoured if you would visit us."

Half an hour later, I walked back to the hotel and left for the airport, in my knapsack a carefully wrapped scroll bearing in scarlet ink on handmade indigo rice paper three Mandarin symbols.

Above was the one for family, below was the one for friends, and in the centre was the one for the heart that binds them close.

Together, they made up the single word for love.

2002

Guyana

Guyana is like the Wild West designed by the Dutch, organised by the British and governed on the same basis as Northern Ireland.

The first because, until 1796, it was a colony of the Netherlands, which built many of the fine wooden buildings which grace the capital, Georgetown. Except that to keep their buckled shoes out of the mud in the rainy season, they added sidewalks which would not be out of place in Dodge City.

The second because the British, who took over from the Dutch, brought such civilising values as cricket, speaking English, driving on the left and, oh yes, the abolition of slavery.

And the third because the country's first reaction to independence in the Sixties was to split into two factions which run it as an edgy democracy until elections, after which the winners celebrate and the losers riot.

However none of this need trouble the couple of thousand tourists who arrive every year to enjoy the tableaux which result from the meeting of several cultures over several centuries.

Like a man shoeing a horse beside a Chinese laundry, across the road from the world's largest wooden cathedral. Or a row of stray dogs sniffing the breeze as they sit on the 280-mile wall the Dutch built to keep the sea out. The schoolboys cutting the grass in the 1924 British military cemetery. More schoolboys playing cricket on the green near City Hall, a building designed in the popular Hansel, Gretel and Addams Family style.

An old man, laden with plastic bottles, trudging past the prime minister's house. The sea cows, introduced by the Dutch to eat canal weeds, grazing in the ponds of the botanical gardens. The sadness of eagles and big cats, imprisoned in the zoo.

All of this to a symphony of *soca* from record shops, car horns honking and the commentary from a live cricket match pouring from countless transistor radios.

However, it is not the wonders of Georgetown that anyone comes to Guyana to see, but the wonders of the interior such as Kaietur Palls, at 741ft the highest single-drop waterfall in the world, to which I flew down the next day in a small aircraft.

Mind you, to describe Kaietur as just a waterfall is a bit like describing Everest as just a mountain. If you can imagine all the lost souls of the world plunging forever into Hades, you are getting somewhere near to the truth. You also have an overactive imagination, and should seek professional help immediately.

Walking back to the little airstrip, I stopped to examine a giant bromeliad, whose spoon-shaped leaves store water all year round.

From its depths, a tiny golden frog stared back at me. He looked as if he was trying to tell me something, and after a while I worked out what it was: get back in the plane and go to Baganara.

This, a luxurious neo-colonial pile on a river island, is an understandable favourite of several celebrities, including Mick Jagger, whose photograph adorns one of the walls. Honestly, Mick, you could at least have buttoned your shirt up.

An hour after I arrived, I had swum, showered and was ensconced in a hammock with a cold beer, watching the sun go down over the trees on the far riverbank. And an hour after that, I was sitting down to a silver service dinner at a table on the beach.

The next morning, I went walking through the forest, which held such delights as the Arara tree, whose toxic covering is used as an antidote to snake poison. Its bark is worse than a bite, you could say if you were inclined towards dreadful puns. Thankfully, I'm not.

It seemed, in fact, as if every other tree the guide stopped at was a source of food, medicine, poison, musical instruments, weapons, luggage, furniture and building materials. It wasn't so much a collection of trees as a branch of John Lewis – albeit a branch populated by thumb-sized insects, bird-sized butterflies and a tasteful ceiling display of tarantula webs, glistening above our heads like a hammock of horror.

It is also a superstore in which the background music is a cacophony of howls, bells, clicks, squawks and melodic convolutions which starts well before dawn and goes on until all the assorted creatures responsible knock off for a tea break.

It is also, it must be said, a superstore in which more care should be taken with the labelling: 10 years ago, eight workmen on the island mistook the bark of the Aromata, which is phenomenally toxic, for the Turu, which is used for making tea.

All eight died in agony.

Staying as far away from trees as possible, I tiptoed carefully back to Baganara.

About two miles down the river from the resort is a camp which the British Army uses for training, but as I sat down to lunch, I couldn't help but think that this was more the sort of tough jungle adventure I preferred: struggling to survive on Banks beer and three meals a day.

In fact, everything was going just about perfectly until Bjorn sat down opposite me at dinner.

I should have suspected the worst when he told me he was a Swedish engineer who lived in Singapore and specialised in deep bore drilling.

It was a talent he carried through to his private life, as for the next two hours his penetrating voice drilled into my head everything I had ever wanted to know about the courtship rituals of the white-crowned manakin, but had not known who to ask.

Finally, he yawned loudly, having wearied even himself, and picked up his dog-eared copy of Hilty's Birds of Venezuela.

"Well, must be off to bed. You have to get up at dawn to catch the really interesting birds, you know," he said, wandering off into the night.

I looked at my watch. I could have sworn that several years had gone by, but it was only nine o'clock. I ordered another rum, and very carefully destroyed all the brain cells containing any information whatsoever on the white-crowned manakin.

The next morning, I wandered down to the pier to catch the boat to Bartica, only to see as it drew in the dread sight of

Bjorn trotting up, a state of the art telescope draped around his neck and his copy of Hilty tucked under his arm. I stood aside politely to let him board first, then sat as far away as possible, lest he suck the will to live out of me like a sort of emotional black hole.

At Bartica, I breathed a sigh of relief as he stepped ashore and disappeared into the jungle. I headed in the opposite direction, down the village's only thoroughfares, loftily named First and Second Avenue, lined with bars filled with lumberjacks and gold miners happily spending their pay.

It was only mid morning, but the temperature and humidity were already over 100. I waited for the next boat downriver in the shade of a dockside bar, surrounded by locals drinking rum and watching a Pakistan v India cricket match. It was like being an extra in a Bacardi advertisement rewritten by Graham Greene.

Inevitably, as the boat appeared, so did Bjorn, looking pleased with himself at a sighting of the Lesser Bowlegged Sandpiper or some such.

"You should sit over this side. Better view," he shouted above the roar of the diesel, patting the seat by his side. I mimed a cheery deafness, and sat several yards away.

An hour later, the boat pulled in at a little wooden jetty, and I saw with relief the car waiting to take me to the Cara Lodge Hotel in Georgetown. I slipped gratefully into its air-conditioned chill, only to look around and see, to my horror, Bjorn jumping in beside me.

"You know," he said, resetting his chronometer, "that journey took exactly 59 minutes and 13 seconds. You don't mind if I share your lift, do you?"

Thankfully, for the entire journey he talked to the driver,

Belinda, about the lack of litter and chewing gum in Singapore.

I watched her carefully in case she nodded off and killed us all, until suddenly a dreadful thought struck me.

"Bjorn," I said as casually as I could, "what, er, hotel are you staying at in Georgetown?"

"The New Tropicana. Look, there it is. My wife thinks I'm crazy to stay at cheap places, but to me, a bed is just a bed," he said.

I breathed a short prayer of thanks to God, Allah, Buddha and the Seven Sainted Sisters of Constantinople as he got out, informed me in passing that the car journey had taken one hour, 10 minutes and 28 seconds, and strode into the foyer in search of fresh victims.

At the Cara Lodge, I had the blissful experience of dinner on my own, several beers and no information whatsoever on the mating habits of any birds anywhere in the universe, and the next morning I left for the interior: an eight-hour drive down a dirt road, through blizzards of suicidal white butterflies who whirled towards the windscreen like snowflakes.

Our destination was Iwokrama, a wildlife research station deep in the jungle at which we were met by the splendidly named resident biologist Waldyke Prince.

His assistant was called Edghill.

"My mother actually called me Adrian, but the priest who baptised me was deaf," he said by way of explanation.

"Anyway, you're just in time for a refreshing stroll up the mountain," said Waldyke cheerily. I dumped my bag in a log cabin, sprayed myself all over with insect repellent and followed him into the jungle.

Almost immediately, the sunlight disappeared. Far above

our heads, vampire bats slept, awaiting the destiny of the night. In front of me, Waldyke waved a stick to stop us accidentally logging onto a tarantulas's website.

"Careful of that bullet ant," he said, pointing to an inch-long creature sitting on a branch. "It's called that because that's the effect its sting has."

Ah hour and a half later, we finally reached the top of the mountain to find a view of the following: an electrical storm raging over the Venezuelan mountains on the horizon; millions of trees; one river; and a reflection of me in the water bottle, weary and soaked with sweat.

As experiences go, it was almost as good as the shower and beer when we got back, in increasing order of both coldness and satisfaction.

Dinner was served on a terrace by a shy Makushi teenager. As she padded to and fro with rice and chicken, bats flitted above her head, an emerald green insect crawled up the wall, and there came from the shortwave radio in the office the hiss and crackle of fractured signals from the distant, alien civilisation of the modern world.

The next day, I found myself eating chicken soup in a native village, watched intently by a three-year-old called Michael.

"Are you going to the jungle?" he said.

"Yes, later."

"Big black snakes in the jungle."

"Oh dear. How big?"

"This big," he said, holding his finger and thumb as far apart as he could get them.

As I finished my soup, three donkeys appeared in the doorway, followed by Milner, the head man.

"Right," he said brightly, "time to walk to the camp. Only two hours."

I sighed, shouldered my pack, assured Michael I would watch out for big, black snakes, and set off. Just before dark, tired and soaked in sweat, we arrived at a hut by a river and put up the hammocks and mosquito nets. Oh well, I thought, at least I can have a swim in the river to cool off.

"I wouldn't do that if I was you," said Milner as I stripped to my shorts and trotted down the riverbank.

"Why not?"

"Piranhas."

It grew dark. We ate chow mein and crept into our hammocks, surrounded by the sounds of creatures waking, going out for a refreshing stroll in the moonlight, and eating each other.

After five minutes, I realised I needed to go to the toilet. I reached down for my torch, something unidentifiable ran over my hand, and the torch rolled out of reach.

Below the hammock, I could hear more unidentifiable things scurrying about. There was no way I was putting my feet out there without the torch. And a pair of Kevlar wellies.

All night long, as I lay awake, the howler monkeys wailed with a sound like a banshee convention.

Next year, I thought as dawn broke over the jungle, I may well stay in The Ritz.

2004

...and Greece

In AD95, just before the Queen Mother was born, the Roman emperor Domitian banished John the Evangelist to the lonely island of Patmos.

"Don't worry," said John's friends as he set sail armed with a pen, a notebook and his pet frog Fred, "it's not the end of the world."

"Huh," said John, "that's what you think."

Arriving on Patmos, the bearded one climbed a mountain, found a cave and, as an act of revenge, penned a scenario in which the Romans, and all the other non-believers, got their comeuppance on the Day of Judgement.

Like the work of that other visionary loon, St Paul, the Book of Revelations has inspired those from the more lunatic fringes of Christian fundamentalism ever since.

John's legacy lives on today as far afield as the militarists of rural America holed up in the hills with their shotguns and survival manuals, and is preserved closer to its spiritual home by the Greek Orthodox Church, whose latest paranoid pronouncement is that bar codes are the mark of the Beast and part of a Jewish-Masonic conspiracy in fulfillment of Revelations.

However, in St John's cave on the day we arrived, things were a little quieter. An elderly monk was busily polishing the icons with a bottle of Zak and dusting the silver frame of the hollow where the saint laid his head between doom-laden scribblings.

Up the hill in the monastery built in 1088 by the scholar-cleric Khristodhoulos, between a remarkable medieval Cretan chapel and a museum holding an even more remarkable 5th Century Gospel of St Mark, sat another monk, the silvery tip of his beard swaying in time with the prayer beads swinging from his fingers.

At his feet, a black kitten idly played with them, and from the chapel came the rising song of voices raised in prayer.

We had dinner that night at a little fish restaurant down by the harbour, and as the full moon rose over the bay, wondered out loud that it had only been five days since we arrived at Rhodes Airport and, due to the fact that the baggage handlers had gone home, were left with two hours to ponder some of the great mysteries of travel.

Like why do fat people wear tight clothes? Or what exactly do middle-aged blokes wearing Italia shirts think it says about them? Or why do young Englishmen feel a desperate need to remove their shirts they moment they set foot in an arrivals hall?

We finally collected our bags and set off through the streets on tiptoe, fearful of moths.

The male tiger moth of Rhodes, you see, is a fragile beast, so timid that a single loud noise can put it off sex for weeks. Thus it was that we hardly dared utter a sound, for fear of being attacked by a herd of myths, as female moths are called, deprived of their conjugal rights.

All around us were the archetypal sights of Greek life: gnarled fishermen chatted on their mobile phones, yuppie couples drank designer beer from designer bottles and, in spite of the late hour, the traditional island shops such as Marks & Spencer and Harley-Davidson were still open plying their simple wares.

It seemed, now that I thought about it, that Greece had changed a bit since the days when you arrived on the ferry from Piraeus to be engulfed in a stygian tsunami of matrons, each offering identical rooms containing one chair, one bed and a toilet into which you deposited the paper on pain of death.

As a result of all this activity, the Greeks now have more mobile phones per capita than anyone else in Europe, and have dropped from first to fourth worldwide in frequency of sex. Americans are first, since you ask.

However, we still lead the world in drinking, so when we finally arrived at Anna, the handsome little motor cruiser which would be our home for the next week, to be greeted by Captain Nicos with an offer of beer, wine or ouzo, we took him up on all three.

The next day, a walk through the old town, with shops selling everything from Rolex watches to Harry Potter beach towels, confirmed our suspicions that Greece had changed.

Heaven knows what the Knights of St John would have thought of it.

That merry band of medieval troubadours, having foolishly sworn themselves to chastity and poverty, ended up so bored as a result that they built a fleet and went off sailing around the Med.

Today, all that remains of their courtly, clanking presence in Rhodes is the cobbled Street of the Knights, in which they lived in the Inns of England, France, Auvergne, Provence, Italy, Spain and Germany.

The ground floors, where they stabled their horses, now house sleepy civil servants who chew their pens, make occasional and languid phone calls with urgent requests for work which will never be done in this heat, and gaze out of the window, dreaming of a more noble calling.

We returned to the Anna to find that the other 14 passengers had arrived, and that every single one of them was German. Apart from the Dutch couple, and possibly us.

Now, I speak German and can get by in Dutch, but a week of starting sentences on a Monday and finally arriving at the verb by Thursday was not my idea of a wild time.

Strangely, though, after several glasses of wine that evening, not only did my German improve, but everyone else's English got better.

But not their stomachs, it seemed: at five the next morning, before we had even left the harbour, two of them woke Iolanda, the affable cruise leader, and demanded their money back because they were seasick.

She resisted the temptation to throw them overboard, and they were still there that afternoon when we docked at Mandhraki, the little port of Nissyros. On the wall of the sole hotel, a sign boasted of showers and ice cubes, although not simultaneously.

Just down the road was a monastery designed personally by the Virgin Mary, who had apparently appeared to the builder with her ideas in a vision. Nice job she did, too, so if you're ever stuck for a simply divine classically trained architect, you can get her on 0800-HEAVEN, extension 4.

Apart from showers and ice cubes, the main tourist attraction on the island is the volcano, which last erupted in 1933, but which still hisses and gurgles spouts of menacing steam into the sulphurous air. Local legend has it that these are caused by volcanic activity, but of course the truth is that they are the groans of Polyvotis, a titan crushed here under a huge rock by Poseidon.

We returned for dinner on the boat, and strolled afterwards through the cobbled streets, eating a peach from the orchard, to the Knights' castle on the hill. Cats dozed, children played and elders hunched over glasses of milky ouzo, all beautifully indifferent to us. We stopped and had a glass ourselves, at a table beside a window which was a song to simplicity: red rose, white sill, blue shutters.

The next day, in Kos, we found the 700-year-old plane tree which is allegedly the great- grandson of the one under which Hippocrates invented medicine in the fourth century BC.

Before that, people didn't know what they died of.

Today, of course, doctors still honour his memory when they sign the Hypocritical Oath, promising to eat, drink and smoke more than their patients.

That evening, an ice cream sunset ended the day, as swifts dipped across the still bay, their shadows tangling up the fishing boats in wakes of dreams.

"Groovy chickens," said Cate. "Fancy a beer?"

We had dinner under a lemon tree, as at our feet a puppy played catch with its tail.

The next day, lunch was a massive barbeque of some Teutonic jollity, set to Bavarian rap music and Hamburg Country and Western.

Afterwards, all the Germans went swimming and sank immediately to the bottom.

"Don't worry, I will catch them," said Nicos, the splendidly bonkers captain, heading aft with his fishing rod.

All safely gathered in, we weighed anchor an hour later and set off again across the briny depths – although some are not so briny, since we were passing directly over one of the mysterious freshwater channels of the oceans, which whales use for transmitting messages hundreds of miles.

I imagine they say things like: "Having a human of a time. Wish you were here."

By dusk we were on Kalymnos, once famous for its sponge divers, who once set out in 80 boats every spring and returned with their booty in September.

Today, many of them are dead or crippled by the bends, and many of the sponges have been killed by a viral disease, so the sponges in the island shops are mainly Egyptian and Libyan.

The island's sponge museum was closed for a holy day, so instead we went for a sponge cake and *kaitifi*, that delicious pastry which looks like Dougal from The Magic Roundabout doused with honey.

As we walked back towards the boat with our German shipmates, who were entirely friendly in spite of their taste in music, you could see, in the faces of the older men who sat on benches, their walking sticks a legacy of the bends or the war, a palpable bristling at our voices.

It was little wonder: during the winter of 1941-42, the German army requisitioned all the food in Greece, and half a million Greeks starved to death. Over 150,000 were shot to discourage resistance.

You could see anger in the faces of the old men, and a lingering sadness, too, that while their former invaders wandered around with Nikons and Sonys, they were left with a walking stick, a park bench and a glass of ouzo to kill the empty night.

And yet, in the midst of all the darkness that was the war, there was one small story that shone like a candle.

I had heard it before, and remembered it as we stood at the top of the hill in the town of Symi, on the island of the same name.

It was here, in December 1944, that the retreating Germans decided to pile all their munitions in the beautiful old Church of the Ascension of the Virgin and blow it up.

Unfortunately, they decided not to tell the hundreds of townspeople who lived around the church.

Enter, then, Rudi, a tall, blond Bavarian. As he and his comrades toiled up the hill with boxes for four days in the hot sun, Rudi would stop islanders and say to them: "Hey, Symiot, when is the celebration of the ascension of the Virgin?"

"Why, August 15, of course."

"Wrong. Quite wrong."

Finally, on the fourth day, when the whole town was talking about Rudi's mystery, anyone who passed him was told: "Tonight, at eight, the Virgin will ascend."

All that afternoon, as quietly as mice, the people of Symi moved themselves out: the young ones on foot, carrying what valuables they could, the old ones on piggyback, the babies in baskets, the birds in cages and the cats which had not been eaten padding along behind.

At just after eight, the Virgin did indeed ascend with an earth-shattering roar, taking with it only an 80-year-old named Maria who had refused to move.

The next day, the Germans left on a boat. It sank an hour later, hit by a torpedo or a mine. Of the 400 on board, only 17 survived, and Rudi was not one of them.

I looked out for a long time that afternoon at the azure waves beneath which his bones still lie, then went for a walk along the harbourfront at Symi.

In a little bar, Rudi will be pleased to know, Germany were playing in the semi-final of the World Cup, watched by his countrymen and the natives of the little town he saved, sitting side by side at last.

2002

H is for Himalayas, and the hunt for Rommel Albuquerque

On a blistering hot day in 1998, I sat on a Royal Enfield in front of the India Gate war memorial in Delhi just about to ride the 7,000 miles home to the UK.

I had only passed my bike test two years before, and only ridden 30 miles on a bike in my life, and as I nodded at my mate Paddy Minne on his Enfield and we set off into the chaotic traffic, fear and excitement were fighting for victory in my heart.

Excitement won, and several bike adventures later, such as Route 66, Chile to Alaska, around Australia and around the world, I sat again on an Enfield in front of India Gate about to recreate some of the same journey.

This time, though, I was not so alone: around me were 71 other riders about to set off north on the 11th annual Himalayan Odyssey to Leh and back, a round trip of 1700 miles.

And this time I was on a modern Enfield with electric start, fuel injection and solid engine and five-speed gearbox, as opposed to the dear old one which I still have, but on which every bit that could shake, rattle and fall off on the way home did, since Enfields back then were made of little more than tinfoil and hope.

Blessed by three Buddhist monks and with the white silk scarves they had given us fluttering like a Biggles convention, we set off past a park in which even at 7.30am a cricket game was in full swing, the click of cork on willow mingling with the soft putter of Enfields which is more than anything the heartbeat of India.

And if I needed any more proof where I was, before long out of the city I met a horse walking the wrong way down a dual carriageway. We nodded at each other politely, and went on our respective ways.

North of Panipat, Paddy and I had dined on vegetable masala from a flyblown roadside shack. This time, a group of us had lunch at a charming little place called McDonald's, presumably run by some Scottish expats. They will do well, if their chicken burgers are anything to go by.

It was 46C, and the afternoon sun beat down so hard that even the Indian riders were struggling, but in the midst of the heat and dust, women in kingfisher-bright saris sashayed along the verge, carrying small forests or haystacks on their heads. These days, though, most of them were chatting away on mobile phones.

At last we began to climb into the cool of the mountains, as welcome for us as it had been for the sons and daughters of the Raj when they escaped the unbearable season to their hill stations, and it was a weary but grateful bunch who climbed off the bikes in Parwanoo.

"Well, Geoff, how was the ride?" said Santhosh, the man from Enfield.

"Santhosh, get those bikes fitted with a desk fan and refrigerated grips immediately," I said.

"Come on," he laughed, slapping me on the back, "time for a beer."

The next day, we rose to the balm of a cool and misty morning, and riding to be enjoyed rather than endured: twisty mountain curves overlooking scenery which would have had Switzerland hanging its head in shame.

The Enfield was in its element, purring sweetly along as I swung it through bends in an elegant waltz which is a much more gentlemanly way of proceeding than the frantic tango of sports bikes.

Well, except for one rider, who would hurtle past like a man on a mission, stop to take a photograph, then hurtle past again.

"Santhosh, who is that guy?" I said at lunch.

"Rommel Albuquerque."

"What?"

"No one knows where he got his name from, but everyone calls him the Desert Fox."

I made a note to get to the bottom of this mystery, and on the stroke of teatime we pulled up at an Alpine chalet hotel and had tiffin on the veranda as the golden light caressed the orchards and cedar woods below.

It was a perfect evening, followed by a night which I spent being comprehensively sick from both ends, slept for about five minutes, then staggered groggily to the morning briefing to discover that our planned route had been blocked by a landslide, meaning a diversion over the Jalori Pass.

Which meant 9,000ft up on a dirt track, then down the other side. Naturally, at one stage I passed Rommel, identified by the No 79 sticker on his bike, taking a photograph of a goatherd tending his flock as an Indian Air Force jet roared past in the distance, a perfect image of the vast variety that is India.

There are days when you love this country, and days when you hate it, and by late afternoon this was one of the latter: the crap roads, the chaotic traffic, the idiotic drivers trying to cram into a space already full of everything from buses to goats on their way home from a hard day's bleating. Why they can't design a fast-flowing system like the M25 is beyond me.

It was early evening by the time we rode by a winding river and fell gratefully into Manali, and having not eaten all day, I went out for dinner with my room mate Dave from Manchester.

We ate delicious river trout at Johnson's Café, founded by the progeny of a player in the Great Game who had retired here aged 70 and married a local 19-year-old, as you do. All around us, the Indian riders were tucking into pizza.

We were joined by Deepak and Shivam, who like many of the Indian riders in the group, had saved up for years for their Enfields, which at prices starting from £1,800 in India and with a year's waiting list, are the bikes to aspire to over the ten squillion Hero Hondas used as daily transport or the handful of Harleys ridden by rich kids or bank managers.

"I've wanted one since I was a boy, and it's like a dream come true to own one. My wife says I love it more than her," said Deepak.

"I was actually thinking of a Honda, then I walked into an Enfield showroom, the salesman started the engine, and I was hooked by that sound," said Shivam. "I sometimes start it just to listen to while I read."

Outside the window, the streets were thronged with Indian holidaymakers, journeyman Rajasthani tailors, Tibetan refugees, Buddhist monks, trekkers and hippies, while street hawkers peddled everything from roasted chestnuts to candy floss, buskers busked and the shops were ablaze with light, selling pashminas and genuine fake adventure kit.

The winding road out of town through an Alpine landscape next day was lined with ramshackle shops selling snow gear, with Shop No 328 doing a special deal for 50p a day. French resorts take note.

At the 13,500ft top of the Rothang Pass, after a two-hour traffic jam, Indian tourists were taking full advantage, rolling around in this strange substance, making snow angels and throwing tentative snowballs at each other.

"Wow," said Vijay, who was from the south. "I have seen photos of snow, but never the real thing."

We stopped for lunch at a roadside shack where the choices were momos, the delicious steamed dumplings, or omlate, sic.

"The folks in the north east don't speak much English, but they give their children English names they've picked up at random, so the poor kids end up being called things like Toilet and Litter," said Vir, a larger than life journalist from Mumbai.

By dusk, soaked from above by rain and from below by countless river crossings, we camped in the grounds of a Buddhist monastery inhabited by a single ancient monk.

It was bitterly cold, and wrapped up in every item of clothing I had, I slept, as above a full moon glittered on the snowy slopes.

The next morning, as I edged past a petrol tanker bearing the hand-painted warning Hingly Infalammle on the back, I could not help but notice that one twitch of the driver's steering wheel would send me plunging from my little shelf of sand and gravel a thousand feet into the abyss below.

We rose and fell through mountain passes, splashing across rivers so swollen with snow melt that the water was knee-deep and icy cold, so challenging and yet satisfying that as we stopped for chai, that addictive blend of tea, sugar and condensed milk, I've never seen so many happy bikers with soaked and frozen feet.

All around as we rode, rested and stopped for photos, the mountains fisted to the sky, either yearning for heaven or angry that no matter how much they yearned, they would remain forever earthbound.

Unlike the eagles who soared above their peaks, mocking us all with their effortless grace.

At Sarchu, we camped in a beautiful deserted valley at 13,000ft, and since there was nothing to do but drink rum and watch the sun go down, French rider François Barrois taught me useful phrases such as: "Pissing in a violin", which is what French people do when they piss in the wind, and: "Do you take my bladder for a lantern?" (Do you take me for a fool?)

Thus educated, I wrapped myself up in thermals and blankets, tried to sleep in the thin air, and failed. I was not alone, as I gathered from the groggy faces of other riders over breakfast of omelettes and tea at dawn.

Still, getting on a motorbike and setting off makes us all feel better, and we saddled up and rode on, over passes as high as 17,480ft and past the cheesy safety signs of the Border Roads Organisation, with slogans such as "Hug my curves, but not too tightly", "Driving after whisky is always risky", and the splendidly antediluvian "Don't gossip. Let him drive".

You could just imagine an office at BRO HQ with Department of Cheesy Slogans on the door and a Big Cheese sitting behind a desk inside.

Suddenly, the door bursts open, and an excited junior clerk rushes in.

"Sir! Sir! What about...Don't lose your nerves on the curves?"

"Splendid! You will go far, young Vijay," beams the Big Cheese, and makes a note.

The many trucks we passed bore their own slogans: Blow Horn, Use Dipper at Night, Keep Your Distance, and once, the bittersweet Alone but Happy.

Which was more than could be said for the unluckiest man on the trip: one of the Indian riders who soaked his boots at a water crossing, changed into his shoes and tied the boots on the back of his bike to dry.

At lunch, discovering one had fallen off, he threw the other one way as useless and rode on. Only to find at the end of the day that the support truck had picked up the first one.

The night, impossibly, was even colder than the one before, and in the morning, the effort of washing in the small bucket of warm water presented to us was so great that we just splashed our faces, and rode on.

After two hours of chewed up road, we stopped at Pang, a hamlet of shacks, and cupped our shivering hands around cups of chai.

The sun came out, and life seemed possible again, but then, as we rode over Thanglangla at 17,584ft, it began to snow and the road turned to deep mud and slush.

And then, after a day of mud and snow and the worst surfaces imaginable, the evening blessed us with a perfect road, sweeping down to Leh by a river reflecting the roseate glory of the dying sun.

Only for dusk to take it away again, leaving us bumping into town on an unmade road in darkness and dust, with trucks coming the other way with their headlights off to save the bulbs. It was, to use that word which encompasses everything from mildly disconcerting to near-death experiences, interesting.

The next day, after the bliss of a hotel bed and a hot shower, hundreds of other riders descended on Leh for the second annual Himalayan Reunion.

Dancers danced, bands played, bikers and mechanics tested their skills in competitions, and I somehow found myself coming second in the Himalayan Open Arm Wrestling Contest to a Sikh gentleman by the name of Mr Singh who was 6ft 4ins in every direction.

"Well done," I said, shaking his hand with what was left of mine.

"Thank you, brother," he said, crushing my ribs in a mighty bear hug.

World peace assured, I looked around at the happy throng of riders drinking beer or rum, the band on the stage, the giant screen beside it showing footage of the trip we had made and the posters advertising forthcoming Enfield rideouts, social events and races.

And in that moment, I felt a deep and heartwarming sense of happiness, that the old and venerable make of motorcycle I had ridden home all those years ago had now become turbocharged with coolness, and that although Indians were proud of its British heritage, they were even more proud of the fact that it was now firmly an Indian brand with its sights set on a great future.

"You know," said Vir, appearing beside me with two cold beers clasped in his mighty paw, "when I was growing up, my dad had an Enfield, and it was the only type of motorcycle you could get, but it was still cool. Now it's even more so."

The next morning, veteran rough riders by now, we bounced our way up the steep and sinuous climb to Khardung Pass, at 18,380ft loftier than Everest base camp and the highest motorable road in the world.

As I got off the bike, my breath taken away by both the altitude and the view, I spotted a familiar figure taking a photograph, and walked across.

"Rommel," I said, "tell me the story of your name."

"The surname is Portuguese, and my first name because my mother was watching a movie about Rommel when she went into labour."

The mystery solved, I shook his hand, climbed on my bike and began the long ride home.

2014

…and Honeymoon

I have a confession to make: I have slept with a married woman. My only excuse is that I was far from home, and she was lovely. Oh, and she was my wife.

Anyway, the circumstances were made for romance: a turreted castle in the Slovenian mountains, a circular bed 10ft wide and a bottle of vintage champagne chilling on ice.

It was the first night of our honeymoon, and the setting of Castle Mokrice, a medieval pile on the Croatian border, could not have been more romantic.

In fact, it was so perfect that we drove past it twice, thinking we could not possibly be staying there.

When we finally realised we were, they showed us up to a circular room in one of the turrets, so big that to go to the bathroom, you brought your passport and crossed two time zones.

Not only that, but it came with a series of antechambers, in one of which was to be found a grand piano.

We drank some champagne, had that most delicious of adult feelings of dressing and going down to dinner in a grand hotel, and the next morning woke to sunlight and church bells through the open window.

Butterflies flitted between sunflowers and a fox loped across the road into a cornfield as we wandered aimlessly, stopping to potter by rivers and lift our faces to the sun.

Above our heads, the birches whispered and the swifts were tossed to and fro by the dying breaths of the *borja*, a wind which every September gathers itself up in the Aegean, vents its rage on hapless sailors in the Adriatic, dries the washing of grateful Croatian housewives, crawls over the top of Mount Sneznik and finally falls exhausted on the rolling hills of southern Slovenia.

This, like much of the country, is a pocket paradise in which the view in any direction has all the elements of a children's fairy tale illustration: the village, its gardens awash with flowers, the white church with its terracotta spire, the wooded mountain topped by the turreted castle. All you do is bring your own prince or princess.

In the lilac dusk, we found ourselves in the 13th Century church of Pleterje. Vespers bells rang in the cool Gothic spaces, and behind the monastery walls beyond, the monks flitted to and fro, lost to the sight of all but God. We bought a bottle of their plum brandy from a little shop nearby, and escaped to more secular pleasures.

And the next day, even more, in the shape of two hours of sybaritic pampering in the spa at the Hotel Terme. Honestly, it was all I could do to drag myself to the bar afterwards.

After such sloth, the least we could do the next day was to go for a hearty walking tour of Ljubljana, a capital so Ruritanian that old ladies still grow vegetables in the centre, and a kindergarten sits in the middle of the grand embassies of the diplomatic quarter.

It was hardly surprising, then, that when we arrived at Lake Bled the next day, we emerged from the Toytown railway station to find the stationmaster tending his cabbages.

In a land of picture postcard beauty, Bled is the ultimate snapshot: as if the surrounding forest and the castle on the clifftop were not enough, in the middle of the lake sits a wooded island topped by a white church. It is to this island that young Slovenian grooms row their brides, then carry them the 99 steps up the church and either call for an ambulance or ring the bell three times and wish for a happy and successful life together.

Remarkably, being neither young nor Slovenian, I managed the 99 steps in one go. Ah, there's life in the old knees yet, I thought, carrying Cate across the threshold of the Okarina, the nearest restaurant, to celebrate.

In fact, we celebrated so splendidly that at three the next morning we found ourselves with Leo the owner and the manager of the Villa Bled plotting to blow up the Vatican. Don't tell the Pope if you see him, since it's meant to be a surprise.

I was not a well man the next morning when we set out for the drive across the high mountain pass to Soca, built by 10,000 Russian prisoners during the First World War.

Mind you, my headache was not helped by the fact that we found ourselves in the middle of a classic car rally, with Ferraris and Porsches, Jaguars and Morgans hurtling past us all day with an expensive howl and a cheery wave.

We arrived at our destination, an isolated farmhouse in a valley, as the moon rose over the mountains.

Fortunately, it was surrounded by other isolated farmhouses and an isolated inn, and as we were sitting down to dinner at a rough table, I was approached by a tall man with a congenial air about him.

Naturally, he turned out to from William Blackley from Cookstown in Co Tyrone, on a mountain hiking holiday with his mates from the patent office in Munich.

"I was living in Edinburgh, but I was getting too settled, so I moved to Munich and got too settled there instead," he said by way of explanation.

Lost in the mountains, we passed the next few days in medieval pleasures: admiring horses, petting goats, improving our archery, eating roasted pigs and carousing.

Descending heavily at last to the sea for a spell, we wandered for a day around lovely old Piran, then caught the boat to Venice: glorious, doomed Venice, forever sinking under the weight of its own decadence while admiring itself all the while in an ornately carved mirror.

And after days of living like lords for pennies in Slovenia, we staggered from St Mark's Square, muttering in shock: "Twenty five euro for two coffees? Seventeen per cent commission at the bureau de change? Good grief!"

We took refuge in a walking tour, letting facts wash over us until we realised they were no longer facts, but raindrops.

Drenched, we hid in the Piero Mauro, a little jewel of a comer bar, all mahogany and brass and mirrors, and spent the rest of the perfect afternoon there, steaming gently over hot chocolate and brandy.

Outside, the thunderstorm sent Japanese tourists in fluorescent macs fluttering to and fro, like a species of tiny, endangered butterfly.

We returned to our room at the Duodo Palace Hotel, a painstakingly restored hymn to opulence, and spent the early evening, before we went out to dinner, sitting on our balcony watching gondolas whisper to and fro.

The next morning, a varnished launch took us direct from the hotel to Santa Lucia station, where, high above the echoing concourse, the clickety-clack board was showing the most evocative of departures: Venice-Simplon Orient-Express, London via Paris.

I felt the same thrill as I had when, about three decades earlier, I had stood at London Victoria, an Inter Rail pass in hand, looking up at the departures board with my heart full of the infinite possibilities of life.

We boarded, and were organising ourselves in our little compartment when Bruno, the steward, stuck his head around the door.

"Listen, the room next door is empty," he said, opening the adjoining door and giving us a suite.

After a while we made our along the train to a languid lunch. Which was followed at length by afternoon tea.

It was the most sybaritic of pleasures, even if being on the Orient Express leads you into the strangest of conversations.

"Sorry I took a while, dear. There were three of them, with knives."

"Were you hurt, darling?"

"Good grief, no. Although the last one was obviously a black belt in dim-sum trained by the great master Shi-Tsu."

"Good heavens. Did you throw him off the train?"

"No, I'm saving that for after dinner."

In between times, we read, or, wrapped up in a cocoon of luxury, simply gazed out of the window at the modem world flashing by, like a parallel universe to which we never wanted to return.

As darkness fell, we returned to our compartment and found Bruno lighting the wood-fired stove at the end of the carriage for heat and hot water.

And so, the honeymoon ended as it had begun: dressing up and going down to dinner with my wife, as beneath us, the tickety-tack of the rails sang to us with the rhythm of paradise on earth.

2004

I is for Italy

A short history

500,000 years BC
Neanderthals arrive and swan around in designer mammoth furs with matching clubs, setting standards which have remained to this day.

736 BC
Greeks arrive, bearing vines and olive trees. Italians make wine and olive oil, then sit around scrubbed wooden tables waiting for pasta to be invented.

600BC
Rome invented by Romulus, Remus and a working party of wolves, starting an empire which will last almost a thousand years.

65 BC
Julius Caesar crosses the Rubicon and takes the city, only to be murdered by Brutus. Mark Antony takes over, gets distracted by Cleopatra, loses battle of Actium and commits suicide, to be followed by Caligula, Claudius and Nero, best known for his hobby of persecuting Christians.

3rd Century AD
Christianity gets its own back by being named state religion

455
Roman Empire ends, issuing in centuries of assorted Popes and Emperors

1401
Filippo Brunelleschi invents perspective, allowing people to walk to the end of the street for the first time, and ushering in Renaissance, in which all the geniuses in the world seem to live in one street.

1886
Italy decides to become an empire again by invading Abyssinia and Eritrea

1886, half an hour later
Campaigns a disaster. Italians give up war.

1939
Mussolini persuades Italians to have another go, helping Hitler to take over the world.

1945
War ends in disaster. Italians string Mussolini and mistress upside down from petrol station in Milan, then give up war for ever and go back to designing cars, motorbikes, clothes and furniture, in between sitting around scrubbed wooden tables laughing and drinking in pasta advertisements.

Rome and Florence

T he mist was draped seductively between a cleavage of hills, the rising sun caressing its slopes and sliding towards the dark woods below.

As the plane sank towards Rome, it was easy to see why Italy was a country where art is love, and love an art.

And talking is a performance.

It is impossible to speak Italian with your hands in your pockets, and waiting at Rome airport for a transfer to Florence, it became obvious why: although Italy stretches from the frozen Alps in the north to shimmering Sicily in the south, the population is about the same as the UK.

That's because everyone is waving their arms around so much that there's no room for any more.

The Italians are also indelibly stylish. It is quite normal, I hear, for families to leave ugly or badly dressed relatives out in the heat to die in the same way as the Eskimos leave the elderly out in the cold.

Alternatively, they can just leave them in the street to be run over. For anyone who says that Italian drivers are a bit mad is a liar. They are, in fact, raving.

Simultaneously engaged in a stormy marriage with the throttle pedal and a passionate affair with the brake, Italian drivers view pedestrians with the same sort of hungry scorn that lions view three-legged wildebeest. Hardly worth the effort, but may as well kill them anyway.

A foot sticking over the edge of the kerb? Fair game, *grazie*. A spot of lane discipline, old chap? Not today, s*ignore*. One hand on the wheel and an air of languid machismo? *Si, si*, that'll do nicely.

After 15 minutes of a car chase which involved only our taxi, we screeched to a halt, paid the driver and, trembling slightly, staggered into the Grand Hotel Baglioni, a magnificent pile with buttery ochre walls, ancient oak doors, arched vistas, a rooftop restaurant with a view of the famous Duomo, and a stiff drink in the bar. The latter was the most welcome.

My room had a bathroom with ancient brass fittings, a toilet flush which was like a bell push set into the wall, and a huge, soft bed.

I checked it for taxi drivers, and finding none, decided it was safe to go to sleep.

The next morning, lightning rent the sky and thunder rattled the terracotta roof tiles.

Splashing through the narrow streets towards the Duomo, it was easy to see why when Stendhal first came to Italy at the start of the last century, he staggered around Florence in a perpetual stupor of delight, fainting regularly and having to be revived with copious draughts of the local brandy.

The art, the culture, the intense, almost spiritual devotion to beauty. And that was only the shoe shops.

There is a tangible sense of infinite satisfaction as you walk through the streets of Florence. Even the golden light on the faded ochre and terracotta buildings makes your heart beat faster and gluts your senses to the extent that you feel giddy with euphoria.

And when you finally stand in front of the Duomo, the shock of its brightly patterned marble exterior is so arousing that you feel you will have to go home and confess to your wife that you have become a duomosexual.

The interior is as plain as the outside is extravagant, which helps calm you down enough for the delicious experience of wandering through the streets in the torrential rain, sniffing air redolent with the nutty aroma of coffee curving o from cafés here and there.

And then arriving at the green river and walking along, deliberately not looking back at the Ponte Vecchio until you cannot resist any longer the temptation to turn and drink in the view.

Objectively, the Ponte Vecchio is just an ancient bridge holding up a collection of patchy ochre, dun, orange, terracotta and duck egg blue jewellery shops which have been there since 1593.

But subjectively, like everything else in Italy, it fills you with the joy which comes from having each of your senses filled to the brim first thing in the morning then topped up all day.

Who knows what causes it? The light on the crumbling paint, the statues everywhere. The food, the clothes, the happy, relaxed marriage which Italians have had with beauty for three thousand years.

Not the rain, which in 1966 fell for 40 days and nights and flooded the city - some believe in divine retribution for letting England win the World Cup, and which by now had become so heavy that we jumped on a bus up the mountain in a vain attempt to get above the clouds.

On board, by a complete piece of serendipity, Paul, one of the group, met Susan, a friend from Dublin who was in Florence studying history.

Although she had only been in Italy for 10 days, she had already acquired a patina of ancient romance, wearing a great black rain-pearled cloak wrapped around a *quattrocento* air of noble frailty.

She took us to the Ristorante Mario in the piazza at Fiesole, where we had salami, crostini, panini, ravioli and fettucini washed down with chianti until we were completely stuffini.

Outside, the sky was slowly clearing, and the drying, opalescent light dripped through the window onto a wooden trolley whose wheels were hooded in curved chrome, sitting on an ancient tiled floor. Beauty, everywhere you looked.

Up the hill, the Monastery of San Francesco offers a stunning view, in colours which seem to reach out and embrace you, of the basin in which Florence sits. It is a view which has changed little since the 16th Century, seen daily by the monks, still padding about in brown habits and sandals, who have changed little since the 16th Century either.

Even older is the 3,000-seat Roman amphitheatre and baths just around the corner, which have apparently been around since Roman times. They come complete with a vomitorium, the stone trough in which hedonistic guzzlers deposited the contents of their stomachs before returning to the feast.

Still, at least they enjoyed themselves, which is more than could be said for John, one of the group who had spent the morning moaning to the tour operators because they had given him a free diary halfway through February, because the flight had been too long, because the hotel hadn't had rashers for breakfast, and because it was raining.

"You wouldn't have a spare tie, would you?" he said after we had returned to a city washed clean by rain, under a sky the colour of shotguns and buttermilk. "Apparently we need one for the bloody restaurant tonight."

I dug out my favourite tie and handed it over in the manner of St Francis of Assisi, who said that to give was to receive.

"It's a bit loud, isn't it? Doesn't really go with my jacket," he said.

"Here, take this one, then," I said, giving him the one I was wearing.

"I hope they don't give us too much for dinner. I'm stuffed enough as it is," he said, knotting it begrudgingly around his neck.

Before I could offer to help him tighten it, the woman standing beside us suddenly noticed that she had torn her tights. Luckily I had a spare fan belt with me.

Sitting before dinner with Alessandro, the manager of the Plaza Hotel Lucchese, it was easy to see why almost every woman in the world wants to sleep with Italian men, although not necessarily to marry them.

Alessandro was wearing an olive linen suit, a powder blue cotton shirt and a silk ochre and burgundy tie, and was so genuinely warm, contended and stylish that although I am profoundly heterosexual, it was all I could do not to go over and snuggle up to him.

Or maybe that was just to make up for John, who was entertaining him with a description of how only the Chinese were worse at organising things than the Italians.

The hotel, meanwhile, was an unconsciously flamboyant combination of gold curtains, wood and marble floors and pink armchairs.

If you are the sort of person who loves dressing up and making a special occasion out of life, for heaven's sake come to Italy. You can drape your cashmere coat over your shoulders, adjust your fedora to a suitably rakish angle and feel perfectly at home, since everyone else will be doing much the same thing - except with such a genuine love of life that they make the equally stylish French seem frigid and stuffy by comparison.

You may mock the Italians for wearing fur coats and fedoras on a wet Tuesday morning, or claim that their army is more interested in the design of their uniforms than their guns, but more power to them, I say.

Their dressing up has all the happy, guileless innocence of childhood, and if every army paid more attention to suiting than shooting, we'd all be a lot better off, hurrah.

That night, possibly as a result of several grappas at the Plaza Lucchese, I dreamt that I went to see Michelangelo's David in the nearby Galleria dell'Accademia, but when I woke up I was still in bed, and when I went to see the real thing I discovered that it was half-term holiday and half the schoolchildren in Italy were standing in the queue for the Galleria.

The other half were standing in the queue for the Uffizi, thus denying me the chance to see Italy's finest collection of paintings by Botticelli, Leonardo da Vinci, Michelango, Titian and Piero, who lived in a house that was never cleaned, kept a garden that was never tended and ate nothing but hard-boiled eggs.

There was nothing for it but to take the train to Rome through countryside so seductively curved and lit that if it was a woman you would want to marry it and have its children, never mind the pain.

At Rome station, the taxi driver raced off as usual, then screeched to a halt in the middle of a busy intersection, leaped out and, ignoring hoots and gesticulations on all sides, helped a bus reverse around the corner.

"I was a bus driver myself for 10 years," he said by way of explanation as we sped away through streets with cars lined with cars squeezed into spaces so small that the people inside could not get out, and were reduced to gesticulating wildly at each other.

Parking is such a problem in Rome that the inhabitants have taken to driving around in smaller and smaller cars like the Fiat Bambino, a wonderful little car so utterly Italian that it would look perfect painted in patchy ochre with laurel green wooden shutters.

Or new city cars with a single seat.

Or, best of all, the ubiquitous Vespa scooters, which even in the early hours of the morning can be heard buzzing everywhere like a storm of angry bees. They are, naturally, ridden without helmets, since that would ruin one's hair.

Even petrol stations have been squeezed to fit onto pavements, with a tiny attendant sitting between two bijou petrol pumps, a bucket, squeegee and mop on his knee and a toolbox resting at his feet.

And squeezed in behind him are hordes of Japanese tourists taking photographs of each other outside the designer shops before whipping out their trembling credit cards and diving in en masse, emerging several hours later laden with bags.

The reason why most of Europe is filled with Japanese tourists is very simple. It is because Japan is so overcrowded that there isn't room for everyone to be there all at once, so the government has set up a system where at any given time half the population is touring around Europe.

At least the fact that they're in the shops buying Gucci, Versace et al means that the Vatican is empty.

To get into this monumental tribute to man's sense of his own importance, you have to pass through airport-style scanners which remove all traces of Protestantism, before being frisked by armed nuns for Orange sashes, King Billy campaign medals and up to date DUP membership cards.

Inside, the scale of St Peter's is almost as stunning as a souvenir shop where the Italians' normally impeccable sense of style has momentarily deserted them.

Here, you can buy everything from 3ft high plastic virgins to holograms which turn from Jesus to Mary and back again.

From far above, if you listen, you can hear God weeping quietly.

Much better to be at the Trevi Fountain, where Anita Ekberg cooled off in La Dolce Vita. Like everything else in Rome, it is better than even the most gadabout optimist could imagine.

Well, almost everything. Later than night we found ourselves at the Fantasie Theatre, where on stage several chaps in drag and women in authentic polycotton peasant costumes were singing Italian marching opera folk pop songs to an audience which consisted entirely, apart from our table, of Japanese people politely chewing salami.

It was so surreal that the only answer was to drink several glasses of wine very quickly and slide under the table as all around members of one of the most ancient, civilised nations in Asia who had abandoned their spiritual inheritance for a pair of Gucci loafers and a Burberry scarf watched as members of-one of the most ancient, civilised nations in Europe who had abandoned their cultural inheritance for a pair of yellow stockings and brown velvet knickerbockers belted out O Sole Mio into a Sony microphone.

Still, the best thing about it was that it wasn't really Rome.

Rome is walking around a corner in the cobbled moonlight to be stunned to your bones by two things.

The sight of the cool silvery water in the Trevi Fountain splashing on the marble below the warm lamplight on the terracotta and ochre buildings around the square.

And the realisation that you are about to be mown down by the phalanx of Vespas which has just appeared around the corner.

1996

The Amalfi Coast

In England, graffiti invariably refers to the lonely nocturnal proclivities of Jones minor, the strongly held belief that carefully selected football teams are more deserving of honour than others, or the dimensions, in imperial measure, of even more carefully selected regions of both the male and female anatomy.

But the flamboyant white text on the side of the tumbledown farmhouse on the road south from the airport had none of that.

"*Ti amo, Mozart*," it simply said. "I love you, Mozart."

It could only have been Italy.

In Salzburg, the composer's birthplace, such an untidy proclamation of affection would have been met with thinly pursed lips and a wire brush.

But in Italy, there is only one thing more important than love, and that is the love of love. After all, 99 per cent of their songs are about the first, and the rest are about the second.

And when you get too old for all that, there is always the love of pasta. At dinner on my first night in the Bajamar Hotel, a dark and brooding establishment on the breezy coast which is known as the Riviera of Ulysses - not because the Greek paragon ever visited there, but because the local authorities thought it sounded nice - we were served with so many different types that I ran out of fingers counting of the pasta which Italians eat in enormous quantities, but which still does not explain the mysterious process by which Italian women, who are universally slim, delicious and fashionable when they are young, wake up the morning after their wedding night as completely spherical mammas dressed in old black army blankets.

Or, indeed, the equally mysterious process by which Italian men, who before their marriages are popularly perceived to be demon lovers with 18in hips, afterwards are becoming impotent in such large numbers that in March 1993 the national newspaper, *La Stampa*, devoted a large article to the subject, offering no more helpful advice than that the chaps affected should listen to more music.

Indeed, I often find that there's nothing like the soundtrack to *The Sound of Music* by the Dagenham Girl Pipers for getting me in the mood.

Perhaps the problem for Italian men is that they always compare their wives to their mothers, and no one wants to make love to their mothers in case they end up in a Greek play with everyone laughing at them.

Anyway, where was I? Ah yes, at supper, where the British guests were eating their pasta by laying their napkins very properly on their knees then spending the whole meal wishing they had brought a hand mirror so they could check their chins, shirt collars and new linen suits for sauce splashes.

The Italians, much more sensibly, tucked their napkins into their collars like huge self-empowered toddlers, covered the rest of their bodies with any other napkins which happened to be lying nearby until they looked like carelessly abandoned piles of laundry, then tucked in with enormous gusto, in between talking about cars, families, outsmarting the taxman, love, betrayal, football, shopping, soap operas, food, health, superstition, politics, bureaucracy, corruption and several other national obsessions.

Each of them was studied and discussed with the effervescence, known in Italian as *allegria*, which shows that it is not for nothing that the word company comes from the Italian *con pane*, or with bread, meaning to break bread with friends.

In fact, so animated did the discussions become that after a while the outside of each trembling mound of napkins began to flicker and glow so that we shrank back in alarm, fearing that we were about to witness the first ever case of self-immolation by enthusiasm.

It transpired, however, that it was just the reflection of the fireworks across the bay to mark the start of the annual festival of Erasmus, the diminutive 16th Century Dutch humanist who, for reasons which in spite of some investigation I never discovered, had been adopted as patron of Formia.

It seemed as baffling a moment as any to go for a walk on the beach and fall into bed, where I woke at half three, switched on the television and found a choice which included a dusty professor demonstrating differential equations on a blackboard, Bonanza, Alec Guinness in The Lavender Hill Mob, Star Trek and an erotic chat line advertisement which consisted of a series of rather too earnest nymphomaniacs grimly gyrating under a large declaration saying: "*Non sono una puttana*" (I am not a whore).

Strangely, according to the address at the bottom of the screen, all this was taking place in the third floor offices of a company called Baubells based at Athol Street in Douglas in the Isle of Man.

Now, I've been to the Isle of Man and I've never seen woman that interesting, but by the look of things on the screen they didn't possess much more than a few scraps of clothing, a large double bed and a whip.

Poor dears, they were obviously saving up to buy some clothes so they could get out a bit more and visit some of the island's excellent rural heritage museums.

I zapped the remote control and fell asleep again, vaguely troubled by the fact that according to official government statistics, if everyone in Italy actually got up, walked over to the TV and switched it off properly rather than leaving it on standby, the country would save enough electricity to build a new power station every year.

But then, if God had meant Italians to walk, he would never have invented Alfa Romeos.

The next day began badly.

I killed a mosquito at dawn, then realised that I was in Mafia country, and spent the rest of the morning worrying that as I was eating lunch, or enjoying a post-prandial grappa this evening, a petite black limousine would draw up and several mosquitoes, dressed in immaculate dark suits and with little fedoras pulled down over their diminutive sunglasses, would emerge and, with a set of exquisitely matching machine guns, unstitch me at the ankles with a hail of tiny bullets.

The Mafia, or more correctly its sister organization the Camorra in this part of Italy around Naples, has been around since the beginning of the 19th Century, waxing and waning, but never going away.

In Sicily, the birthplace of the Mafia, it almost disappeared under the Fascists, then was restored by the Allies, who relied on Mafia intelligence in the battle for Sicily in 1943 and maintained political control of the island by entrusting 62 of its 66 districts to mafiosi or their kin.

Today it controls more than half the world's heroin trade from Palermo and deals with official purges much as it has always done, by killing the officials involved and leaving behind a trail of what the Italians call with moribund elegance *cadaveri eccelenti*, or illustrious corpses.

But none of this explained, as we drove away from the hotel this morning, why I was worrying so much, when I normally worried less than anyone I know.

Maybe I was worried about being 41 and not having 2.54 children, a Labrador and a Volvo estate bought on one of those strange schemes where you pay for the car for two years then give it back to the dealer.

Or maybe I did have 2.54 children somewhere that I didn't know about. But then, I'd always practised safe sex by keeping my eyes closed when I was doing it.

So there was little point worrying about anything, really. Maybe I should just worry about worrying, and cut out the middleman.

Thankfully, at this stage my metaphysical reveries were interrupted by our arrival at Sperlonga and its well-known mausoleum, which is, as we all know, where German mice are buried in tiny vaults which they reserved by laying down their beach towels several years earlier.

In between their discreet cadavers lay the remains of Monazio Planco, founder of Lyon and the governor of this part of Italy under Julius Caesar.

The most important Roman site in the area, however, is the nearby villa of Tiberius, uncovered when workmen building a road in 1957 started uncovering enormous marble legs, arms and torsos buried underground like the aftermath of a massacre by giant mafiosquitoes.

Tiberius moved here in 14AD at the age of 55 to get away from an ancient nagging mother in Rome, surrounding his new villa, grotto and swimming pools with statuary representing the adventures of Ulysses, like a sort of Pop-Up Odyssey.

Magnificently reconstructed in 1958 by the winner of that year's Italian 3D Jigsaw Open, it is now the centrepiece of the simple, refreshing Sperlonga museum, which also possesses a wonderful film of the 1957-58 excavations, showing excitable workmen holding up a bust, shouting "Head, head", then all rushing off in a group to see if it fits on the torso they discovered that morning.

If you can, get an interpreter to sit through it with you - the script is spontaneously hilarious.

Just down the hill are the walls and floors of the slaves' and soldiers' apartments, the terrace where Tiberius and his guests would take their regulation 40 paces after dinner to aid digestion, and the pools.

In one of them, Tiberius kept his pet crocodiles, presumably for guests who passed the grapes the wrong way after dinner, and in the other he swam with his minnows, the young boys and girls he liked to cavort naked with of an afternoon.

Ironically, although much of the slaves' and soldiers' quarters are still standing, the luxurious villa which stood on the hill above was partially buried in a 19th Century landslide, and today it is nothing but dust. Looks like Hamlet was right after all.

Of course, Tiberius wasn't the only out-of-town obsessive to visit the area - in 1541 Il Barbarossa sacked the entire coast on the instructions of Suleyman the Magnificent to find and bring back to Constantinople the legendary beauty Princess Julia Gonzago of Fondi.

Tens of thousands died in the subsequent war, and only 37 escaped, among them the Princess.

At various stages before and after that this part of Italy was in the hands of the Etruscans, the Greeks, the Romans, the Barbarians, the Byzantines, the Lombards, the Franks, the French and the Spanish before Italian unification in 1871.

Today, the only invasions are from ten squillion German tourists every summer, but in late spring the little square at the heart of Sperlonga village is only half empty, or half full depending on whether you're an optimist or a pessimist, and is a perfect spot for sitting outside the Nibbio gelateria tucking into one its famous ice creams and a café latte while watching the plums, figs and peaches slowly ripen on the market stall nearby.

Sperlonga itself is a pearl among places, cradled in the palm of the mountains and perpetually offered to the blessing of the sea below.

But if you can bear to tear yourself away and plunge inland, you will be well rewarded by the Circeo national park, full of migrating birds who arrived and never left, filled with a combination of Mediterranean torpor and fear that the moment they cleared the park's boundary fence, an Italian sportsman, dressed in the most exquisite tweeds and bearing an intricately worked Purdey 12-bore with a walnut stock which his grandfather purchased as part of a brace in London in the Twenties, would, in the most elegant, gentle and apologetic manner possible, blast them to pieces.

At one end of the park, and a fine venue for lunch to boot, is the rather exclusive hotel of La Stiva, which possesses the most automated toilets in Italy.

I walked in and the light came on. I put my hands under the tap and water came out. Then the water stopped and was replaced by hot air.

I should explain at this juncture that I always wash my hands before going to the toilet, on the basis that since I have been out and about doing all sorts of things with them, they are actually much more filthy than the part which I am just about to touch with them, which has been innocuously nestling in freshly laundered cotton minding its own business all the while.

Anyway, after I began performing my micturations and the urinal started flushing, I half expected a pair of mechanical hands to reach out of the wall, give me the regulation two shakes, tuck me away and zip me up, but in the end I had to do it myself, sadly.

So it was that, fed and watered and with everything back in place, I drove south down the coast, following the route of the Appian Way and passing from time to time shops with signs outside saying *Mozzarela di Bufala*.

Now, someone had actually told me once that proper Mozzarela was made with buffalo milk, and I had dismissed it in the same way that someone told me that the Israelis were going to set up an official dairy industry and call it Cheeses of Nazareth.

Now, it appeared that it could actually be true, but it was difficult to know how to ask someone. If it was the case, they would think I was stupid for not knowing something so obviously true, and if it wasn't, they would think I was stupid for asking something so obviously untrue.

Still, if I was stupid it was too late to do much about it now, so I did ask, and it is true. Which leads to yet another question. How on earth do you milk a buffalo?

By some sort of miraculous process, presumably, similar to the one which according to local legend caused the cliff at nearby Gaeta to split into three at the very moment that Christ died on the cross.

Fifteen hundred years later, a chap from Cassino named Filippo Neri abandoned the ways of the world and came to live, not in the biggest split, which was too draughty, nor the smallest one, in which you could not even have swung a German mouse, but the middle one, which was just right.

Today the site is, naturally, a shrine and a chapel which combines the worst features of Renaissance, Gothic and Baroque architecture and which is best avoided if you suffer from good taste. Even the candles are electric and coin-operated, and there is a box nearby for the appeal fund, but whether the funds are to be used wisely for demolishing the chapel or foolishly for restoring it is unclear.

Outside, stalls sell little glass bowls which when turned upside down engulf tiny plastic Popes in a flurry of snow.

It is strange how the Italians, normally such paragons of style, occasionally fall into such black holes in which their entire sense of beauty is sucked off whole, like the souvenir shop in the Vatican.

But then, you only notice the rain when you've been standing in the sun, I thought as I walked down the hill to the much more impressive medieval Chapel of the Immaculate Conception and its matching orphanage, which has in the middle of one wall a night safe for children in which distraught mothers would place their unwanted bundles.

The nuns, hearing the infant's cries, would flutter down the stairs like doves to fling open the wooden doors and reveal their latest tiny burden.

Although Gaeta was mightily pillaged in the Second World War, this chapel was saved by an enlightened German officer who arrived ahead of his troops, fell in love with it, and planted ersatz "*Achtung - Minen!*" signs around the building.

Although his name has been lost, the embodiment of his spirit lives on in not only the building, but an interior which contains a deeply moving 16th Century series of panels depicting the life of Christ but an interior which shows that the dialogue between different architectural styles need not always descend into argument.

Unless, that is, it involves the Neapolitan architect Guarinelli, who in 1848 was asked by Ferdinand II to design a magnificent cathedral, using only the finest of materials, to replace the little church which had stood on the hill above the Chapel of the Immaculate Conception for centuries to celebrate the 1222 visit to Gaeta of St Francis of Assisi.

Instead, Guarinelli used half the king's money to build a magnificent villa nearby, then invited the king to the villa-warming party.

"Nice pad, eh, king?" he said when the king sauntered up halfway through the evening.

"Do you take me for an (expletive deleted)?" replied the king.

As a result of Guarinelli's duplicity, the facade of the cathedral is, indeed, a splendid hymn to marble, but the rest was built with the cheapest local rock. You'd better see it soon, before it falls down.

Or even better, treat yourself to the luxury of returning to your hotel by evening boat, leaving behind a town in which the soft golden light of early evening was blessing one by one buildings painted variously the salmon pink of the 18th Century Bourbon dynasty and the buttery yellow of the Pope.

And, in the harbour, a collection of strange white pointed objects which were slowly bobbing ashore.

A day which had begun with the threat of death by mafiosquito was ending with the threat of death from the underwater division of the Ku Klux Klan.

It was, it has to be said, a good time to leave.

In the morning, I took the ferry from Formia to the Pontine Islands. Shame it hadn't been running in Cicero's day.

He could have hopped on the 8.30am hydrofoil, spent a very pleasant day out of town and avoided being murdered by Mark Antony's soldiers for opposing the triumvirate that succeeded Caesar.

He doesn't know what he missed, for the islands are much more pleasant than being hacked to death by a bunch of burly legionnaires.

The hydrofoil docks at the hillside village of Ponza, painted in the delicious Italian colours of faded terracotta, buttery ochre, indigo and white, so that all I wanted to do for a while was collapse into a café chair, admire the view and ask for a cappuccino and acqua con gas while all around indolent teenagers prowled with an air of what they hoped was brooding menace but which actually looked like the result of premature haemorrhoids.

Except there was no gas.

"*Non abbiamo gas,*" said the proprietor with a sympathetic shrug.

The island was having a bubble crisis, so we were reduced to drinking still water while in the villas in the hills behind the village, disenchanted widows presumably sat tapping their dessicated fingers impatiently on the marble edges of flaccid Jacuzzis.

Beside the cafe where we sat, at the end of a row of the usual tourist shops, was an interesting establishment selling scuba diving equipment and, quaintly, a black plastic sack with a nozzle attached describing itself as a solar shower.

"Simply rinse with one teaspoonful of baking soda, fill with water, leave in direct sunlight, and after three hours you should be able to have a relaxing hot shower," said the instructions on the front.

Below that was a discreet pile of bright yellow packets of something called laundry tablets. Did you eat them then watch the molecules of grime leap off your shoulders like lemmings?

Sadly, I was never to find out, for at this moment a grizzled veteran in a South Sea Islands shirt and brown trousers turned up and offered us a chance to potter around the coast in his boat for a fiver each.

It seemed too good an offer to refuse. From time to time, as we explored deserted inlets and coves over the next couple of hours, the coastguard launch would drift idly by, rendered incapable of chasing smugglers by the weight of the medals which the captain had, ironically, been awarded for valorous chasing in the past, and which he now wore as a sort of paramilitary clothesline stretched proudly across the left breast of his tasteful pale olive uniform.

From time to time, also, there would speed past fat speedboats of the sort advertised in American boys' comics of the Sixties, driven by men in dangerous sunglasses who I imagined were highly placed mozzarella smugglers on their way to a cartel to fix the price of buffalo milk artificially high.

In their mysterious wake as they unzipped the tranquil surface of the Tyrrhenian Sea they left huge waves which almost engulfed our tiny craft, leaving us in turn gazing down into the bottomless blue then up into the endless sky, and although most of us on board were indifferent Protestants, leaving us crossing ourselves and praying to Neptune, St Erasmus, Our Lady of the Aquatic Grottoes, Robert Maxwell and anyone else connected with disasters at sea, who might be able to put in a good word for us.

And miraculously, when we opened our eyes, a deserted beach had appeared before us. We splashed ashore, fell to our knees, partly in gratitude for our lives and partly because walking on sharp shingle is an art which requires years of practice, and undressed for swimming, each according to our nation.

The Dutch flung off all their clothes without a thought, flung guttural consonants over each other to ward off the cold - with that peculiar Dutch way of speaking which in an Amsterdam accent sounds like someone trying to swallow a reluctant goldfish and elsewhere sounds like small hedgehogs being beaten to death with cucumbers - and flung themselves in the water.

The English undressed so slowly, taking such infinite care to cover every inch of flesh with towels, that by the time they were ready it was time to leave and they had to content themselves with a quick paddle.

And the Italians draped themselves so elegantly with a single white towel in the manner of Augustus addressing the Senate that by the time you had finished admiring them they had magically donned swimming costumes so up to date that by the evening they would be unfashionable and would have to be replaced.

They were led into the water by Gigi, our guide, a noble, white-haired patriarch so...so...

Sorry, I ran out of adjectives there and had to nip down to the thesaurus shop to get some more. Happens a lot in Italy...so magisterial that as he breast-stroked across the bay he looked for all the world like Moses parting the Red Sea, so that rather than take the boat back to Ponza for lunch, we simply walked after him down a corridor of water lined with baffled bream and fretful octopus parents on one side who had temporarily become separated from their little octopi on the other.

We shuffled hastily by with eyes averted, knowing that we were going to eat their second cousins for lunch, in a dockside restaurant in which as the meal went on the noise levels from the tables around us gradually rose to the level which in other countries would have had someone reaching for either earplugs or a handgun.

But Italian is the most beautiful language to listen to, unlike other languages such as German, in which most words ends with a plosive sound which leaves the speaker in such a state of tension that they can never relax except by driving their Porsche faster and faster down the autobahn until they crash into a Trabant in a welter of torn metals and slowly deflating egos, and which leaves the listener with such a feeling of being violently besieged that even someone says: "I love you" in German, your immediate reaction is to punch them in self-defence.

In Italian, however, each word is stressed on the penultimate syllable, a stress accompanied by a slight raising then lowering of the shoulders which for the speaker creates the feeling of cycling up a gentle hill on a fine summer's afternoon - on the latest designer racing bicycle from Turin, naturally - pausing briefly to admire the view, then coasting gently down the other side.

For the listener, meanwhile, the inevitable reaction is to fall into a hypnotic torpor in which they want to remove all their clothes and be made love to with beautiful, almost unbearable tenderness for the rest of that same summer afternoon.

Tragically, there was no one around to make beautiful, almost unbearably tender love to, so I had to content myself with a tour around the island.

You can do this on a scooter, which will cost £20 a day, or, if you are clever enough to take with you on holiday the entire Royal Corps of Signals motorcycle display team and split the cost with them, 95p.

Or you can just jump on a bus, which is a lot less bother.

The island of Ponza was inhabited in turn by Romans, monks, no one and Bourbons, whose 2,000 descendants drive around in quaint three-wheeled vans while wearing woollen bobble hats, both of which have been banned from the mainland for not being stylish enough.

Highlights of the splendid coastal drive include the cliffs from which Lucia Rosa, a beautiful local girl, threw herself because her rich parents disapproved of her lover because he was so penniless that he could not even afford a bobble hat, never mind a Reliant Robino.

Other strange forms of transport on the island include Citroën versions of Second World War German Kubelwagens and a red Fiat Strada convertible whose interior the owner had imaginatively replaced in its entirety with wicker.

Below the white and periwinkle blue houses are cliffs dotted here and there with the giant cactus onto which in the 19th Century the Bourbons used to fling their enemies, then use them as watering cans.

Actually, they didn't. I just made that up to pass the time on the hydrofoil back to the mainland on which one of the more unusual passengers was a nine-foot swordfish in a body bag, obviously the innocent victim of the feud between the mafiosquitoes and the Ku Klux Klan underwater division which I had predicted the night before.

"I'll never forget the halibut I had in Kiev," said Gerbert, the man from Amsterdam who was sitting opposite me at breakfast.

He was silent for a moment, becoming as misty-eyed as a Frenchman would about his first mistress, an Englishman would about his Morris Minor and...well, a Dutchman would about a halibut.

We were at breakfast, discussing our trip later in that day to Naples, a city so close to social meltdown that only a few years ago hospital patients having a seizure would pick up their mobile phones and dial the emergency number 113 rather than waiting in vain for a nurse doing her rounds.

Not only that, but there wasn't a decent halibut to be had in the whole city. Margaret Thatcher, who not only lionised the

195

cult of self-reliance to the extent that she said society had ceased to exist, but failed to mention the halibut in any of her major speeches, would have loved it.

Even before then, the city was once so decadent that for a couple of centuries it was the sex capital of Europe, giving rise to syphilis in such quantities that the expression "See Naples and die" took on a much grimmer meaning than originally intended.

Today, Naples is returning to normality, although of a sort so chaotic that Neapolitan drivers say there are only two types of traffic lights in the city - those that are there for decoration and those which are merely a suggestion.

Locals will also shrug with proud helplessness as they relate how street urchins will unscrew your car numberplate at one set of traffic lights and sell it back to you at the next. It actually happened to a friend of a friend of theirs, in fact.

To get to the city, you drive through countryside where more escaping British prisoners of war were caught than in any other European country.

Their home-made suits fooled the Germans, but the Italians took one look and knew that not even Germans could dress that badly.

We arrived and decamped at Garibaldi Square, where it is said that at any one time, one in three of the occupants are major criminals, and the other two haven't been caught yet.

And indeed, as we got off the bus, two youths on a Piaggio were being frisked by a carabinieri while his colleague and a sniffer dog checked their scooter for illicit halibut,

Standing nearby with an expression which suggested that he had seen this all before was Antonio the guide, who with his shaven head, luminescent green eyes and slightly pointed ears, looked like the result of a night of unexpectedly illogical passion between Sinead O'Connor and Mr Spock.

Indeed, so otherworldly was he that he established an immediate telepathic link with my preconceptions about his city, and began to apologise for them before I had said a word.

"It's a bit unfair," he said. "No matter what the city's social and political problems are, it had a very cultured and civilized reputation until after the Second World War."

Sadly, my concentration on his subsequent eulogy about the city's moral worth was disturbed at this stage by the sight of a passing pigeon so devoid of self-worth that it had given up flying and was hitching a lift on top of a bus.

"Of course, you must be careful with your belongings when walking around," Antonio was saying. "It's understandable - we have a large number of unemployed people, and they can't eat air. And another thing..."

Tragically, what he was just about to say - that we were standing in the middle of the Galleria Umberto I, an astonishing *fin de siecle* plaza in marble and mosaic now occupied by an eclectic mixture of shops and businesses, including one intriguingly advertising Intercontinental Investigazioni Private - was drowned out by the piercing whistles of a passing march of policemen protesting about low pay.

"Since Antonio Bassolino was elected as mayor in 1993, things have become much better in the city," Antonio was saying after the din died down. "For example..."

Tragically, what he was about to say - that Bassolino had attracted the G7 summit in 1994, cleaned up the city centre, dealt effectively with its traffic problem and was tackling the stranglehold of organized crime - was drowned out by a group of well-dressed businessmen nearby shouting at each other at the tops of their voices while waving their arms around so extravagantly that it could only be a matter of time before one of them took off and rammed one of the few pigeons who still bothered flying in Naples.

"What are they arguing about?" I asked Antonio.

"They are not arguing. They are discussing last night's football match," he said. "Did you know that..."

Tragically, what he was about to say - that Napoli had won the Italian championships in 1987 and been celebrating ever since - was drowned out by a rattle of paperwork as a traffic policeman booked a passing motorist for stopping at a red light, thus causing such a cacophony of horns that we had to step into the Church of Gesu Nuovo for a bit of peace and quiet, only to find a wedding taking place in the midst of a riot of baroque which was the visual equivalent of the noise outside.

Indeed, as we stepped out through the streets again, the only respite from the constant racket that is Naples was in the occasional nuns who flitted about with patiently baffled expressions, and in the narrow and deeply shadowed side alleys, draped with washing, in which many Neapolitans still live in windowless one-room *bassi*.

Paradoxically, though, the most silent object in Naples is also its most menacing - the brooding, truncated hulk which sleeps under a blanket of cloud to the east of the city.

Vesuvius.

The volcano, apparently the only one in the world designed by Germans, since it has erupted with clockwork regularity since it buried Pompeii in 79AD and is just about to pop again, as a result of which a team of scientists monitors it 24 hours a day.

Although 20,000 people lived in Pompeii, most of them had scarpered after several days of ominous rumblings, and it was only the city's 2,000 optimists, who put the noise down to indigestion and. were in any case reluctant to leave a town containing 25 brothels, who were left.

What the eruption did leave behind, apart from 18,000 smug pessimists, was the world's most perfectly preserved Roman town, buried under 27ft of soft ash which, like an early neutron bomb, killed the people and saved the buildings.

And happily, the optimists did not die in vain, because even their most gloomy counterparts today are bound to be astonished by Pompeii, with its almost complete forum, basilica, baths with detailed stucco and frescoes, its streets of shops staffed by Greek slaves, its amphitheatre, gymnasium and stadium where Gladiators II v Barbarian Thirds would draw capacity crowds every week.

You cannot help but be astonished - by its scale, by its beauty, by the spooky feeling as you round every corner that you will come chest to face with a fully armed centurion, looking just as surprised as you do.

But there are no living people in Pompeii today, apart from the tides of tourists who ebb and flow.

There are just the plaster casts of the bodies caught as they swam or napped, or curled up to escape the fatal rain of ash.

Strangely, many of them have a peaceful expression which can only be gained from the sort of optimism which takes the rumbling of a volcano as a spot of indigestion.

And which believes that you can find a decent halibut anywhere outside Kiev.

1997

J is for Japan

A short history

660 BC
Emperor Jimmu founds country, which over the centuries adopts and adapts Chinese script and Buddhism.

794-1185
Heian era, of peace and poetry.

1185
Start of Kamakura era established by Yoritomo, the first Shogun, who rules over a spartan military regime of feudal lords and their samurai, known for quaint traditions of ritual suicide and chopping heads of anyone who annoys them.

1274 and 1281
Mongol hordes of Kublai Khan driven back by typhoon, which Japanese christen kamikaze, or divine wind, a name which will return to haunt American sailors centuries later.

1549

Portuguese missionaries arrive, bringing religion and guns. Japanese, more interested in latter, take them away and, in a sign of things to come, improve them.

1637
Realising that Christians are taking over the country, Japanese expel them, shutting the country off from the outside world until 1853.

1853
US Commodore Matthew Perry arrives with fleet of black ships and forces Japan to open its doors to foreigners, resulting in the end of the shogunate in 1867.

1868-1912
Meiji era, ending feudal and class system and bringing huge modernisation and a craze for all things Western, including beef, christened "mountain whale".

1926
Inauguration of Emperor Hirohito, who chooses the name Shōwa, or Enlightened Peace, for his reign, then invades Manchuria and attacks Pearl Harbor.

1945
Atom bomb brings defeat and American occupation. Japanese, unused to both, take a deep breath and decide to make the best of it, eventually creating Sixties economic miracle, symbolised for Japanese families by the "three sacred treasures" of fridge, TV and washing machine.

1980s
Three treasures become 3Vs – video, villa and vacation abroad.

1998
Recession. Japanese smile inscrutably and wait for new technology and internet boom.

Japan

Hai! I had finished the 3,564-page manual on bowing, graduated with honours from the four-year degree course on ways to avoid saying no and finished the evening classes on the correct way to hand over a business card.

I was a black belt in origami, and could kill a rhinoceros at 40 paces with a carefully folded sheet of foolscap.

I'd had the lyrics to Yesterday and My Way tattooed on the inside of my eyelids so that I could go out to karaoke bars and sing with the best of them.

I could work 28 hours a day making widgets for a Nissan Sunny, drink whisky all night and pick up a single grain of rice with a pair of oiled chopsticks.

In fact, I was absolutely indistinguishable from most Japanese people, apart from being 6ft 7ins and blond.

So why was I so nervous?

Perhaps because the more I read on Japan, the more baffled I got. It was a paradox, in a country full of them.

A country of sumo wrestlers and women like reeds in the wind. Of monstrous urban architecture and the delicate beauty of a tea cup.

A country which loves nature and the changing of the seasons, but which pours millions of tons of effluent into Tokyo Bay annually.

A country where Buddhism advises the letting go of all earthly desires, but which buys 40 per cent of everything that Chanel produces, and where the profits from selling the grounds of the Imperial Palace in Tokyo would buy California.

Perhaps I was nervous because I was standing at the end of a very long queue of people trying to get onto the overbooked BA flight from London to Tokyo.

All around me were tiny Japanese women clutching Louis Vuitton purses and Prada handbags, and Japanese men in the navy suit, white shirt and sober tie of the salaryman, except for one, who was dressed from head to foot in English tweeds, complete with deerstalker.

Miraculously, I got on the flight. Even better, I got an upgrade. Delayed for three hours by fog, we finally rose into the evening and tilted east.

Below us, earnest Scandinavians munched pickles and downed vodka in their saunas, while outside the night gathered around and inside the food and club class champagne passed to and fro so that by the time the brandy and chocolates arrived I had convinced myself I was quite fluent in not only Japanese, but Sanskrit, Swahili and left-handed Urdu.

It was a conviction increased not only by watching all of Braveheart in Japanese, but by a successful transfer of business cards with my neighbour, Shigehito Kawasaki, according to the rigid rules of Japanese business etiquette – hand card over with both hands, English side upwards so that you pay the other person the compliment of accepting that he can read English, bow slightly deeper than he does, which is difficult, since he's trying to pay you the compliment of doing the same thing, accept his card with both hands, study it carefully, feel the paper and nod approvingly at the quality, graciously accept his denial that it is anything special, place his card lovingly in your wallet, and when you thank him profusely, do not look him in the eye for too long, since it will be seen as a sign of arrogance.

In fact, by the middle of the night I had become so Japanese that I stood for three minutes outside a toilet which turned out to be unoccupied, quite unable to push the door in case there was someone inside who had forgotten to lock it and to whom being discovered in mid-ablution would be such an unacceptable loss of face that they would rush to the cockpit, wrest the controls from the pilot and send us all plunging to our deaths.

There's a lot to be said for politeness, I thought as I finally fell asleep, vaguely troubled by the fact that although I was apparently cocooned in an endless limbo of blankets and brandy, I was in fact hurtling across Russia with Vladivostok just emerging over the lilac horizon.

And beyond, already dimly lit by the rising sun, a land chaotic with impregnability.

However, possibly the thing that was troubling me most was that I had just realised I was going to the most expensive country in the world and had somehow forgotten to go to a bank and get some money.

Dawn broke to reveal the Japanese Alps below in bright sunshine and the pilot telling us that if we looked out of the starboard window we could see Mount Fuji.

I looked, but all the mountains seemed the same.

However, it was hardly surprising in a country which values harmony above individuality and where even the smallest Japanese schoolchild knows the proverb that the nail which sticks up gets hammered down.

As we landed, I was for some reason still incredibly nervous. I couldn't think why - after all, I was only arriving tall, blond, penniless and almost illiterate in the most expensive, alien, cultured, vertically challenged and trichologically stygian country on earth.

Perhaps it was because the ancient samurai code of conduct was known as *bushido*, the way of the warrior, and for me it was going to be the way of the worrier.

However, the reason soon became clear. Following the signs for the Narita Airport tourist information office, all I found was a pile of brochures and a sign telling me to take a bus to Terminal 2, where the office was on the second floor.

After an hour of wandering around the vast, echoing second floor of Terminal 2, all I had found was an information screen which no matter what buttons I pressed gave me only a delightful scenic view of the airport.

In the meantime I found two banks, each of which refused to give me any money but directed me with unfailing courtesy back to the other one.

I sat down and wished with all my heart that I could go back to my mummy, get a sensible job in a bank and give up this travel writing lark.

Then a small light bulb came on above my head. In Japan the ground floor is called the first floor, so their second floor was our first floor.

So I went down to the first floor, and somebody there told me the tourist office was on the ground floor. Simple, isn't it?

A quick phone call to Seiko Taniguchi in the Japan National Tourist Office in Tokyo to explain that I'd been delayed, a successful raid on a third bank and I was off to

Tokyo on a bus, a song in my heart and a page of directions to the JNTO in Japanese for a taxi driver.

This may seem superfluous, but in Tokyo houses either have no numbers, or numbers which refer to when they were built rather than their position in the street.

As A result, addresses go something like "Turn left at the train station, go past the soft drink vending machine, right at the post office and third left at the little noodle shop on the corner." The handy thing is that you can use the same directions for almost any house in Tokyo.

At Mrs Taniguchi's office, I was served a bowl of green tea by an office lady who was probably better educated than I was, but due to the male domination of Japanese office life, was destined to spend her working days serving tea to people like me until she married that nice salaryman in the corner, preferably before her 25th birthday, after which her friends would start calling her Christmas cake, since it's no good after the 25th either.

The unfortunate state of Japanese women is pretty much the fault of Confucius, who set down the strict hierarchy of obligation which still governs Japanese society.

The 17th Century Confucian scholar Kaibara Ekiken set down the following maxims after his master: "A woman should look upon her husband as if he were Heaven itself. She should never dream of jealousy. If her husband be dissolute, she must expostulate with him but never either nurse or vent her anger. Should her husband become angry she should obey him with fear and trembling."

Yes, quite.

Mrs Taniguchi, who was obviously not a Confucian, was making three phone calls at once in four different languages and simultaneously handing me huge wads of cash to pay for the inns in which I would be staying.

For a people so rich, the Japanese have a strange distrust of credit cards, preferring instead to walk around with loads of dosh sticking out of their wallets, a habit which makes them very popular with pickpockets when they go abroad.

And so it was with a thousand quid in crisp yen secreted about my person that I bowed carefully and set off, suddenly nervous again.

For I had just realised that I was about to experience the Tokyo subway at rush hour.

Still, in Japan, even the subway is polite.

The machines thank you for putting your honourable ticket in them, and once you are on a train a cheery female voice and a series of brightly lit arrows make sure you know where you're going.

You'd better be sure, because once you're on in the rush hour, there's no getting off.

Everything they say about the Tokyo rush hour, like the white-gloved attendants politely shoving 10,000 people into a space designed for three men and a small dog, is not only true, but falls far short of the truth.

If you can imagine being stuck up to your chest in quicksand, unable to move your arms to wipe the sweat trickling down your face because you've been stupid enough to wear an overcoat, you have some idea what it is like - and I wasn't even on the busiest line.

I looked out over the packed glossy blue-black heads, and felt like a daffodil in a bowl of olives.

On one side of me, a girl who had been clever enough to get on with her hands in the up position read a picture comic called Be Love, and on the other side an advertisement for

Guinness suddenly appeared on a station wall, as surprising as the face of a dead friend at the window.

At Asakusa station, squeezed to three inches wide and nine feet high, I was borne by the crowd to the exit beside Thunder Gate, which marks the entrance to Asakusa Temple.

The temple, which contains a 4in gold statue of Kannon, the Buddhist goddess of mercy allegedly hauled from the Sumida River in 628, was built the same year and is the oldest temple in Tokyo.

However, by this stage my armpits felt as if they'd been around for a lot longer, and what I really needed was a bath at the Ryokan Shigetsu.

Ryokan are traditional Japanese inns, where you sleep in a simple room with sliding paper shoji screens and tatami matting on the floor, upon which the maid will lay your futon at night.

And like everything else that is simple in Japan, ryokan are very complex. When you enter, for example, you take off your shoes, leave them pointing towards the door and are given a pair of slippers which you wear at all times when you are in the ryokan.

Oh, except for in your room, where you are only allowed bare feet or socks on the tatami.

Er, and in the toilet, when you put on a special pair of toilet slippers.

Ah yes, and outside, for which you get a special pair of outdoor slippers called geta.

Anyway, where was I? Ah yes, at the reception desk, behind which stood a small, exquisite woman wearing a small, exquisite kimono.

"*Konbanwa. Hiru desu,*" I said, surprising both of us.

"*Ah, Hiru-san. Irasshaimase*," she said, since she'd obviously read the same phrase book.

Exhausted by having used up practically all my Japanese vocabulary in one go, I sat down and started to take off my shoes.

"Oh, *Hiru-san*," she said - Hiru being the closest you get to Hill this far east of Belfast, and san turning me into an honourable Hill - "you don't need to do that."

I laced up hastily and was whisked in a space-age lift to a room which contained a normal bed, carpet on the floor and a TV in the corner.

Oh well. At least there was a beautiful blue and white *yukata* on the bed. Light cotton kimono for throwing over your shoulders after a bath, these are not to be confused with *yakuza*, the Japanese gangsters identifiable by flashy suits, permed hair, tattoos and a little fingertip missing as a punishment for a minor misdemeanour like not killing enough people in a gang fight.

Try throwing a *yakuza* over your shoulder after a bath and you'll lose a lot more than a pinkie, dear.

But first - the bath! Tying my *yukata* left over right in the approved manner I strode manfully up to the sixth floor for a dunk in the *o-furo*, o being the respectful prefix which is also attached to rice and chopsticks.

Japanese baths, naturally, come complete with their very own set of rituals. God forbid that you should   actually wash yourself in one; that's all done beforehand, sitting on a little wooden stool and soaping yourself all over, and then rinsing from a wooden bucket and tap or a shower.

Most modem Japanese baths have a soap detector sensitive to one part in a million and linked to the nearest police station, so that should you enter the bath with the merest whisper of suds behind your ear, the local cops will nip around and drag you stark naked and screaming to the airport for the next flight home for being such a barbarian.

So, rinsed thoroughly, you ease yourself down into a communal bath in which the water is just on the right side of scalding.

There, you lay your head on the edge, watch the neon of Tokyo twinkle ever the rooftops, and imagine that you are the hero of a post-modern James Clavell novel, just about to elope with the receptionist downstairs, live in a little wood and paper house in the mountains, swim naked in forest pools every morning and have 15 children with blond hair and olive skin who give themselves a happy surprise when they look in the mirror every morning.

And after you've dreamt all that, you can come downstairs glowing gently, make yourself a nice bowl of green tea and come over all Japanese.

After a while I pulled a padded cotton jacket over my *yukata* and went for a walk, finding myself sitting in the shade of a moonlit cypress tree watching a woman in a pale blue kimono making an offering at the shrine below the great squatting roof of Asakusa temple, her head bowed in silent prayer.

Nearby, a white cat snoozed inscrutably in spite of the fact that it was the dog walking time of the night, and assorted poodles, collies and rottweilers were passing within feet of its nose.

A day which had begun in the turmoil of a late arrival in Tokyo, a battle through the subway and a sincere desire that I had stayed at home and got a proper job had ended in peace.

For me, for the cat and for the bank, with whom I would not now be taking up employment after all.

Breakfast the next morning was delicious, whatever it was. Mind you, the fish looked even more surprised than I did - but then, I'd never eaten a whole fish with chopsticks before.

From sneaking a glance at the people kneeling at the next table, who were slurping down beer, noodles and pickles with relish, it looked like the correct technique was to work back along the spine from the head to the tail, finally leaving something on the plate which looked like the piscine equivalent of Thunderbird 2.

The rest was spicy miso soup, glutinous rice, pickled this, that and the other, tiny strips of dried seaweed, cubes of tasty tofu and steaming bowls of o cha, or green tea.

Stuffed, I had to sit in the lobby of the ryokan for a while before I could make it up to my room. Framed by the open front door was a white wall, a simple red lantern, a black wooden beam and the autumnal branch of a maple tree.

Suddenly into this rectangular poem strode a passing salaryman, a Japanese white collar worker, on his way to another brutal 12-hour day at the office.

As his footsteps receded, the scene began to slip back into the past, not stopping as it reached one hundred years ago, or two, or even three.

In Japan, life is art and the past is the present. Every day is filled with moments of the most extraordinary beauty, and you are often uncertain which century you are in.

Later that morning, I stood at the shrine in Yoyogi Park built in 1920 for Emperor Meiji. Like almost every shrine in

Tokyo, it had been burnt down during the war and rebuilt to the last detail.

A traditional Shinto wedding was taking place, with the bride wearing a flawless white silk kimono and cowl and the groom in layers of black and grey.

They were flanked by two huge wooden drums, below which sat four white lanterns and above which two black rooks spiralled in a clear blue sky.

At the entrance to Shibuya Park, only 10 minutes away, a young woman in a kimono hurried below a giant TV screen blasting out continuous pop videos, while just down the street two red British telephone boxes stood outside the Walt Disney store.

Everywhere, old met new and east met west, nodded peremptorily to each other and went their separate ways.

Six hundred feet above our heads, visitors to the Metropolitan Bureau building were enjoying the staggering view. Or rather, they were thinking how staggering the view would be view were it not for the smog. On a clear day, they say, you're not in Tokyo.

After a few minutes not admiring the view, they made their way to the lifts, where white-gloved attendants made sure they were all gathered safely in, thanked them for their honourable custom and wished them a pleasant descent.

Most then made their way to the Imperial Palace. The palace itself is only open to the public on Emperor Akihito's birthday, December 23, and New Year's Day, so for the rest of the year visitors must content themselves with 100 acres of punctiliously trimmed grass, black pines and a lake filled with the imperial carp.

Carp are much admired by the Japanese because of their tendency to swim against the current, probably because most Japanese people spend their lives doing exactly the opposite.

But since there is no current to swim against in the imperial lake, the carp just amble aimlessly about, bumping absentmindedly into each other then bowing and apologising.

The emperor, who has nothing much to swim against either since his father Hirohito was forced to renounce his divinity at the end of the war, has applied himself a little more diligently than the carp, working hard to make the royal family a little more human.

However, no matter how low key he becomes, he is unlikely to break his father's record for the understatement of the century when Hirohito went on live national radio after the bombing of Hiroshima and Nagasaki and the unconditional surrender of the Japanese armed forces and announced: "The war situation has not necessarily developed to our advantage."

By this stage, too, the daylight had not necessarily developed to my advantage, and as darkness fell I returned to the ryokan, passing on the way the following things.

An old woman reading palms by torchlight.

A small man in a lime-green shell suit being taken for a walk by a huge white husky.

A cigarette vending machine urging me to Speak Lark.

A man in purple tweed plus-fours, orange socks and a turquoise turtleneck pushing all his worldly goods in front of him in a shopping trolley.

A nightclub doorman who asked me in Japanese what height I was.

"*Ni hai*," I said, meaning two metres. I'm not sure if it was grammatically correct or not, but it was quite comforting to know that although I was the tallest person in sight, I was still only ni hai to a Japanese person.

Back at the ryokan, I found on the television a cookery programme in which a man who looked like a Japanese Marcello Mastroianni was sailing out of mist-shrouded harbours to hunt shark, plundering fish markets at dawn in search of giant crayfish and crashing through aromatic forests to dig up mysteriously phallic mushrooms, accompanied all the while by stirring music and a Babe from Heaven in a mini-skirt who took photographs of him while he cooked the lot then ate it with astonished gasps and sensuously quivering sighs.

Like most Japanese women, she had no bottom, which probably explains why most women in the rest of the world feel they have more than enough bottom to be going on with.

Another thing the Japanese have very little of is the word No.

According to Michihiro Matsumoto, an expert in the matter, there are 145 different ways in which the Japanese can say no without actually saying no.

Even Richard Nixon, no slouch himself at being economical with the truth, complained when he visited Japan in 1970 that President Sato failed to live up to a firm promise.

But as Sato explained, what he had actually said was: "I'll handle the matter with prudence."

Other variations include: "Mmm, your suggestion is very interesting," which means: "What a load of old borrocks," and: "I will almost certainly look into this possibility," which means: "The moment you leave the room I will throw your proposal in the bin and go out to that little karaoke bar on the corner with Tanaka-san."

Of course, we do it as well: "I'm sorry, he's in a meeting," "I hope we'll still be friends" and "It's been interesting meeting you - let's have lunch sometime."

It's just that the Japanese do it much better.

Which is why I think that although they claim that the new offices lining Tokyo bay are built on landfill, it is in fact a vast pile of unused Nos and women's bottoms.

In the morning, I rose at the stroke of nine and set off to Tokyo's Ueno Park intent on going straight to the Shitamachi Museum of Life in the old town and calling in on what the guide book referred to quaintly as the zoo logical gardens, which presumably meant that the animals were arranged in alphabetical order and the zebra was always last to be fed.

But then I got waylaid by Mr Wadaka.

It happened like this. I was standing listening to an outdoor karaoke and wondering how the same singer could tunelessly murder John Lennon's Imagine then produce a tone-perfect rendering of an old Japanese folk song, when an elderly man who was wearing a floppy hat and listening to a Grieg piano concerto on his Walkman came up and bowed.

"So sorry, but would you like me to explain what's going on?" he said.

"Ah, certainly, please, yes," I said, having apparently become illiterate in English as well as Japanese.

"It's karaoke. It will be the death of us yet," he said with a grin. "Let me buy you a beer."

Mr Wadaka had learnt his flawless English in junior school before the war.

"We learnt English properly then, but after the war young people didn't really bother," he said, tucking into the Sapporo and pickles he'd bought us from a noodle stand.

"During the war I was in the army in Indonesia serving as a mechanical engineer, then when we lost I worked for the American Air Force."

After that he spent 15 years with the Nippon Electrical Company and 10 years selling cancer insurance - the Japanese, with their almost exclusively seafood diet, have one of the highest rates of bowel cancer in the world.

"Now I get up at five every morning and walk for four hours listening to music. My wife complains she never sees me, but she should come with me, especially in the autumn when the trees are changing so beautifully like this."

"Your English is perfect, Wadaka-san."

"Thank you, thank you. But I'm 76 now, and I think I will die soon. Bit of a shame, since I'd really like to visit Norway and Finland for some reason. Still, in a couple of weeks I'm off to Sendai in the north to visit my brother."

"By train?"

"Oh no, I have a Suzuki 100cc motorcycle. Bit small for 400 kilometres, but it'll get me there. The milk's very good up in the north, and the beer's even better."

He drained his Sapporo, shook hands, bowed and set off at a brisk pace for the remaining two hours of his walk around Ueno.

In the national museum at the end of the park, they were having a special exhibition on flowers in which I spent a happy hour wandering around studying displays of ikebana and impressing the Japanese people around me by breathing in sharply through clenched teeth, nodding wisely then muttering: "Ah, astanubate," a nonsense word I had somehow remembered from phonetics at university.

At the other end of the park in the Shitamachi Museum, upstairs you'll find a wonderful collection of everyday artifacts like fridges, tin toys, televisions, comics, early Sony tape recorders, Godzilla posters and Pentax cameras.

Downstairs is a small but perfect recreation of the maze of tiny streets, wooden houses, tatami mats and shoji screens which was Tokyo until the great earthquake of 1923 and the firebombing of 1945.

Take off your shoes, sit on a cushion on the tatami in the prescribed knee-twanging position, and you could be one of the characters in James Michener's Sayonara.

Except, that is, for the thunderous noise of the open air rock concert on the other side of the lotus pond, so loud that it made old ladies on their bicycles wobble in the gaps between the cedar trees.

Perhaps, in spite of all its perplexing past, Japan is just the same as other countries - young people playing bad music too loud, and old faithfuls like Mr Wadaka wondering why they can't get up at five and listen to Grieg like any civilised person.

But enough of Tokyo. It was time to take to the mountains, by bullet train, mountain train, funicular and boat.

To Hakone, specifically, a popular Japanese getaway since 1590, when Toyotomi Hideyoshi first ordered hot springs to be opened there for his samurai to rest their battle-weary bones.

The last part of this journey starts on a little train which has been puffing and panting its way up the mountains since 1919.

All around us on the steep journey up, the trees burned with autumn fire, and in the near distance the black mountain steamed with white smoke-wraiths. Looking like a Hokusai print., it was the strangest of sights - the cold trees looked hot, and the hot mountain looked cold.

From Soun-zan it was a giddy cable car ride across the yawning valleys to Owakudani, where I had a lunch of black eggs boiled in volcanic mud - repulsive, it has to be said - and that canned Japanese soft drink peculiarly known as Pocari Sweat, as all around the mountain boiled and steamed and a few miles away that most famous of Japanese symbols and home of the world's highest Coke vending machines, Mt Fuji, made a rare public appearance from bchind the cloud which normally shrouds it.

They say you're wise to climb Fuji once and a fool to climb it twice, but I was going to get the chance to be neither, since the climbing season had ended on August 31 and the Japanese are very particular about dates. Air conditioning, for example, will not be switched on until June 1 even if May is the hottest month on record.

Instead, burping gently from the volcanic reaction the eggs had caused, I swayed onwards across another valley then, to a chorus of cheery "Harros" from schoolchildren in the cable car going the other way, descended into Togendai and took the ferry to Moto-Hakone, settling back in a clean seat with a freshly laundered cotton headrest as a female voice on the intercom informed us all that we were on a ferry of the Izu-Hakone Railway Line, pointed out that the ferry operated all year around so that we might fully appreciate the changing seasons on beautiful Lake Ashi, added by the way that the traditional Japanese pile on our left was the Hakone Prince Hotel Annex, which was perfectly asymmetrical, and urged us to relax and enjoy the rest of the voyage.

Which I did, as burnt orange Shinto arches rose out of the dark waters to a backdrop of forests which were a peaceful riot of colour.

Come to think if it, I had had a perfectly asymmetrical day - travelling by bullet train, mountain train, funicular, cable car and boat, arriving nowhere near where I'd left and still feeling at home.

It seemed appropriate to round it off on foot, docking at Moto-Hakone and toddling
down the Tokaido Highway, the ancient route used by shogunate samurai but today only a little side road filled with memories, falling leaves and the occasional Toyota Corolla.

I bought some noodles and checked in to the Moto-Hakone inn, only for the innkeeper to vanish before I could borrow some chopsticks off him, reducing me to sitting on a bench outside eating the noodles with my toothbrush and inventing a new Zen koan riddle in the manner of What is the sound of one hand clapping - What is the sound of one chopstick eating?

Replete, I went up to my room to find a shrink-wrapped telephone and a strange electrical plug with a small foil package attached to it.

It looked for all the world like an electric condom warmer in the same tradition as that other great Japanese invention, the heated toilet seat.

And so, with a full belly and an empty mind, safe from the threat of cold pregnancy and hot pursuit by samurai, I had a beer and fell asleep on the futon, in a perfectly asymmetrical sort of way.

The bullet train, which I found myself on again the next day, was originally conceived in March 1941, but the little matter of a war put it off for more than two decades.

Finally, after months of slow-speed trials, the engineers were given the go-ahead on March 3 1963 to sink the pedal to the metal - which they did, setting a new world rolling stock record of 160mph and leaving behind the light plane which had been sent to record the event.

Hats were flung in the air with the sort of controlled hysteria which is one of the characteristics the Japanese share with the English, along with living on an island, driving on the left, drinking lots of tea, being rained on and firmly believing that cold showers and a damned good thrashing never hurt anyone.

On the Tokaido line between Tokyo and Osaka, it makes 230 runs a day carrying 300,000 passengers.

On several occasions the network has moved one million people a day, and the system has not had a single fatal accident.

You can also set your watch by it, whereas in some countries you'd be lucky to get away with a calendar. Not to mention the fact that your ticket tells you precisely where to stand on the platform for your carriage, and when the train pulls in, the white-gloved stationmaster trading a formal salute with the driver, the door stops opposite you to the nearest inch.

However, the statistic most of interest to me on this particular morning concerned Seat 4A of Car Four in the Tohuku and Yamagata Line Shinkansen to Utsunomiya, because I was in it, whispering along without that familiar clickety-clack of train journeys elsewhere, since the lines are continuously welded to ensure a ride so smooth that if you balance a 100-yen coin on the end of your nose at the start of your journey, your nose will still be there when you reach your destination.

At Utsunomiya, the ticket collector followed me all the way to the platform to make sure I got on the right local train to Nikko, home of several dozen historic sites, the quaintest of which must be Deity with Sedge Hat presiding over Prayers with Deadlines.

And just up the hill from that is the Toshugu shrine, built by 15,000 artisans in the 1630s.

The home of 42 buildings, 5,147 carvings, two and a quarter hectares of gold leaf and three monkeys, the shrine was in questionable taste when it was built, and goes so completely against the Japanese grain of chaste minimalism that the effect of suddenly seeing it at the top of an avenue flanked by quiet cedar forest is as shocking as if a nun's habit had slipped aside to reveal a scarlet basque.

Among its more wonderful sights are two elephants sculpted by an artist who had never seen one, and which look like what you'd get if you threw all the animals in the world into a pile, picked out the fattest and ugliest bits, and glued them together.

Slightly more realistic, part of an allegorical series depicting the life of the monkey, are the original hear no evil, see no evil, speak no evil threesome.

In the innermost courtyard, though, was a sight more beautiful than wonky elephants or indifferent monkeys.

It was the shrine attendants in snowy robes and deep red overskirts, covering the sacred offertories with pure white cloths then taking out brooms almost as tall as themselves to sweep the temple grounds.

I wandered off into the forest by the river, where the air was damp and sweet with the afternoon rain, past modern houses where fathers were outside tinkering with recalcitrant motorcycles, wives were inside kneeling on the tatami setting the table for supper and children were playing in the road with that mad, excited joy for life that Japanese children have before they are sent to school.

And on into the aromatic gloom, until even the ubiquitous vending machines had vanished.

On, as the road became narrower and darker and the houses became wooden ones with folding shutters of the sort which have been built in Japan since the time before time.

It was the twilight time of day when colours seem brighter if you look away from them a little, so that the forest seemed to burn darkly as I walked on until the houses vanished and I was alone among the trees, sure that time had been unmade and I was standing in a Japan where the present had not yet happened.

A Japan in which the hurtling sound from around the corner was a Tokugawa samurai - galloping back in a fury from a fruitless meeting with a member of the *bakufu*, the shogunate civil service, in an attempt to get planning permission for his bonsai - who would decapitate me in about five seconds for not being prostrate in the ditch as he passed.

Which probably explains the stupid expression on my face as a white Toyota estate appeared around the corner and sped past on its way into town before the shops shut.

In the morning, on the train to Kyoto, the girl opposite me was carrying a knapsack bearing the timeless legend Flash

Bowl American Football, like a leopard finding a game. We are longtime friend of sportsmen, let's form a scrummage together.

While this may seem strange, it was not, for the Japanese are one of the most cultured, civilised and literate people on earth - until it comes to their slogans, which are a fascinating mixture of nostalgia, postmodern angst and gibberish. Over the 12 days I was there, examples I saw included:

Tissue of kitten — on a box of paper handkerchiefs

America takes nature for a friend - sweatshirt slogan

Funk the peanuts – radio station jingle

U-boat team — T-shirt on a toddler

Love and aids - graffito in Tokyo

Please let me know all about yourself – T-shirt slogan

Every day you need goods, Junior In Bag, For boy and girl young beet – on the side of a leather bag in Ueno Park, Tokyo, where I was charged £9 for a hot dog, a boiled egg, a slice of tofu and a can of beer

Joyous — on a shopping bag

Shot at close range – a hunter's sweatshirt

This is the White Corner. It's the bright, fantastic and sophisticated urban life - sign on cigarette machine

Let's Kiosk - name of a railway station shop

Moto Fizz motorcycle good Napoleon Air Valve System — on a punk's knapsack

FIDS: Fresh Information Delivery Service - on the back of a tracksuit

Spilt coffee has a sad remembrance of old — on a shopping bag

I like two wheels. Have a nice life with motorcycle and scooter — plastic motorbike cover

Fall in love with Twinkle Heart and she become charming, happiness for a while — on the side of a vacuum flask
Buy More Socks – girl's sweatshirt
Live Asahi for Live People - beer vending machine
Enjoy refreshing drink while taking part in a good chatting – Coke vending machine
Scandinavia Natural Roman Best Bread Message - shopping bag
Ones I missed, as spotted by Mark Gauthier, author of Making it in Japan, include:
International Baseball – The Baseball player I am very good at fighting. He is a man of ability. Fighting Monkey! Don't Give U-p Nice Batting – on a sweatshirt
Women are making bread on Sunday with the high quality milk and powder lie on their face and turn up their sleeves sweat is falling down on the trough Women's finger, hand, and body hot just like burning their blouse seems to be burst swing their rich breast - on a bread wrapper
Forcible. Beetle. I am pleased at your honesty Bebe - T-shirt
A lamb must be dreaming happy dreams - sweatshirt
The trouble is, it's catching. In a ryokan in Tokyo one night, I found myself muttering: "Yokohama mamasama. Oh yes, I'm running around like a lovely young chicken, then I'm going to bed to have a fine rich time, isn't it?"

Anyway, where was I?
Ah yes, on the train to Kyoto, where that evening, I found myself on Gion Corner, watching the most expensive women in Japan for nothing.
   They were geisha and maiko, their apprentices, dressed in the most formal style of the country's most formal city - from their elaborately coiled hair held up by antique ivory

pins to their snow-white faces and cherry lips, to kimono and obi in the most understated silks, to their simple white cotton *tabe*, split socks and lacquered *geta* sandals.

They were on their way to appointments, and they do not come cheap.

If you want them to dance and sing a little, to pour your sake as you eat and to laugh from behind a politely raised and perfectly manicured hand at your bad jokes, it will cost you at least £600.

And, naturally, money alone is not enough to procure the company of these most refined hostesses for the evening. So sorry, honourable guest, but you will also need an introduction from a patron.

The institutions to which they were tripping were probably specialists in *kaiseki*, or stone on the stomach cuisine, named after the warm stones Buddhist monks held against their stomachs to end off hunger during the long hours of meditation, and which developed into plain meals with tea, and then into one of the most ritualised forms of eating in a country where ritual is all.

In the best of establishments, the bill per person is unlikely to be much short of £300.

You can see why I was sitting on a fence with an £18 ticket for the Gion Corner Theatre in my back pocket.

Gion Comer, an evening of traditional arts, is the poor man's night out with a geisha, down a back alley which was so tricky to find that I finally asked at a police box. This is always a good way to get directions in Japan, except that no one ever knows how to get to the police boxes.

First onstage, after a lot of relaxing plinky-plonky music from a traditional 13-string koto - not to be confused with the relaxing plinky-plonky music from the three-string shamisen - was the tea ceremony.

Not to be confused with nipping out to the kitchen for a cuppa during the commercials, this was perfected in the 16th Century by a Zen priest called Sen no Rikyu as a means of achieving inner peace through simple surroundings and graceful ritual.

However, since the original ceremony took place in a small four and a half tatami room, the surroundings just disorderly enough to seem uncontrived, it is difficult to achieve the desired serenity in a theatre filled with foreigners with big feet, itchy beards and trains to catch. You might as well try to read a poem at a football match.

After some more relaxing music on the koto, there was a display of ikebana, or flower arranging.
There are about three thousand schools of ikebana, from vastly complex ones involving entire forests and gardens, to the school we were to see this evening, *nageire*, where the flowers are literally thrown in.

If you ever want to make a joke at a Japanese dinner party, study a large ikebana display which obviously took several years to arrange and then announce wisely: "*Ah - nageire.*" This will either have your hosts doubled up with laughter, or have you doubled up with pain after they give you a dig in the dongles.

Next onstage was a bunraku, or puppet theatre in which although no attempt is made to hide the puppeteers, they soon become invisible to you as you are wrapped up in the story of Kichiza, a page boy, and his sweetheart Oshichi, whose love finally overcomes their parents' attempts to marry them off to someone else.

I do like happy endings, I thought as I wandered home, had some noodles and beer with a Dutchman living in Washington, a Frenchman living in Uppsala and a Swede living in Berlin, and went to bed under a Kyoto moon.

At nine the next morning, waiting outside the inn just as she had promised was Sei the guide, a slim, exquisite girl in her twenties who was here to take me on a walking tour of Kyoto.

Autumn is the perfect time to do this, in an ancient city full of stories as sad as the falling of the leaves.

And one of the saddest of all is the tale of Kenreimon-in, last empress of the Taira clan.

The ruling Taira were defeated by Minamoto no Yoritomo, first shogun of Japan, in the great naval battle of Dan-no-ura Bay in 1185, and it is said to this day that the patterns on the backs of the crabs in that bay are the ghostly faces of the slaughtered.

Seeing that all was lost, Kenreimon-in flung herself into the sea with her mother and her infant son, only to be pulled out by the hair. She was the only member of the Taira to survive.

Taken back to Kyoto, she shaved off the treacherous hair which had saved her and became a nun, living in a bare hut until it was demolished by an earthquake and she came at last to Jakko-in, the temple which was to be her home for another 27 years.

In the spring of the following year, the noble priest Go-Shirakawa arrived unexpectedly from Kyoto to find her returning from picking flowers, her appearance so bedraggled that his entire retinue was moved to tears.

They talked all that afternoon of the vanity of human ambition and her happiness as empress.

"I gladdened my eyes in spring with the blossoms of the imperial cherry tree. In the hot months of summer I refreshed myself with crystal streams, and in autumn I viewed the moon in the midst of my ladies," she told him.

"In the cold nights of autumn, soft bed-quilts were heaped up to warm me, and I thought that I had only to wish for the draught of immortality. . .for it to be immediately forthcoming. So full was my life of joy and happiness that perchance even in heaven nothing could surpass it."

When the time finally came for him to leave, neither could hold back their tears as she stood at the top of the stone steps of Jakko-in and watched his procession until she could see it no more.

Although the feudal system established by Minamoto was to last for 676 years, civil wars continued on and off in Japan until 1603 when Ieyasu Tokugawa conquered the whole country, establishing the Tokugawa shogunate which was to rule Japan for 268 years by the simple principles of closing the country to foreigners and maintaining a rigid, unchanging order within.

There is no greater symbol of that order than Nijo Castle in Kyoto. The feudal lords, or daimyo, who had originally sided against Tokugawa got no further than the outer reception rooms, where wall paintings of ferocious tigers and leopards gave no uncertain message that they were to stay in their place.

More trusted daimyo were allowed deeper and deeper into the building to be granted an audience in rooms where the paintings were designed to relax rather than intimidate them.

In every room used by the shogun, bodyguards sat permanently behind ornate doors set into the walls, and even the corridors between the rooms were specially designed so that the floors creaked to warn of intruders.

Today, the so-called nightingale floors are still creaking; even when the Japanese do something badly, it seems, they do it well.

The most impressive room in the building is the huge inner sanctum in which only the most trusted lords would be allowed to gaze upon the imperious figure of Tokugawa, alone in his frugal majesty on a raised platform at the other end of the room.

We walked away across the creaking floors, and had lunch in a little inn nearby.

As I handed Sei the noodles, our hands brushed, and our eyes met, for exactly a second too long.

"What fine hands you have, *Hiru-san,*" she said.

Nijo is in its way a sad indictment of the fretsome nature of power, especially when compared to the Katsura Rikyu villa built in 1624 for the emperor's brother, Prince Torihoto, where the gardens are a miniature landscape of chapels and tea houses which has possibly contributed more to the ascetic elements of contemporary architecture than anywhere else in the world.

Each of the tea houses is the very essence of restful simplicity - a little entrance, four and a half tatami mats and an alcove for the display of ikebana or calligraphy.

One house is designed so that you can sit and enjoy the moonlight on the waves of the pond. "How beautiful it would be to take tea there on an October night, wrapped up in a padded cotton robe against the autumn chill," said Sei.

She was right. There is a sense of immense peace to be gained from this type of architecture, without the CripescanIaffordit syndrome which you often get when confronted with the best of Western design.

It is a sense of peace continued elsewhere in Kyoto at Daitoku-ji Zen temple, where I arrived to find the wonderfully mad abbot singing *Deutschland über alles* to a departing German tour group, giving them a quick V for victory sign and wishing them *Auf Wiedersehen* individually as they left.

When he heard I was from Ireland he whipped out a remote control, pressed a button and brought an illuminated globe descending from the ceiling with a hum as he launched into a word-perfect rendition of It's a Long Way to Tipperary.

Outside, we stopped in front of an ancient cherry tree.

"This tree is very famous," said the abbot.

"Oh? Why?" I said.

"No particular reason," he said, and wandered off, having thus filled his quota of Zen moments for the day.

Funny old thing, Zen, I thought as Sei and I wandered into one of the gardens and watched the sun set through the trees, casting ever-changing shadows on the raked sand.

It is very difficult to explain in words the feeling you get when looking at a Zen garden, which is probably why attempts to explain Zen since it was established in the 12th Century has been met with snorts, guffaws and claims that it is a huge fraud.

But being in the presence of it creates such a sense of peaceful contentment that you can only feel that whatever it is, it must be right.

We said goodbye to the abbot, who saw us off with a cheery rendition of The Soldier's Song, and finally, as darkness fell, we found ourselves at the temple of Jakko-in, where Kenreimon-in spent the last 27 years of her life.

For some reason I was thinking of another sad sight I had seen two days before in Kamakura - hundreds of tiny grey statues on a hillside overlooking the sea of Jizo, the patron saint of children.

Many of them had been draped with unused baby clothes by women who had lost a child and who came there in the misty morning or in the long shadows of evening, bearing with them their unbearable burdens of a futureless past, then walking away down the desolate path, as alone as it was possible to be.

And now I was standing at the top of the long flight of stone steps in Kyoto where Kenreimon-in had stood on an evening such as this and watched the procession of the priest Go-Shirakawa wind its way back towards Kyoto until it had disappeared, taking with it the light of the mortal world that she had known and loved.

And then she would have turned and walked back into the tiny bare cell where she was to spend the next 27 years in the darkness of solitude until she died.

We stood there for a long time as night crept by, then hurried home, the autumn leaves tumbling down like the tears of Kenreimon-in.

As we walked away, I looked at my watch. It was coming up to eight.

"Sei, may I buy you dinner?" I said.

"Of course," she laughed.

We found a little restaurant, and had beer and teriyaki, and talked and laughed, and then she walked back with me to the inn.

"You know," she said, as we stopped outside, standing close together in the breathing dark, "we have a saying in Japan that when we travel, we leave shame behind."

"I have heard that," I said, looking at her and knowing exactly what she meant. "What a pity that I am travelling, and you are at home."

"No. Tonight I am travelling," she smiled.

I looked at her, thinking how stunning she was, and then thinking of my girlfriend back home.

"Oh Sei, you are lovely, but I cannot," I said, and hugged her.

She smiled again, kissed me on the corner of my lips, and walked slowly away.

I watched her disappear into the night, honour and desire wrestling in my heart, then went into the inn and slept the sleep of the just, but only just.

And since my girlfriend later left me, I have regretted it ever since.

I said right at the start that Japan was a land of contrasts, and I could not have asked for a greater one the next day, when I went to see Cecil.

Cecil gets free beer, free lodging and free massage, but I wouldn't trade places with him for all the tea in Japan.

For when you look at Cecil, you are looking at 2,000 of the most expensive steaks in the world.

He is, in fact, one of the famous Kobe cattle bred by the likes of Mr Kakushi Ikeda, who collected me at the train station in a small green floppy hat which seemed to deny his

233

status as a millionaire, and a very large black BMW which seemed to confirm it.

Ikeda-san, a big cheese in the cattle world, is the current holder of the award for the best beef in Japan, as he proved to me when we arrived at his farmhouse by producing not only a diploma containing a photograph of a huge slab of beef, but the breeding certificate of the bull which produced it.

A sort of passport for dead cows who want to travel abroad, this contains all the details of their mum and dad, favourite beer and a large black and white rectangle which looks like the tributaries of the Ganges but is actually an ink print of a bovine nose.

Ikeda-san buys Kobe calves for £2,000 each, spends 30 months breeding them then sells them at auction for up to £31,000. Translated into steaks, that works out at £30-60 a shot. Translated into Mr Ikeda's bank account, it means the manager stands up when he walks in.

We leaped out of the BMW and wandered around the cowshed with Chijiki Imura, the interpreter. A huge yellow, green and black spider scuttled through the rafters, and all around us, black, furry cattle the size of small elephants   sat around munching finest quality American corn and wheat blended to Ikeda-san's secret recipe, looking at us with damp, oily eyes as he discussed their relative merits.

"That's Cecil in the corner. Eh, that's a nice fat arse on him, like a pig, don't you think?" he said as number one son arrived back from the winery in a new pick-up truck.

For, not content with bringing home the beef, Ikeda-san is now producing the wine to go with it. Over 80,000 vines have already been planted, a small research laboratory built and Ikeda-san junior packed off to France to learn his Chablis from his claret.

With the way the Japanese usually go about developing original ideas, I'd give it about 10 years before we're all standing around at dinner parties chattering away about how Tesco are doing a lovely little Chateau Kobe 2004 for only a fiver, darling.

"Here, let me show you around the winery," said Ikeda-san, ushering me into the BMW and tearing off up the lane only to become distracted by the sight on the way of the Kobe Beef Pavilion, inside which we found a series of wall posters showing the intriguing process of embryo transfer, in which the startled expression on the face of the receiving cow can probably be explained by the fact that the eggs are stored at -196 Centigrade before transfer.

I wrote politely for 20 minutes as Mr Ikeda explained in great detail the whole messy business, then realised that the only reason Mr Ikeda was still talking was that I was still writing.

I put my notebook away and stared politely at a grove of plum trees, then we both gave a sigh of relief and walked across the road into the local pottery, where small, wonderful women were producing small, wonderful pots.

And so to lunch, where the local wine proved as soft as a Mazda gearchange and where Cecil...well, I'm afraid Cecil turned out a bit like Prince Andrew must have felt about Sarah Ferguson - very sweet, but slightly fat and not worth the expense in the end.

Ikeda-san, meanwhile, was asking me increasingly complicated questions about agriculture in Ireland, to which I gave such increasingly obtuse answers that I'm sure by the time dessert arrived he was quite convinced that our main exports were De Lorean cars filled with mangoes and driven by Kashmiri goats.

We drove to the station, bowed deeply to each other and left in different directions and similar confusions.

At the station, Chijiko asked me where I was heading next.

"To Osaka, to catch the Midosuji line tube to Namba," I said.

She sucked in her breath sharply, as Japanese people do when faced with anything very difficult or upsetting. .

"*Ah so desu ka*? Osaka subway is very complex, *ne*?" she said, giving me directions which went something like this – take shinkansen to Shin-Osaka, local train to Osaka on Kobe line, go down steps, turn right, cut through food section of Daimaru department store, take sharp left at radishes, slow down for chicane through persimmons, handbrake turn at those little green furry things from New Zealand, straight on at sour plums, exit at pickled ginger then sharp left through Hanshin store and look for door beside women's perfume counter.

She drew me a map which looked like the wiring diagram for Apollo 13 and left, still shaking her head at the unutterable complexity of the Osaka subway system.

When she was finally out of sight, I dropped the map politely in the bin, took the train to Osaka, followed the signs like everyone else, and found myself eventually at the Ebisu-so ryokan, an inn so gloomy that the two ancient women who ran it seemed to have become almost transparent, like those spiders which live in very deep caves and never go out.

I asked one of them about the possibility of breakfast the next morning, a suggestion which reduced both of them to helpless cackling.

When they finally straightened up again, one of them led me up a dark and creaking staircase and down an even darker corridor to a three-tatami room which contained walls apparently covered in fur and a black Bakelite telephone with no dial.

I sat on the floor and wished that I had followed Mrs Imura's directions and got lost after all. It served me right for being so ungrateful to her.

But after a while I decided to make the best of a bad job and go out for an evening in Osaka. Osaka is the Birmingham or Glasgow of Japan — miffed that Tokyo is seen as more important and determined to look, talk and act bigger than the capital.

Walking through it even on a Monday evening, you get the impression that half the people of the city have been told they're going to die in the morning and they should dress up, go out and enjoy it while it lasts, and the other half have been ordered to use up a year's worth of electricity before dawn.

Beneath entire buildings covered in moving neon and giant TV screens, shops were selling everything it was possible to buy, pachinko arcades plinked and plonked and cigarette vending machines urged me to Speak Lark.

Men in Armani suits huddled together on street corners in flickering wreaths of cigarette smoke asking each other how much they earned today, and women wearing outfits just in from Paris rode to and fro on shiny bicycles, languidly discussing on mobile phones which date to accept for the evening.

I went back to my room, had a hot dog and a beer and slept fitfully, dreaming that I had forgotten to cut my nails.

But in the morning they were fine. I checked out and walked away down the street in the morning sun, the plastic dog on the doorstep barking at me all the way to the corner.

And then I took a train to the mountains to see some monks.

Funny chaps, Buddhist monks. You'd expect them to spend their time either sitting meditating or wandering about with little bowls begging for alms.

Yet from the 11th to the 16th Centuries, the Japanese ones were a right bunch of mad buggers, either burning down the temples of rival factions or showing their disapproval of Shogunate policies by rampaging down from the mountains and slaughtering everyone in sight.

But then, they were members of the Pure Land school, for whom salvation was simply a matter of nothing more vigorous than repeating the phrase *Namu Amida Butsu.*

Having thus saved themselves, and with nothing to do all day but wander around the mountains occasionally chanting: "Save me, Amida Buddha" just to keep their spiritual insurance payments up to date and checking the north-eastern horizon where evil spirits were supposed to dwell - it's hardly surprising that they found themselves twiddling their thumbs and wondering what else they could get up to.

Finally, one soggy autumn evening in the 11th Century, Kakujin, the 36th bishop of the Enryaku-ji monastery, stuck up his hand and said: "Here lads, what about forming an army just in case we're attacked by someone?"

"Er, like who?" the rest chorused from where they all sat steaming damply around the smoky fire.

"Well, that Nara lot are always a bit dodgy, and Zen's just about to be invented, so you can never be too careful, as my old dad was always saying. You know, my old dad was a bit of a philosopher in his own way. As he often said to me when I were a lad..."

"All right, all right, have it your own way."

Human nature being what it is, of course, it wasn't long before the monk-soldiers got a bit bored sitting around waiting to be attacked, and decided the best policy was to get their defence in first.

Finally, in 1571, Oda Nobunaga got fed up with them. Storming into the mountains, his samurai burnt thousands of temples, killed the monks and left eight centuries of history in smoking ruins.

Today, at holy sites like Koya-san, high in the mountains, there are 120 temples where once stood 1,500.

And the only way that visitors get killed is with kindness.

As I arrived by train and took the cable car, the glorious weather of the morning had broken, bringing rain slanting down from a leaden sky as I caught a local bus up the narrow mountain road and finally squelched through the low wooden gateway of Haryoin temple, sat on the front step and took off my sodden shoes.

A young monk, his head shaved and his feet bare, brought me in and padded in front of me down a polished hall as I schlipped and schlopped behind, leaving huge, damp footprints all the way to a simple room with a view of a garden dripping with rain.

We exchanged bows and I went inside to unpack, listen to the rain on the roof and drink green tea from a little pot in which the leaves were already damp, since the Japanese believe that the best tea is made from leaves which have already been used more than once.

And by then it was almost time for supper.

Kneeling on a cushion in front of a low table, I was served a delicious combination of food grown and cooked by the monks. Known as *shojin ryori*, it lacks meat, fish, onions and garlic, but neither quality nor quantity.

After half an hour of huge portions, I slowly began to realise two things.

One was why the Buddha's belly is so big.

And the other was that I couldn't stand up because both my legs had gone to sleep.

After five minutes trying to work out how to make a dignified exit from the dining room, I gave up and limped slowly backwards on my knees to the sliding door, which was thankfully open, bowing deeply and muttering: "Delicious, thank you so much," in bad Japanese, much to the enjoyment of everyone in the room.

After retreating to the hallway and wriggling my toes until I could feel them again, I decided to celebrate being able to stand again by going for a walk.

And although it was still chucking it down outside, it seemed the perfect night to visit a cemetery.

Borrowing an umbrella from the monk at the gate, I caught a local bus to Okuno-in, where the body of Kobo Daishi, who founded Koya-san in 816, is enshrined.

Twenty minutes later, as the tail lights of the bus disappeared into pouring night, I turned and plunged into the deep, wet blackness of the cypress forest, walking along a winding path lit only by guttering stone lanterns.

Behind them lay the ashes of thousands upon thousands of abbots and priests, bonzes and acolytes who had come here to spend their days on the mountain, to live and then rest at last beneath the tall trees in wait for the western paradise which Buddha had promised them.

A wandering dog joined me, and since he spoke English we walked on together, leaning into the rain.

He was the first to stop. And then I heard it too - the faintest tinkling, deep in the forest somewhere ahead.

It grew and grew, and then suddenly from the flickering dark, carrying tiny bells or lanterns on wooden staffs, came a file of elderly pilgrims dressed in white, as if the dead had risen.

Dog looked at me, and we both shivered, and agreed that it was time we went our separate ways home to bed, where I was lulled to sleep by the rain washing off the roof and the wind howling in the eaves.

And awakened at dawn by the time-honoured temple greeting of Diana Ross and the Supremes.

Eh?

Closer inspection revealed that it was only 2am, and that one of my fellow pilgrims was suffering from insomnia and was either determined to share the experience with us or had forgotten that the reason Japanese walls are paper-thin is because they are made of paper.

Several hours of Motown later, interrupted by bouts of stentorian nose-blowing, the real dawn arrived and it was time for morning prayers in the temple's candlelit inner sanctum.

Prayers began with a gentle dusting all over with powdered incense - which left me carrying around with me for the rest of the day the delightful aroma of chicken korma - followed by half an hour of chanting punctuated by the sonorous tolling of a bell and occasional bouts of spiritexorcising by the abbot, who at last summoned me forward, bade me kneel in front of the sacred flame and wash the purifying smoke over me, then dipped his fingers in the still glowing embers, blessed the back of my neck and bowed me out.

At breakfast, my noisy neighbour turned out to be an Englishman with a wild look in his eye and a crumpled Burberry over his shoulders, who wished me a hearty "Good morning, sah!" then proceeded to go over to the table of everyone else who came in, bow deeply, announce: "My woman - Japanese!" and share their tea. Noisily, naturally.

It was one of those moments when you know it is time to leave.

Sneaking quietly out the door, I pulled on a pair of shoes still sodden from the day before, bowed to the monk on farewell duty and took the first cable car down the mountain to catch the local train.

Down and down, into a scene in which at first the only colours were the white of mist, the sharded green of pine and the bitter red of maple, accompanied by the glorious, living smell of a forest after rain.

And then at last the muddy olive of workers' faces as they boarded the train on their way to work in the valleys.

But best of all was the fact that the train along the coast to Shingu had a stream of hot air blowing out from under the seats which had my feet toasty in no time. As they say, you only appreciate dry and warm when you've had cold and wet.

Bliss. Exhausted by a night of Motown, I tilted my seat back and slept all the way along the edge of the Kii Peninsula, passing in happy slumber the ancient training grounds of the ninja, as in turtles, the birthplace of the poet

Bashō, as in haiku, and the home of Minakata Kumagusu, as in presenter of 300 papers to the British Museum, identifier of 70 new Japanese fungi and master of 19 languages before he died in 1941.

Net to mention the building in Shinawa bearing the legend Fukodo: Bone Setting, which summoned up a curious vision of the people of Shinawa regularly falling over and muttering: "Oh heck, fractured my leg in three places again. Better hop down to old Fukodo and get it sorted out."

Any time I tried to sit up and take more of an interest in my surroundings, however, I fell asleep again. It was all the fault of the muzak section of Japan Railways. Even the jingles preceding announcements that the next stop is approaching are so relaxing that they're liable to make you nod off and miss the stop.

In keeping with the Japanese belief that nothing is more important than *wa*, or harmony, they seem to say: "So sorry to disturb you, honourable travelling guest, but we at Japan Railways are as happy as teddy bears that you have decided to join us this morning. Please feel free to tilt back your honourable seat, loosen your honourable tie and relax. Please be kind to old people, and if you miss your stop, please do not trouble your honourable self, for was it not Buddha who said that it will take many attempts to arrive at our chosen destination?"

It was, in fact, with a considerable effort of will that I dragged myself off the train at Shingu, a seaside resort where I was booked into the Station Hotel, a western-style establishment where I'm ashamed to say I ruined my perception of myself as a cosmopolitan by bouncing up and down on the bed in my room for five minutes saying: "Springs, springs, springs – hooray!"

It was obviously time I got back to being Japanese, which I did first thing the next morning by inventing a koan riddle all on my own.

Q: What do you do if you've got a town so old-fashioned that everyone's leaving it?

A: Turn it into a town so old-fashioned that everyone wants to visit it.

Tsumago, one of the post towns on the Nakasendo Highway which ran between Kyoto and Tokyo between 1603 and 1867, fell into disuse in the early part of the 20th Century.

Then, in the late Sixties, the citizens had the bright idea of preserving the entire town as an open-air museum to the extent of keeping TV aerials and electricity poles out of sight.

And today, millions of Japanese people who when they lived in the country couldn't wait to get out of it, flock to Tsumago every year to see what they have lost.

There are two ways to get to it. One is to take the local bus up the mountain from Magome, but the best way is to come upon it as *daimyo*, or feudal lords, and their retinues would have done in the 17th Century, hiking for hours up the old highway and spending the night in an inn before moving on.

On the bus I took as far as Magome, the girl sitting across the aisle had a wonderfully samurai-like look of petulant anger about her.

You imagined that if you crossed her she would whip out the traditional twin swords and behead you with both of them, leaving a thin slice of homeless neck in the middle.

Sadly, I had no chance to test my theory on her, since my Japanese was still pretty much limited to: "Excuse me, honourable ticket inspector, but where might I find the next bus to Magome?"

Even more sadly, when I arrived at Magome I found that I was two months late for the daily delivery of rucksacks from there to Tsumago, and was forced to walk up the mountain, rather than in the manner of a feudal lord, in the manner of a grumpy snail.

At first, all was well. Bright fritillaries fritillaried about, enabling me to use up all my butterfly vocabulary - "Ah, a Cabbage White! And look, a Red Admiral!" - while all around the afternoon sun glowed brightly on orange persimmons, red maple, yellow birch and green cedar trees.

Streams gurgled down the mountain, as streams will, and rooks spiralled overhead, cawing in English out of politeness. It was the sort of day that made you glad to be alive.

But after an hour's steady climbing, dripping and with a huge blister on my big toe which had chosen this most awkward of moments to commit ritual suicide in accordance with Murphy's Law of Chiropody, I was beginning to regret my impetuosity.

I was beginning to wonder, in fact, why it was that God had made me a Calvinist, halfway up a mountain with a rucksack, when he could just as easily have made me a hedonist, lying in a bath in a Tokyo love hotel surrounded by beautiful young women covered in suds.

But then, as I sat on a wooden bench and mopped my damp brow with an even damper hand, two apple-cheeked farmers' wives with their heads wrapped in white kerchiefs and their teeth elsewhere came out and gave me a brimming bowl of milk.

Perhaps, I thought as I sipped it gratefully, since I was incapable of kneeling and meditating for hours on end without my legs going to sleep, climbing mountains was the rigorous discipline which would lead to my own moment of Zen enlightenment.

So, filled with fresh milk and fresher vigour, I leaped up and plunged into the cool and cypress-sweet forest.

Sweat dried, and above my head the setting sun fell on the tips of the trees, painting them greenish-gold.

I pressed on, keenly aware that for almost 300 years daimyo and samurai, priest and pilgrim, merchant and peasant alike, had walked these very steps, looked up at these same trees and wondered if they would find their inn by nightfall.

What a boyish adventure it was, to walk through forests in the footsteps of such heroes and villains.

And then, finally, as darkness fell, to stagger gratefully up the steps of the Koshinzuka Inn, to have the hottest bath I have ever had in my life, in an ancient cedar tub.

To be given a bedroom whose shoji screens slid back to reveal a pond flickering with moonlit carp, and the river tumbling in the dark forest below.

And then to have dinner in an old wood-beamed room, of tempura of wild vegetables and a rare moss which can only be plucked a little at a time, otherwise it dies.

Of pickles, potatoes, buckwheat noodles, baked fish from the river outside. And *kurumimochi*, the local delicacy of pounded sweet rice dipped in ground walnut sauce and baked over the *irori*, the open fire in a sandpit in the centre of the room, over which a blackened kettle hung from a cantilever of bamboo, pine and plum wood.

And then at last *umeboshi*, tiny sour plums.

After dinner, the woman who owned the inn showed me the old family album, from the pages of which gazed her grandfather, the ancient white-bearded keeper of this same inn who had made the table at which we sat - a 5ft wide slice from the knot of a 350-year-old chestnut tree.

Some of the photographs were fading badly, not so much because of their age but because as the evening wore on the room had been filling so completely with wood smoke that it was quite some time before I realised that my host had actually gone to bed and I had mistakenly been exchanging pleasantries with the stuffed boar in the comer.

In the morning, walking down the mountain from the inn was like being awake at the dawn of creation: dewy grass sparkling in the warming sun, wood smoke rising against the forest green and the barking of dogs echoing through the valley as I came to Tsumago itself, the little town preserved exactly as it was during the Edo period of 1603 to 1867.

It was a strange place. Outside the ancient wooden buildings, lazy waterwheels turned, carp flashed dimly in dusty pools and women washed their faded white smocks in wooden troughs with a rhythmic trash and slop.

And inside, in the Edo gloom, were shelves of Fuji film.

At the top of the town, the street narrowed and rose, and I found as it turned the corner a garden of grass and moss, with an overhanging rock to which a small maple clung.

Beyond it, in a sundappled glade, stood a slim woman wearing the deepest of red dresses and a simple straw hat with a wide brim.

She was holding a wine glass and talking in a low voice to someone unseen.

With her head slightly bowed and her face in shadow, it was impossible to tell whether the conversation marked a beginning, or an end.

Whatever it was, it was one of those moments where you know that the best thing is to go on.

I turned and walked quietly down the hill, and took the bus down the mountain with three farmers and a small pig.

At Nagiso station as I waited for the train, I looked down at my brogues, which were getting a little battered, but they had been through a lot with me, those shoes. They had sat with me through business meetings in London, lain at nights under happy beds here and there, trekked through Yukon snow, been soaked by the rain of the Spanish winter and walked through the Japanese Alps.

A man only needs three pairs of shoes, I thought. Tan brogues for life, black Oxfords for death, and trainers for sport.

And so to Matsumoto, home of a famous castle which was built in 1595 and is entirely black and white, since they didn't have colour in those days.

Near the castle is a museum of Japanese folklore, which contains a magnificently batty collection of hundreds clocks donated by local businessman Chikazo Honda.

I stood there for quite a while thinking of what a strange place Japan is, but I am afraid I cannot tell how long I stood for, because in a room filled with hundreds of clocks, every single one of them had stopped.

It was now my last few days in the country, but at least I had finally discovered the secret of why Japanese women had such lovely little bums.

Noodles.

After two weeks of eating little else, my own had shrunk to a state of such pert splendour that I quite fancied it, and had to keep slapping myself to keep my hands off it.

Still, at least it provided the solution to my overdraft. I'd go home, grab my bum as I was bending over the filing cabinet, sue myself for sexual harassment and settle out of court for half a million to save me the difficulty of cross-examining myself.

My future thus secure, I leapt out of bed and took the next train out of Matsumoto, passing on the way to the station several people wearing face masks, not because of pollution, but in case any of their friends spotted them going to work at the unacceptably late hour of 8am.

It was a bright, cold morning, perfect for warming your hands on some station platform vending machine coffee.

Who would have thought that you could come addicted to coffee out of a can, I thought as I boarded the early train, from which the view as we proceeded north was quite baffling.

The fields below had rice drying in what looked like midsummer sun, the trees beyond were rioting with autumnal colour and the mountains beyond that were heaped with winter snow.

I almost expected to arrive at Yudanaka and find the cherry blossoms in bloom.

But then, it hardly mattered what season it was any more, for I was on my way to find the key to salvation.

The key is contained deep within the inner sanctum of the Zenko-ji temple in Nagano. To get to it, you pass through an immense wooden gate, walk past a No Smoking sign almost obscured by the clouds billowing from the incense burner and climb the steps into the Hondo, or main hall.

Ninety feet high and the largest thatched building in Japan, the Hondo contains statues of the Buddhist trinity of Amida Buddha, Kannon and Daiseishi Bodhisattvas.

However, in 642 Emperor Kogyoku decided that the images were too sacred for human eyes, and since then no one has been allowed to see them. Even the copies are only brought out for viewing every seven years.

At the very front of the hall is the *naijin*, the innermost sanctuary, and to the right is a flight of steps leading down to a winding, pitch-dark corridor beneath the altar. Somewhere along its twists and turns, on the right hand wall, a lock is hung, and on that lock is a key. If you find it as you grope your way along, you are guaranteed entry to the Buddhist Paradise.

But first let me tell you about a strange little creature from Japanese folklore called Tanuki. He resembles a badger, an animal which crops up quite often in the country's mythology.

Tanuki, usually depicted wearing a straw hat and clutching a bottle of sake, has a reputation for saving people by suffocating their enemies with his scrotum, which is of legendary size.

The reason I mention him at this juncture is because when I finally encountered the key, it was with the part of my anatomy least prepared to deal with a large piece of metal sticking out of the wall.

Rather than me being saved by a scrotum, mine had found salvation all by itself.

Painfully fumbling my way to the exit, I emerged with a deep bow which the monks kneeling there took as a gesture of immense respect and bowed back, but which was actually an attempt to walk upright.

Uncertain whether I had been got to heaven or not, I decided to go to hell instead and have a bath with some monkeys.

Jigokudani Onsen, or Hell Valley Hot Springs, lie in the mountains above Nagano. At this time of year, wild monkeys come down just after first light to bathe, preen and escape the cold.

First you take the train to Yudanaka, looking out of the window and realising that virtually every spare inch of the Kanto plain between Tokyo and Kyoto is cultivated – to the extent that you can reach out from the train window and pluck a passing peach.

On the train, a woman came up and gave me a tiny, succulent mandarin, and behind the Uotoshi Ryokan in Yudanaka, where I was staying, I found a session of Zen archery underway.

Wearing plain white kimono and black overskirts, the archers stood on a wide cedar platform using unadorned bows almost seven feet long.

They invited me in to drink green tea, and then they began again, using a ritualised series of slow and graceful movements.

I sat and listened to the creak of the huge bows being drawn, the phhht of the polished bamboo arrows being released, the silence as they arced over the long carp pond and the thwack or plunk as they either hit the small targets or sank into the soft sand 100ft away.

Either way, it did not matter. The important thing was the stillness arrived at through focus and repetition.

An hour passed by, unnoticed. The moon rose above the mountains, splashing silver on the stream tinkling into the pond.

At peace, I left, bathed in a hot cypress tub, ate a little, and slept the sleep of the blessed.

And woke before dawn, to take the bus to Hell Valley. A farmer's wife got on, gave me a plum, then got off after a while, leaving me the only passenger as we rattled up the tortuous mountain road.

At last I got off and walked for an hour through the forest, while geysers steamed and spiders sat on dewy, trembling leaves.

To sit, and wait, until finally the monkeys came, pink-faced macaques padding down through the trees and over the rocks in an orderly procession.

"After you, Yuriko-san."

"No, please, you put me in a difficult position, honourable friend."

"But really, I insist."

"Ah, this will never end."

In their dozens they came, to bathe and preen, looking around from time to time with their almond eyes.

I left them in peace, went downstream a little, took off my clothes and walked into the hot spring for humans.

With my head frozen and the rest of me being boiled alive, I was, as any statistician will tell you, at the right average temperature.

In hell, I was in heaven - a koan riddle which ensured that although I had not discovered Zen, I would at least leave Japan as baffled as I had found it.

1995

K is for Kazoo

It all seemed so simple as I lay in bed that morning at the Rose and Kangaroo.

First of all I was going to be the only person ever to visit Niagara and miss the falls.

Then I was going to drive to Buffalo to try Buffalo Wings and Beef on Week, that city's twin contributions to heartburn.

And finally I was going to polish the day off with a spin down to Eden, home of the world's only kazoo factory. The conversation over breakfast at the Rose and Kangaroo - a Niagara guest house owned by a local woman called Rose and an Australian called Laurie - should have alerted me that the best thing to do that day was go back to bed with a good book.

There was a woman from Ohio who should have had a Space to Let sign above her head, and her husband, who spent most of the time locked in his room.

The other two couples introduced themselves as Gary and Jennifer, and Hi! and Thelma, down from Toronto for the weekend.

"Uh, well, I think given the choice, I'd drink a whole glass of cream before I'd drink a glass of milk," began Jennifer shyly.

"I must say I prefer it in my coffee. It takes the edge off the bitterness," opined Hi! optimistically.

"I like a nice strong cup of coffee myself," stated Gary conclusively.

I made my excuses and fled into town. On Clifton Hill, the town's main street, honeymoon couples strolled past amusement arcades, wax museums and souvenir shops lined with obese pink pigs, debating which of the Rent a Circular Vibrating Bed for an Hour offers to take up.

Above their heads, a plastic model of Blondin, the French daredevil, balanced on a tightrope slung between the House of Dracula and the Guinness World of Records.

And above that, the ghost of Oscar Wilde looked down and thought how right he had been to describe this, one of the world's most popular honeymoon destinations, as the second major disappointment of American married life.

I got into the hire car and headed south for Buffalo. In my rear view mirror, the heavy industries of New York State emptied the contents of their corporate bladder into Canada with a great roar of relief and Japanese tourists flitted to and fro in the polluted mist.

In their opaque yellow capes, they looked like a tiny doomed species of moth for whom endlessly taking photographs of each other was the only hope of survival.

Buffalo had to be better.

Buffalo wasn't.

Buffalo is the home of the only two mail order houses left standing in America. Sold by Sears and Roebuck for £2,000 in the Twenties, they're still lived in.

The price included everything but the kitchen sink, which is where the catchphrase came from.

Buffalo is also the home of Frank and Teressa Bellissimo's Anchor Bar, where Buffalo Wings were invented on a dark and stormy night in 1964 when all Teressa had left in the kitchen when a bunch of starving customers rolled in was a pile of chicken wings fit only for soup stock.

She fired them up, smothered them in spicy sauce, and served them with celery and blue cheese dip, and hey presto, the rest is hysteria.

The wings are eaten with your fingers. Which means they get covered in hot sauce. Which means you'd be well advised to wash your hands before you to go the toilet. Believe me.

Believe me, too, when I say Buffalo was so dull that they close the shops on a Saturday. Even the tourist office had shut up shop, leaving only a dripping sign proclaiming that Millard Fillmore, one of the USA's less memorable presidents, had lived there from 1858 until his death in 1874. Of boredom, I imagine.

Let me put it another way. Mel, the black man I gave a lift into town, was regretting leaving the US Army because they'd threatened to post him to Alaska. Compared to Buffalo, the company of caribou beckoned like endless cocktail parties.

I dropped him off and went in search of Eden, the village south of Buffalo which is the home of the world's only kazoo factory and museum, established in 1907.

The kazoo, the only original American instrument, was invented in the 1840s, and now has 15,000 bands devoted to it, including a classical ensemble called Kazoophony.

Sadly, for the trip to Eden I had picked as my navigator a fellow Omagh man called Dominic McClements who was even worse at giving directions than I was at receiving them.

If you've never driven around rural New York State in the pouring rain looking in vain for the world's only kazoo factory, you've never appreciated how close it is possible to come to the edge of sanity.

At 4.45pm, 15 minutes before the factory was due to close, I stopped at a garage and persuaded the owner to let me use his phone so I could get through to the kazoo factory and persuade the caretaker to stay a little longer.

But by the time Dominic and I got there it was 5.20, she had gone, and I had added the world's only kazoo factory to the list of Great Tourist Attractions I Have Missed, along with Heidelberg Castle and the 10.30 bus to Liechtenstein.

Through the windows of the pale yellow clapboard building, rows of kazoos lay along the shelves, and in the factory at the back, piles of metal ones lay gleaming in baskets.

I had failed to fall for Niagara, and been bored by Buffalo.

But missing the world's only kazoo factory was the worst of all.

I pressed my face to the window as the rain streamed down, and felt like a child locked for ever out of the toyshop of dreams.

1992

L is for Lough Erne

It was a Thursday evening in spring 1978, and I was sitting in the downstairs bar of Queen's University in Belfast and thinking about the love poetry of John Donne, as I did in those days.

Suddenly I saw approaching through the throng Robin and Peter, who these days are very high up in marketing, but those days were scruffy students like all the rest of us.

"Here," said Robin, peering out from behind the giant Afro he sported, "we've accidentally booked a cruiser on Lough Erne for a few days. You don't fancy coming down, do you?"

"Aye, why not?" I said. "I'd only be going to lectures instead."

"Grand," said Peter. "See you outside at nine in the morning."

I had several more pints, went to bed and woke up at a quarter to nine, vaguely aware that there was something I was supposed to do.

Then I remembered, leaped out of bed, raced over to the union and arrived just as they were driving off in Peter's decrepit Mini.

The next few days were hazy. I dimly remember running the boat aground, then losing the chart, the rowing boat and finally Robin, when he fell overboard.

We hauled him back on board and set off that night for a celebratory pub crawl of Belleek, which was so small that we had to circumnavigate it twice to notice any effect.

You can imagine my feelings, then, when I drove into the same village a few weeks ago, an older and not much wiser man, to pick up a cruiser and treat my dear old dad and brother Trevor to a few days messing about on the lough.

We were warmly welcomed at Belleek Charter Cruising by Noel Coyle, who obviously hadn't heard about my previous record, and after he'd shown us the basics, like how to strap ourselves to the wheel in a hurricane, we were off for a gentle potter over to Lusty Beg, where the first day of an international fishing competition was just finishing, and weatherbeaten chaps were standing around talking about their flies, as chaps will.

The sun came out, the sound of a chaffinch drifted across the placid water, and all was well with the world. Dad was playing with his mobile phone, having finally got one at the age of 75, and marvelling at how different it was to the days when he built his own radios.

"I even wound my own coils and variable condensers," he said. "Then I think I built the first transistor set in the Province. I ordered the kit from Chicago, and even though they just addressed it to Bob Hill, Co Tyrone, Northern Ireland, it got to me in five days. That was good going, wasn't it?"

He looked up from the phone, a twinkle in his eyes, and I opened a beer for him.

We had dinner in the cosy wood-lined restaurant, a far cry from the last time I had been there, when the facilities were more like a prefab hut in a field.

All around us, the fishermen were eating the one that hadn't got away.

Dad, meanwhile, was looking aghast at the menu, which was awash with organic fettucini al fungi and Thai prawn salad with a hint of lemongrass.

"Here," he said to Siobhan the teenage waitress, "would there be any chance of an oul country fella just getting a bit of meat and a spud?"

"Steak and baked potato it is, then," said Siobhan. "Would you like garlic butter with that?"

"I can't believe the prices," said Dad when she'd gone. "Eighteen quid for a steak!"

The next morning, we rose at dawn, as manly adventurers do. Then we realised what time dawn was, and went straight back to bed.

All along the shore, when we finally got up, the fishermen were preparing to do battle with the mighty salmon and the unforgiving trout. When they were ready, they lined up and were led along the shore path by a lone piper - why do pipers have such trouble finding friends? - then, on a marshal's signal, raced to their boats, climbed in and set off, like a slow motion version of an ancient Le Mans start.

We had breakfast and set off to Kesh. Dad was following the route in a 1984 chart he had bought in the days when he had a little motor boat, Trevor was at the helm, and I was reading a book about South America.

"You know," said Dad, "I was just thinking there about the promise I made to my father to put up decent headstones on the old family graves.

"I've saved up enough to do it, but the flipping minister won't let me because he says the burial records were lost in a fire," he muttered darkly into his beard.

"I wrote to the Archbishop about that, and he said to go ahead anyway," Trevor shouted down from the helm.

"Did he indeed?" said Dad brightly. "Grand job. I'll order them next week. Tell us, Geoffrey, when we're on the subject, if you ever see a dusky *señorita* selling sombreros on those travels of yours, buy one for me and I'll sort you out when you get home."

"What do you want a sombrero for, Dad?" I said.

"Well, I plan to plant some nasturtiums and sweet pea before the autumn, and I'd like to wear it when I'm sitting out in the sun and admiring them next year"

Bonkers. Don't know where he gets it from, I thought, gazing out through the window and wondering idly whether hearing music in your legs meant that you were suffering from DVD.

It was obviously time for a beer, so we had one and sailed down through the afternoon into Castle Archdale, where a few years ago a London film company called Open Shutter came over to try to find one of the half-dozen Catalinas which was towed out and scuttled at the end of the war because it was cheaper than flying them back to the States.

They found what looked very much like one on the sonar, and planned to come back and raise it the next year, but never did, so the Catalinas are still there, just waiting for their return to the sun.

We didn't have to wait so long for ours: it was a glorious evening as we sailed into Enniskillen just in time for dinner.

The next day, we had a manly lunch of bacon butties and mugs of tea, moored next to Hill's Island so that we could at least view our ancestral heritage, if not actually claim it.

Dad finished his tea, and sat back in the chair, the afternoon wind ruffling his grey hair.

"You know, it's been grand being out like this, with just the three of us. I've wanted to do the circuit of that lower lough for years, and now I've done it, I feel very happy and content," he said.

He closed his eyes, the better to listen to a blackbird singing on Hill's Island, and as the late afternoon sunlight off the lough danced on his face, looked perfectly at peace.

2004

M is for Mongolia. In sparkly tights

I'm riding a Royal Enfield and sidecar across a frozen lake in Mongolia, it's -40C, and I'm wearing a pair of sparkly tights.

I'm sure there's a rational explanation for all this, but at the moment I can't think what it is.

At least I can explain the sparkly tights. I wore them for a fancy dress party (it's a long story), and when I mentioned the trip to a friend, he said he always wore tights on work trips to the Arctic to stay warm.

And since he was formerly a Colonel in the SAS, do feel free to question his masculinity. See you in A&E.

The tights don't have to be sparkly, by the way. They were just the only ones Tesco had in my size. And in my defence, the equipment list for the trip included, and I quote, hot pantyhose. And anti-cracking cream. For the ice, presumably.

As for the motorbikes, I've a long association with Royal Enfields, dating back to when Paddy Minne and I rode two from Delhi to Belfast in 1998 in temperatures which hit 51C in the Baluchistan Desert.

So if nothing else, I'd end up as a Royal Enfield world record temperature extremes holder. Or dead.

On the plane from Moscow to Ulan Bator, Pete the strapping Kiwi sitting next to me was on his way to take part in the Mongol 100 Rat Race, in which 28 competitors walked, ran, skated or cycled across Khövsgöl Lake.

"Aha, same lake as we'll be riding the Enfields on. See you there," I said as the pilot announced in Mongolian that we were descending to Ulan Bator Airport.

It sounded like Klingon in a Dutch accent by someone being strangled underwater. No wonder Genghis Khan's Mongol hordes had conquered Eurasia in the 13th Century: every time anyone saw them coming, they ran away screaming before they were zapped by a disruptor. Or challenged to a game of tennis by the Borg.

Anyway, where was I before I interrupted myself? Ah yes, at the airport, meeting François from Vintage Rides, the French company which organises worldwide motorbike tours, including this aptly named Frozen Ride, his girlfriend Sophie, several French riders and Mark, a jolly former Merchant Navy seaman from Devon turned successful property developer now enjoying the fruits of his labours on motorbike adventures.

Sadly, I didn't meet my bag, which was to spend the entire week in Moscow Airport. You know, the bag with all my cold weather gear, four-season sleeping bag and riding trousers with thermal lining. At least I was wearing my bike jacket and boots, which I hadn't had room for in the bag.

Thankfully, biker camaraderie being what it is, Jean the sidecar designer came up with an open face helmet, Mark had spare thermals and inner gloves and Lauren provided a furry gilet and a balaclava.

Which still meant that my legs were only protected from the cold by sparkly tights, thermals and thin cotton combat trousers. Through the window, a giant poster for Palm Springs mocked me with its promise of balmy warmth.

Still, Scott of the Antarctic wouldn't have complained about a little frostbite, so I stepped out into the ether-cold dawn with a stiff upper lip. If only because it was frozen stiff.

It was soon unfrozen by what followed: 14 painful hours bouncing around in the back of a minibus on the potholed road to Moron, through a bleak, rolling landscape like the Wild West, except here the horsemen herding cattle, horses or yaks wore great dark robes tied at the waist by bright sashes, rather than Stetsons and spurs.

The occasional log cabin or ger, the traditional circular felt tent used by the estimated third to half of the population who are still nomadic, were like the people themselves: squat and hunkered against the cold, with no airs or graces.

Their entrance always faces south, towards the sun and away from the north wind, and they were occasional: Mongolia is one-sixth of the size of the USA, but the population is only three million, half of those in Ulan Bator.

By the time we finally got to Moron late that night, I was suitably moronic, having not slept for 32 hours.

Next morning, the action began. We were introduced to the bikes and the arcane processes of kick-starting a Royal Enfield and riding with a sidecar, which becomes natural once you treat it like a car with handlebars rather than a bike.

The first day was an easy 60 miles on road to a lakeside log cabin, where Lala the interpreter and his team of two mechanics and backup vehicle drivers fitted studded tyres to the bikes and we went down to the annual three-day Khövsgöl Ice Festival.

Hundreds of locals tucked into barbecues, admired ice sculptures, slid down ice slides, skated to and fro, took horsedrawn sleigh rides across the ice or practised sliding their right-hand drive Toyota Prius Japanese imports, the apparent vehicle of choice for Mongolians who've graduated from a horse.

When they weren't doing that, they were asking for selfies with me, although I can't think why, since apart from being 6ft 7ins and blond, I was indistinguishable from everyone there.

And I was lucky Genghis Khan wasn't still around, since he ritually beheaded taller prisoners.

The lake fishing fleet of rusty trawlers was frozen in for the winter nearby, and I wondered where the fish were. Presumably they all went on holiday to the Mediterranean, sending back postcards saying come on down, the water's lovely.

Back at the ranch, Amara, the woman of the house, produced a dinner of chewy mutton and rice, washed down by beer and vodka, while her husband wandered around beaming aimlessly at everyone.

Mind you, women have ruled the roost here since Genghis Khan, disappointed with his useless sons, handed large parts of his empire to his daughters instead.

We slept on the floor around a stove, and wrapped in two thin sleeping bags provided by François, I woke at four to find that the stove had died down. My breath ghosting in the moonlight, I lay awake the rest of the night, too cold to sleep.

A wolf howled outside once, and the local dogs answered it with a cacophony of barking, safe behind their stockade walls.

My spirits revived by the rekindling of the stove and a hearty breakfast of bread, jam and instant coffee, we took to the ice on the bikes at last, and what a hoot that was.

The bike overtakes the sidecar on accelerating, and vice versa on braking, and before long, we were all laughing our heads off doing power slides and doughnuts. Stopping every so often for coffee and to check our temperature, riders and passengers swapped places.

Looking down through the ice, meanwhile, was magical: the deep blue of the water below, interwoven with a delicate tracery of white cobwebs, like the vapour trails of a Battle of Britain dogfight frozen in time.

The island we'd planned to camp on for the night was inaccessible, the ice for a mile around it churned up like a storm-tossed sea, so we decamped to a collection of lakeside gers normally used by a gold and copper mining company as a summer holiday camp for its workers, complete with pub, restaurant and spa, although they were shut for the winter.

Stove lit and beer opened, I went for a wander, gazing through picture windows in wonder at the swimming pool and meeting the world's unhappiest guard dog.

Barking constantly at being chained up and left to sleep in a kennel in the bitterly cold nights, he spurned my hand, then stood looking at me with sad anger in his eyes. I walked away, feeling much the same for him. Poor old dog.

Dinner, prepared by Lala and his crew, was chewy mutton dumplings in soup, followed by chewy beef with potatoes and carrots.

I began to fear that the chances of Mongolia winning a Michelin star were about the same as Elvis, Shergar and Lord Lucan being discovered on the moon. It was like being trapped forever in an Irish mother's kitchen in the 1950s.

We stoked the stove, and went to bed. Waking at four needing to pee, I knew now there was no point putting it off, so reached for my torch. Only to knock it over and hear it roll across the floor.

I tried to switch on my phone to use the light from it, but the cold had killed the battery, so I found the torch using the Murphy's Law method of standing on it.

Stifling a bloodcurdling scream, I limped to the door, only to find that the designer had neglected to include handles. As a result, it took me 4,378 attempts to open it, and twice as many to close it without waking everyone. I restoked the fire, crawled back into bed and tried to sleep, only to yawn a lot and listen to everyone else snoring contentedly in their 14-season sleeping bags.

I finally slept, waking at seven to the welcome sound of crackling wood as François relit the stove.

Outside, it was so cold that Lala was using a blowtorch on the Enfield crankcases to thaw the oil enough to kick-start them.

We rode north, only to find our way blocked by a wall of jagged ice, so that we had to explore for half an hour until we found a way through to the former Soviet holiday camp at Hanh, only 12 miles from the Siberian border.

A faded red CCCP sign still stood beside the gate and an ancient Uaz minibus was parked inside, its bug-eyed headlights making it look like the love child of Thomas the Tank Engine and Herbie the Beetle.

We opened beers and thawed out, sitting in deckchairs and watching the sun set over the frozen lake. Little cracks and groans echoed across the surface as it settled for the night.

"Wonder what we're having for dinner?" said Mark.

"Oh, probably smoked salmon on home-made wheaten bread with a nice glass of Chablis, followed by boeuf en croûte, gratin dauphinois and petit pois, washed down with a bottle of Gevrey-Chambertin, followed by apple crumble, custard and vanilla ice cream with a glass of Château d'Yquem," I said wistfully.

"On the other hand, it could be mutton," he said.

Astonishingly, it was trout and chips. Presumably the only trout in the lake too poor to go to the Med on holidays. It was lukewarm, and the chips were cold, but we still fell to our knees and gave thanks at the respite from mutton.

All over Mongolia, sheep breathed a sigh of relief, said their prayers and went to bed.

Even more astonishingly, the camp had a wood-fired sauna, or banya. I gloried in its heat, gasped at the bucket of cold water I threw over myself, and emerged cleansed to my soul under a starlit sky.

The next morning as we got on the bikes, the camp owner, clad in robe and sash, was chopping wood, his dog sitting patiently beside him.

I gave him a wave. He gave a sadly cheery one back, and we rode off to our privileged lives, leaving him to his.

In the past two days, three cars had fallen through the ice on the west of the lake and their occupants drowned, so we stuck to the east, coming across the racers in the Mongol 100 event one by one.

As we were chatting to their support crew, I heard a sudden cry of: "Geoff!"

It was Pete the Kiwi, striding across the ice in jeans and brogues.

"Afternoon, chum. Why are you wearing the clothes you wore on the plane?" I said.

"I might ask you the same question, mate. Ah, don't tell me – Moscow Airport lost your bag as well."

Back at the miners' holiday camp, we went for a short and bumpy ride through the woods to meet a family of seven living in a ger which they moved from pasture to pasture several times a year with their 500 cattle.

Inside, obsessive tidier Marie Kondo would have had a heart attack. Then scratched her head and wondered what to throw out, for everything had a function, with the men's side on the left with saddles, tools, hunting gear and wolfskins, and the right with cooking implements, children's toys and clothes.

In the middle was the all-important stove, and at the back a little altar and the traditional Mongolian HD TV, powered by a solar panel outside and a window on the world which allowed the family to ask the key questions of the day, like what would happen after Brexit, how we saw Europe's relationship with Russia developing and the price of a litre of milk.

That settled, a bowl of fermented yak's milk was passed around the adults, each running their finger around the rim before drinking and flicking a few drops in the air as an offering to the sky gods, since this part of Mongolia is still richly shamanistic. Mind you, in Northern Ireland we also worship inanimate objects by electing politicians who don't do anything.

Clear and bitter, it was like anorexic vodka with a hint of vinegar.

Back at the ger, Lala and Co rustled up the best meal of the trip so far: tender beef with noodles, followed by one of two Mongolian delicacies, along with blowtorched marmot: a sheep's head from which they cut slices and passed them around.

Surprisingly tasty, they went to gold medal position on the podium of my top three weird foods, ahead of guinea pig in Ecuador and grasshoppers in Mexico.

The next morning, a minor disaster: a raised platform of ice loomed ahead, and Eric, one of the French riders, saw it too late and did a splendid Titanic impersonation, sliding sideways into it, buckling the sidecar wheel and bending the frame.

Handy, then, to have Jean the designer and Lala's mechanical skills to hand, and within half an hour Eric was up and running again.

Naturally, his compatriots passed the time by playing football with the chunk of ice he'd knocked off.

Before Moron, we took a last side trip across country to see deer stones, the 7ᵗʰ Century BC carvings of highly stylised reindeer leaping aloft, their eyes filled with yearning for the sky.

The vast Mongolian sky, a dome of cerulean blue by day and by night filled with twinkling stars, their apparently eternal nature reminding us that our days on earth are numbered; all the more reason to fill them with adventures such as this.

By now, I'd become surprisingly used to wearing the same clothes night and day, not washing, and the, er, interesting experience of using a squat toilet at -40C, but the hot shower and clean clothes in the hotel back at Ulan Bator was a glorious experience.

Particularly since my missing bag was waiting for me.

"And about time too. Nice time in Moscow?" I said to it sternly.

"Lovely, thanks. Had a fling with a nice Louis Vuitton handbag, although I suspect she was fake."

"Hope not. If you two have lots of lovely little handbags, I can sell them on eBay, make a fortune, learn Klingon and open a decent restaurant here."

2019

N is for Namibia

L et me give you two pieces of advice. Never look a leopard in the eye, and always put collapsible water bottles away where you can find them again.

But let me explain. The previous year, I had walked across the Sahara with 123 other lunatics from Northern Ireland to raise £250,000 for Mencap.

Every day, we walked 20 miles in temperatures of 40C, facing blisters, sunstroke, heat exhaustion and 2000ft high dunes.

Every night, we faced sub-zero temperatures, the life or death struggle to find a bed next to someone who didn't snore, and the horrific realisation while halfway across the dunes to answer the call of nature in our bare feet that scorpions only come out after dark.

Every morning at dawn we were dragged out of warm sleeping bags to wash from a tin mug in a bucket of freezing water.

So why, when that nice Ciara Gallagher from Mencap phoned up to ask me if I'd fancied an even tougher trek across the deserts of Namibia, did I accidentally say yes?

Sighing deeply, I made my way up the study, found a guidebook on Namibia, made a nice cup of tea, and sat down to find out, among other things, that you should never look a leopard in the eye, because it really annoys them, and to avoid male elephants when they are sexually aroused, which I generally do anyway.

The politics, meanwhile, sounded even more complicated than Northern Ireland: groups vying for supremacy over the past few decades had included SWANU, OPO, SWAPO, PLAN, DTA, MFC, MPLA, SADF AND UNTAG, as well as a few incursions across the border by UNITA. That stands for the National Union for the Total Independence of Angola, which should really be NUTIA, except that sounds like a vegetarian spread.

The similarity to Northern Ireland doesn't end there: in the early 19th Century, missionaries arrived and gave all the natives guns, thus establishing a link between religion and loud noises with which everyone in Belfast was only too familiar.

However, all this was unlikely to trouble me, since I would be in the desert, where the only occupants are the bushmen of Namibia, one of the few people in the world who have learned to live with no permanent access to water.

In this they are like the indigenous landlocked people of Tyrone, although they make up for it by going on holiday to Rossnowlagh every year.

In fact, being from Tyrone I should be entirely at home, I thought, going to the cupboard under the stairs where I was sure I had left my collapsible water bottle from the Sahara trek.

And failing completely.

Making a mental note to buy another one and not let it out of my sight this time, I returned to the history of Namibia, which was colonised by the Germans when they arrived in 1884 and left beach towels all over the country.

However, in 1914 they wanted the towels back for their attempt to colonise the rest of the world, so they handed Namibia over to South Africa.

In 1990, South Africa handed Namibia back to the Namibians, and in a few weeks the freshly independent nation would face its biggest challenge yet: the arrival of 87 of the whitest people ever seen in the country, who were not only going to go out in the midday sun, but walk across the desert in it.

I arrived at Belfast Airport to find them well prepared with endless supplies of Tayto cheese and onion crisps, entire rucksacks filled with chocolate and, in the case of one large chap whose name tag identified him as Whitie, a stuffed dog.

And then there was me, wearing a pair of old volleyball shoes and pink ski socks, and clutching a book on Siberia.

Still, if God had meant me to be organised, he would have bought me a Filofax.

Tragically, we arrived at Heathrow later that afternoon to find that everyone else in the world had decided to go to Namibia that weekend as well, and there was not a single seat to be had with extra legroom.

Even checking in gave me vicarious DVT, and when I got to the seat I found that the only person who would have been comfortable in it was a legless gerbil.

I think the people who design economy class seats should be forced to sit in them for ever, in the same way that architects who design pebbledash bungalows should be forced to live opposite them, and lawyers who extol the virtues of nightclubs and bookie's shops should be forced to live beside them.

Anyway, where was I? Ah yes, spending an entirely sleepless night on my way to Namibia.

At one stage I went for a wander and found an empty seat in front of the cinema screen, but the only way to get comfortable was to rest my feet on the bottom of the screen, and after a while the steward made me take them down.

This was a bit unfair, since my feet were actually more interesting than the film.

It was called Bedazzled, and if you ever get a chance, don't see it. The only good thing about it was the casting of Elizabeth Hurley as the Devil, since she was entirely bad.

Many hours later, we landed in Windhoek. It was a Sunday morning, but there wasn't a Presbyterian anywhere in sight, except for the ones we'd brought with us.

It was February, but it was summer, and it was the rainy season, but there was no rain.

It was so confusing that the only thing was to buy a copy of the local newspaper, the Windhoek Observer.

The three main stories were a flood, a plane crash and a boat launch, although not simultaneously.

On page 3 was an obituary for Mr Pieter Ignatius Botha.

"Mr Botha died recently," it began, then added, by way of an afterthought: "He was seriously ill."

The more I read it, the more it became clear that all the stories had been written by the same person, a man who had once been introduced to the English language, but had not developed a lasting relationship with it.

Here was another paragraph: "The daughters of the particular mother were active in recent years, and sex, in abandoned rail cattle trucks standing on a loop line, took place and according to the latest allegations, revived."

Inside, things got even better: This was page 11: "Before I tell you the story of Tuesday, a few words on the Marquise de Pompadour. She was indeed beautiful, 27 in 1977, a rather uncommon face, little make-up and she seldom visited a hairdresser which added to her qualities of beauty rather than diminishing her attraction.

"She had a lovely and very firm body, exceptionally nice legs, a quiet person but fiery and principled. Her mouth was slightly too wide but that was not unduly disturbing because in her company a man, and I'm talking of a real hot-blooded one, soon became aware of the vigours in that shapely body.

"Her teeth were good, of high quality, and her hands were not delicate, strong and pleasing to the eye. Her breasts strained against her blouse."

Then, on the back page, in the middle of a report about how run down the town hospital and swimming pool had become: "The hospital is dirty, grimy and everything reminds you of sex because it is one notice or poster after the other of sex.

"The huge municipal swimming pool is in total disuse... at least an Observer reporter when taking the photograph could reflect back to a day in 1959 when he fell in love with a young teacher at the pool, so infatuated with her that he missed his lift with Mr Percy Niehaus, political party leader, to Tsumeb where Mr Niehaus was to address a rally.

"The frantic reporter, after hurriedly and passionately saying goodbye to the young woman searched the streets for a car and lo and behold found Mr Johan Coetzee of Sanlam Insurance with his DKW Sax-0-Mat, a lovely car with a two-stroke engine. Mr Coetzee raced to Tsumeb with the reporter on a dirt road..."

"Anything in the paper?" came a civilised voice from beside my shoulder, interrupting my reverie.

"You wouldn't believe it if I told you. Here, have a look," I said, handing it over to him.

He turned out to be one of the two doctors on the trip, rather splendidly named Titus.

"After Andronicus or Oates?" I said.

"The family dog, I fear," he said, opening page 24 to reveal four photographs of topless women which I had missed. I looked more closely, but none of them resembled the Marquise de Pompadour.

We climbed aboard a bus and set off for the oldest desert in the world, decamping some hours later in exactly the middle of nowhere and setting off across the blazing sands.

Two hours later, as the shadows lengthened towards the sharp violet and orange of a desert dusk, we found camp. I unrolled my sleeping bag and began the minutiae of winding down a day in the wilderness: washing in half a mugful of water, setting out a clean shirt and socks for the morning and, most important of all, taping up toes before they had a chance to turn into blisters.

Above my head as I finished and went to bed, the sky slowly filled with stars.

There are many more stars in the southern hemisphere than the northern, because they all drift down with gravity.

By the time I fell asleep there were zillions of them, and on each one, someone was standing looking up at Earth wondering two things.

What the chances of intelligent life here are, and what became of that girl by the municipal pool.

What seemed like only five minutes after I had nodded off, I was being awakened by the cheery voice of Daz the guide announcing: "*Mesdames et Messieurs*, wakey wakey, rise and shine, it's another beautiful day in the desert, breakfast in 15 minutes!"

Ah, I had forgotten the joy of being woken before dawn, crawling out of a warm sleeping bag and washing in half a teaspoon of freezing water.

I pulled back the tent flap. All around, happy trekkers were emerging in the misty dark and making their way by torchlight like a procession of glow worms to a welcome breakfast of bacon and eggs, toast and coffee.

As we shouldered our packs, dawn crept around to reveal that the mist had sprung the desert into life. Along the river bed that we had camped in, everything from acacia trees to rock lichen glowed vibrant green, and at my feet a small black basking beetle sat with its rear end in the air, the rivulets of mist slowly running down its carapace into its mouth to give it water for the day ahead.

From the cliffs all around came the sweetly strident cries of the rock dassie which, believe it or not, is a descendant of both the elephant and the guinea pig. One of them, presumably the guinea pig, must have had far too much to drink that night. Let's just hope he got to be on top.

We climbed out of the river bed onto a high stony plain filled with remarkable sights.

There was a locust, looking so much like the pebbles around it that Kevin almost stood on it before it jumped.

There was a chameleon, its eyes swivelling independently at our intrusion.

"Are you looking at me?" several of us said simultaneously, then laughed.

Past it was a Left Ear Tree, whose pale green seed pods looked, funny enough, exactly like left ears. Or right ones, if you were walking the other direction.

There was even food, from the plant the bushmen call ostrich salad, which tastes like fish and chips with extra salt, but without the fish or the chips, and desert melon, which is like a lemon marinated in TCP.

Spitting it out, we strode on and down into the trapped heat of a river gorge, where no breeze ventured. All around, the heat had twisted and cracked the granite rocks into fantastical shapes by Henry Moore out of Dali - whales, frogs and once a giant Venice Carnival mask. Astonishing, and much cheaper than drugs.

Halfway through the morning we were joined by Joe, a lean South African guide who had just got back from a kayak trip to the Mozambique islands.

"One afternoon the kayak got ripped from stem to stem and started sinking. Then half a dozen grey sharks turned up for their lunch. I got it patched up, but by the time I got to the next island it was pitch dark. I got to the beach more by feel than anything else, and fell onto it in agony with cramps from my head to my toes," he said, carefully sidestepping a small sand snake.

"Heavens," I said, "what did you do then?"

"Went for chicken and chips. They do a great feed at the beach hut there," he said as we came upon the lonely graves of two German officers, Ferdinand Zarp and Robert Kirchgatter, who died on the 26th and 27th of June 1895, and whose dusty skeletons lay beneath our feet clothed in the tattered remains of their Imperial Army uniforms and topped by two tarnished pickelhaubes.

There were no particular wars being fought that year, so they must have died, in all their colonial finery, from the most common of insects, the most humble virus, to be brought here and laid in the parched earth half a world away from the morning sweetness of mountain pine.

I left the wind whistling through their iron headstones, and hurried on to catch the rest of the group, who had stopped to observe a rather large chameleon.

If you pick these up very gently, they will at first hiss at you, revealing a mouth the colour of a fresh lemon, then relax and slowly change to the colour of your palm.

Which made me wonder: how on earth do chameleons find each other to mate? Or do they end up going out with rocks and branches for three years before finally going for chameleon counselling?

"She's just so passive, doctor. At first I thought she was just naturally quiet, but the funny thing is, I'm beginning to quite get used to it, a bit like Tom Hanks and the volleyball in that film Cast Away."

Mind you, a chameleon would never say that: since they don't have any pockets for change, they couldn't go to the cinema to see Tom Hanks.

However, at this moment my thoughts were distracted by the welcome sight of camp, in the shady gorge of a river bed.

We collapsed gratefully in front of our tents as Daz came trotting up, looking far too cheery.

"Here, if we climb that peak over there," indicating with a nonchalant wave a 2000ft mound of granite rising nearby, "we'll get a great view of the sunset."

Now, you'd think after a day trudging 16 miles across the burning sands in temperatures nudging 50C, we would have playfully garroted him then pegged him out for the ants covered with a little honey

However, my little honey was at home in Belfast, so along with all the rest I said: "Yeah, why not?" and climbed the mountain.

And yes, the sunset from the top was worth it.

But the cold beer at the bottom even more so.

As I was examining my toes with a torch before tucking myself in for the night, a middle-aged chap with the sort of expression which comes from being comfortably set in your ways trudged gloomily past.

"Are you all right?" I said in the spirit of St Francis of Assisi, who said that to give is to receive, although to be fair, he was speaking in the days before income tax.

"Can't seem to find a space in a tent," muttered the chap, who turned out to be called Jonathan.

"Well, there's space in this one, although it'll be a bit cramped," I said, flinging back the tent flap as generously as a sheikh.

Tragically, I was to discover that the reason he couldn't find anyone to share with was because he snored like the offspring of a sinusoidal horse and an asthmatic turkey.

The man in the tent next door, meanwhile, seemed to be working his way through every page of the Kama Sutra.

"Mmmm, ohhhhh, mmmmm, yes, oh yes, pfhwoar, wow, ormph," he went all night long, building to a crescendo around four in the morning.

It was like being trapped in a musical of Animal Farm written by the Marquis de Sade, and it was in a sleepless and disgruntled state that I staggered into the frozen dawn.

"Hope I wasn't snoring," said Jonathan, emerging cheerily well rested from the tent. "My wife says I do when I'm knackered or if I've had a few beers."

Even worse, the previous day's trek had produced a rather painful chafing on the bit where I sit, and no amount of Sudafed cream seemed to sooth it.

I breakfasted heartily on toast and peanut butter, applied a large tub of Vaseline, and walked off into the sunrise like John Wayne.

I was with a new group this morning, led by Tony, the sort of quintessential blond and aquiline Englishman who during the war would have carefully folded his pyjamas and gone off to die nobly in a blazing Spitfire. Just ahead of us was a bunch led by JoJo, a former ballet dancer who was built like a small gazelle and who had most of the chaps in her group dreaming of dying nobly in a pair of blazing pyjamas.

"Right," said Tony, "before we proceed, let me remind you to drink far more water than you think you need. Your pee should look like champagne. If it looks like Smithwicks, you're in trouble."

"What happens if it looks like champagne and tastes like Smithwicks?" came a voice from the back.

It was Kevin, who was going to come in very handy in half an hour, when we discovered the skull of a zebra, with the rest of it nowhere in sight.

"He must have been doing some speed when he hit that rock," said Kevin.

"He was probably run down at a human crossing," said someone else.

Five minutes later we came across the rest, half skeleton and half rug.

"Is he dead?" said Phelim.

"No, but it's the worst case of anorexia I've ever seen," said Kevin, who had now been our resident zebra expert for, oh, five minutes.

Five hours later we stopped for lunch by an abandoned diamond mine. The sun had risen to its zenith, and with it the temperature. Kevin's thermometer rose steadily to 50C, went off the scale, theft expired with a weary pop.

"God, I could murder a nice cold pint," said Peter, a veteran of the previous year's Sahara trek who had kept his indigo Tuareg headscarf, and was now wearing it at a jaunty angle. "A really cold one, with those little beads of moisture on it, it's so cold."

"Peter?" said Andy.

"What?"

"Shut up, shut up and shut up," said Andy as we came around a rock to find a herd of zebra who were as surprised to see us as we them.

"Here, do you think zebra's white bits stay cool and their black bits heat up in this sun?" said Kevin.

"Aye, but every minute they take a step forward to equalise the balance," said Andy.

We marched on, through the shimmering heat of the afternoon into the blessed cool of early evening, finally arriving in camp to discover to my delight that I actually had enough clean T-shirts to last me to the end of the week.

Honestly, when you're knackered at the end of a hard day in the desert, you wouldn't believe how happy it makes you to know that you don't, have to wear a dirty shirt the next day.

In fact, I was so content that rather than take up Daz's kind offer of climbing another mountain to watch the sunset, I dragged a folding chair over to my tent, in which I was blissfully alone, had a beer and read my book about Siberia.

And so to dinner, a splendid feast of oryx spaghetti Bolognese followed by fruit salad and custard, washed down by a very nice South African red.

Honestly, I don't know why chameleons look so fretful all the tame. Life in the desert is a doddle, as long as you've got custard.

Even better, the next day was the last, and we set off with a song in our hearts and a spring in our steps, only to come face to face with a 6ft wide Welwitschia Mirabilis, a plant which is unique to this part of the world and has a lifespan of about 1,500 years.

The Welwitschia is the Little Shop of Horrors of the desert As you walk up it, you expect it say: "Feed me, Seymour", eat you and produce a belch which will still be echoing in the hilts by sundown.

It is, what's more, the ugliest plant in the world, although it does not realise it, since there are no mirrors in the desert. Not surprisingly, it reproduces asexually.

"Astonishing," I said, then hurried to catch up the rest of the group, who were having the daily competition for the person with the most embarrassing story.

The top three so far were:

1. Being sick over the statue of the unknown soldier at Westminster Abbey;

2. Being followed by a gay stalker;

3. Falling out of a changing cubicle into a shop after getting both legs stuck in a pair of trousers he was trying on, then hiding in the cubicle for half-an-hour only to find that the staff had captured the whole thing on video.

Even more strangely, all three had happened to the same person, although obviously I can't reveal who it was in case I embarrass Peter.

Chuckling at random, we set off again and ran into the next group gathered around Tony, who was holding up a small grey object about the size of a well-fed peanut.

"This," he said, "is an oryx dropping, and it is a Namibian tradition that on the last day of a great journey, there is a competition to see who can spit one the furthest."

Well, we're the sort of group who'd believe anything, and after several minutes of intensive oryx poo spitting, Kevin emerged as a clear winner with a rather impressive effort of just over 10 metres, which will stand him in good stead if it ever becomes an Olympic sport.

We wandered on. I'm not sure what the rest were thinking, but I was thinking that if Cate ever got to hear about this, she'd never kiss me again. So if you ever see her, don't say a word.

In the afternoon we paused on a high rocky outcrop for another last day tradition, in which we all sat apart and took a few minutes of silence to reflect on what the trek had meant to us, and to those less fortunate for whom we had done it.

We sat, and were still. The peace gathered around, vast and true, and from it came a honey bee, thrumming past on its way to some imagined meadow of my childhood.

How strange, I thought. Exactly the same thing had happened at the same moment on the last day of the walk across the Sahara a year ago, like a little leitmotif of contentment and completion.

We rose, and strode on into the last two hours of the day, our steps quickening as we descended into the burnished cauldron of a river gorge and saw in the distance the finishing line.

A breeze sprung up from nowhere, and it was with the wind in our hair and a grin of blessed relief on all our faces that we crossed the line, dropped our packs and sank onto the hot sand.

"Well done," said Mark, the leader of the guides, handing me a plastic cup filled with champagne.

"Say that to Kevin," I said, draining it in one gulp, "he's the new world oryx poo spitting champion."

"Oh no. You didn't fall for the old oryx poo yarn, did you?" he grinned.

2001

O is for Old Blue Eyes: to Palm Springs on the trail of Sinatra

The Fifties. Ava Gardner was diving naked Into Frank Sinatra's swimming pool in Palm Springs, and I was growing up in a field in Tyrone. Frank was having martinis with Carmen Miranda, and I was drinking National Health Service powdered milk. He was leaving Lauren Bacall, and I was leaving for school.

The Fifties. When the American dream was pure, and Americans were perfecting the art of endless childhood which they continue to this day: the instant friendships, the artless lack of irony, the wearing of bright clothes well into senility.

The corollary of that, of course, is arrogance and selfishness, unthinking generosity, hedonism and the inability to defer a pleasure if it can be had right this minute.

Frank Sinatra was the epitome of all of those, and Palm Springs was where he perfected them. As a result, the ghost of Sinatra is everywhere in this California town. You go into a bar, and his voice is sailing through the air without a breath to disturb the arid desert air. You talk to a man in that bar, and discover that he was Sinatra's dentist. You order a cocktail, and Sinatra is in the glass, in the effortless cool of late afternoon beneath the palms. You talk to a man outside, and Sinatra paid his father's medical bills. You check into a hotel, and the owner says of course Sinatra had a temper: he was short and Italian, so what did you expect?

A town of 45,000 souls, eight thousand of them millionaires, Palm Springs has had many lives. A thousand years ago it was the home of the Cahuilla Indians, who retreated to the nearby canyons in the heat of the summer.

In the Thirties it became Hollywood's hideaway, and from the Forties to the Sixties everyone from Elvis to Liberace stalked the streets and gathered for cocktails in the tangerine dusk, which for many of them was not long after breakfast.

In the Seventies it became a retirement town in which the average age and temperature were both about 88.

In the Eighties, hordes of libidinous teenagers descended on it every Spring break, making it more hip than hip replacement until Mayor Sonny Bono banned the testosterone tearaways.

In the Nineties the gap left by the students was plugged by gay tourists who stay in luxury private resorts where the rooms naturally, start at standard queen size.

Appropriately enough, I arrived in this perpetual mecca of cool at the cocktail hour, falling from a lilac sky to a desert the colour of powdered brick.

I picked up my convertible at the airport and pressed a button by the seat. The hood tilted back, and the heat of the night filled my bones. I pressed another button, and the music from the radio poured into my veins like honey.

It was Sinatra, singing Lady (pause for effect) Luck.

"Sinatra, who died a year ago today," said the announcer, when the song had finished. "All this week in the valley he loved so well, we will be making sure that his flame bums (pause for effect) forever."

By the pool, a waitress was waiting with a gin martini.

The darkness crept around, draping me with the scents of bougainvillea, jasmine and orange blossom. I could not sleep, and read a novel late into the night.

And the next morning, I had a Californian breakfast conversation.

Me: "Hi. And what sort of mood have we on offer this morning?"

Waiter: "Well, we got sunny, sunny, sunny or extra sunny."

Me: "I'll take extra sunny with coffee."

Waiter: "You got it. How would you like your coffee... hi-caff, low-caff, decaff, or no caff?"

Me: "Extra caff with milk."

Walter: "Absolutely. And will that be hi-fat, lo-fat, no-fat, soya or goat?"

Me: "Cream."

In the Los Angeles Times on the table in front of me, nine of the top ten in the best sellers list were self-help books. The tenth was the restaurant guide to Southern California.

And then, before I went looking for the ghost of Frank Sinatra, I had an appointment to meet Morgan.

Morgan was, in fact, the Sinatra of the desert: cool, confident and brilliant, but known to mix with some nasty types.

In Morgan's case, they're the critters you meet on her jeep adventure tours of the desert and mountains, which were apparently coming down with rattlesnakes, tarantulas, black widows and lawyers protecting their weekend retreats.

However, all I could see were lambs, and since this was California, we weren't allowed to stop and play with them because a sheep therapist had apparently proved that it causes lambs stress. Although not so much as mint sauce.

Morgan, however, was astonishing. Half scientist, half-philosopher poet, half raconteur -I know that's a lot of halves, but there was too much in there for just one brain – she talked almost non-stop for over three hours about the wilderness, and if I ever get lost there, I want her by my side. In about a day she'll have a house built, curtains sewn, soap, aftershave, shampoo, moisturiser, a complete medical kit and a five-course meal all made from cactus, and we'll be lying on a rabbit fur rug in front of a fire sipping home-made tequila.

Handy hint: a sheet of sandpaper is a useful substitute for expensive maps when visiting the desert.

If you prefer your wildernesses filed alphabetically, there's always the Living Desert: 1,200 acres which include an African village, a hospital which treats 20,000 sick animals every year and a daily show in which guides, owls, golden eagles, rats, porcupines and cervils do that talking, flying, swooping, scurrying, prickling and pouncing thing they do.

It is, of course, the closest you're likely to get to a rattlesnake or black widow spider and live to tell the tale, but all the logical arguments in the world about education and salvation from extinction fade, for me, with the sadness of being two inches away from the cougar who looked at me through the glass with terrible beauty and heartbreaking boredom. A bit like those TV presenters some people keep in little boxes in the comers of their living rooms.

I looked at my watch, and realised that it was the cocktail hour again, and that I had a date at Sorrentino's, Sinatra's favourite restaurant in Palm Springs. In the Fifties, when the Guadalajara Boys played mariachi here, there were seatbelts on the bar stools and the men bought dolls from the barman and gave them to the hooker they wanted.

This evening, Sinatra was the background music, as it would never have been in his day: anywhere he went out he insisted that his songs were never played.

There was even a Steak Sinatra on the menu, still served the way he liked it, with mushrooms and bell peppers. But since Sinatra's idea of good food was pork and beans out of a tin, I gave it a miss and had sand dabs with lemon and a glass of Chablis.

Hermann, the waiter, had served Sinatra here for three decades, not to mention every star in Hollywood and several presidents, and Sinatra had been persistently generous to him and his children in return.

"My best customer? Mr Sinatra. He was always pleasant and helpful. My worst customer? Mr Sinatra when he didn't get exactly three coffee beans for luck in his after-dinner sambuca or a bottle of Chateau Lafite '56."

Indeed. It was a very good year.

The owner, Billy Sorrentino, came over to the table and talked all evening. And talked. Everything he said was fascinating, but his voice was like a sheet of sandpaper, so that all I was left with was a map of the desert.

At the end of the night, I went to the toilet, and suddenly realised that I was probably using the same urinal that Sinatra had. But then I noticed another one, so I used that as well, just to make sure.

Sinatra, of course, was not the only celebrity to pee in Palm Springs, and several tours will take you around the weekend retreats of those with vast wealth., from the house up in the hills which Bob Hope built just for parties, seating 350 for dinner, to the row of four adjoining houses which author Sidney Sheldon bought: two to live in. one as a guest house and one as a gym.

Or the old Liz Taylor home, bought by a young couple who park their Rolls-Royces outside, one a convertible with the registration RR CONV, presumably in case they can't work out what it is by themselves.

I woke before dawn and went for a swim in the heated outdoor pool. In the duck-egg light, mist wraiths ghosted on the surface of the water and the tiny black birds known as Phainopepla sang with their soft, insubstantial call, like the love song of a soufflé.

It was five in the morning. At six I was due to meet a pilot in a hotel lobby out in the desert, and we were to go flying in his balloon over the warming sands to the mountains where snow still lay in the curves below the peaks.

Twice before in my life I had risen at five for a balloon flight, only to find when I arrived at the takeoff site that the flight had been cancelled due to high winds. I had, in fact, become an expert not-air balloonist.

But this morning was as calm as a nun. I drove for an hour, with the hood down and Sinatra on the radio, to the hotel.

In the lobby there was no sign of a balloon pilot.

"Is this where I'm supposed to be?" I asked the night porter, a large man with a small way about him.

"Balloon flight's been cancelled due to high winds," he said.

"Haven't I met you somewhere before?" I said.

Unable to get into the air, I drove back into town and spent a vicarious couple of hours in the Palm Springs Air Museum pottering around assorted Thunderbolts, Bearcats, Corsairs and Spitfires, and noting with British disdain that Mustangs were fitted with air conditioning: "Base, I gotta problem – the air con's busted and my shades are misting up."

Outside the window, the midday heat was shimmering off the runway where Sinatra used to land with the rest of the Rat Pack in his private plane, then walk straight to a waiting helicopter to take them to Villa Maggio, the mountain retreat he built in 1968 and named after the Oscar-winning role in From Here to Eternity which relaunched his career.

A modest little log cabin with nine bedrooms, 13 bathrooms, two saunas, pool, spa, tennis court, petrol station, heliport and separate guest house, this has been beautifully restored by a tax fraud lawyer and his wife who moved to Palm Springs from San Diego - "We didn't like the people: you say hello and they're stuck for an answer" - bought this as a weekend home, and were now selling it for $2 million.

The house is full of the flotsam of fame: you're leaning on Al Capone's old table and a Shi-tsu comes snuffling by your ankles.

"That's Harold Robbins' old dog," said the lawyer's wife. "We got her when he died a year ago."

Sinatra spent his early years in Palm Springs, though, in Twin Palms, a house down in the valley which he built in late 1947. A perfect example of mid-century modernism, it has now been immaculately restored by former landscape gardener Marc Sanders, who only discovered its famous history when he dug up some old planning permits.

In the heat of the afternoon we padded through the house, followed by Marc's miniature terrier - what is it with rich people and small dogs?

Here was the pool into which a drunken Ava Gardner dived naked in front of Sinatra's party guests.

Here was the room where Garbo stayed, arriving in midsummer in a heavy coat and scarf and only emerging to swim topless in the pool, clad only in a pair of baggy khaki men's shorts.

These icons passed before my unblinking eyes. But something was wrong! I had lost interest in the past, in history, in all that old stuff.

I was turning into a Californian, that's what it was.

I said goodbye to Marc and went for a drive in the convertible, the wind whipping in my hair and Sinatra on the radio, as he would be all week. I checked in the mirror. I was tanned. I filled up the tank, drank a bottle of low-sodium energy supplement and ate a diet loganberry yoghurt, then went to a car dealership to look at some pre-owned low mileage Rolls-Royces. I felt better.

On the way back to the hotel, I was overtaken by two teenagers in a vintage Jaguar and a bald pensioner in a red Corvette.

That night I went out to the old Plaza Theatre to see the Fabulous Palm Springs Follies, a bunch of retired showgirls and boys between the ages of 54 and 86 who've put their dancing shoes and their singing hats back on for a last hoof through the twilight years of vaudeville.

It may sound like finding out your granny's become a kissogram, but it was in fact, brilliant, and by the end of the evening I had fallen in love with not one, but several of the dancers.

Ah, if only I was an older man.

The next day I went to the Joshua Tree national park, 800,000 acres of desert, rocks, cacti and the strange trees given their name because the Mormons who travelled west through here in the 1850s thought they looked like the prophet showing them the way to the promised land.

If they were right, Joshua was a ra-ra girl, eternally holding aloft several handfuls of pom-poms.

Late in the afternoon I drove over to Desert Memorial Park, the final resting place of Palm Springs' rich and famous, to see Sinatra's grave. It is just a simple plaque set in the grass, bearing the inscription The Best is Yet to Come, Francis Albert Sinatra, 1915-1998, Beloved Husband and Father.

His several wives, especially Nancy, would probably have something to say about the beloved husband bit, but after reading so much about him, it sent a shiver up my spine to actually stand on the grave where he finally sleeps with all the stars of Palm Springs. Much as he did in life, really.

That night I went to see Sinatra: My Way, the tribute show by Frankie Randall, a friend and fan of Sinatra's for 38 years, in which Russ Loniello is a better Dean Martin than Dean Martin ever was, Louie Velez is a splendidly dreadful Sammy Davis Jnr and Randall... well, good he is, Sinatra he ain't, as he would admit himself.

I sank back in my seat, and realised the back of my neck was sunburnt.

I had been in his homes, I had stood on his grave, and now here I was listening to his music live on stage in his town.

In the darkness, I drifted away.

In the dream, Frank was cooking pasta in the kitchen. Dean Martin was lying drunk on the sofa, Ava Gardner was swimming naked in the pool and Greta Garbo was sitting on the floor in the comer, wearing an overcoat.

I looked at Garbo and her eyes closed, and with them the past.

The next morning I drove to the airport in the indigo dawn. On the radio, the Sinatra week had finished and they were playing Smooth Operator by Sade.

I climbed into an aeroplane and rose, high above the palms, into the endless curve of a Sinatraless future.

1999

...and Oman

Touring on a motorcycle and living on the way is a glorious sport that sets the blood tingling, that clears the mind. He who has never rolled with a softly purring engine between his knees, stopping at the heights to drink in every detail of scenery, has not yet tasted of a simple, wonderful joy'

Harley rider Theodore J Werle, 1913

Deep in the Omani desert, Cedric and Gertrude were relaxing under a palm tree after a hard day of being camels.

Cedric had just finished reading a fascinating article in Camel Monthly headlined "Lose that Unsightly Hump in only 30 Days!" and was tackling the crossword, and Gertrude was catching up with her knitting, as camels do.

Suddenly Cedric put down his magazine and pricked up an ear.

"I could be wrong, dear, but that sounds like a Harley," he said.

"And one of the big cruisers, since that's definitely Born to be Wild blasting out of the infotainment system," said Gertrude.

"Ah, that's the word I was looking for," said Cedric, filling in 14 Down: Milwaukee mobile music, 12 letters.

And the funny thing is, they were both right, for not only has Harley been making motorcycles since 1903, it's also been encouraging riders to go on motorcycle tours on them more recently, and Oman's the latest one.

It was, as you can imagine, tough going: on the first morning, I woke at the Banyan Tree resort just outside Dubai in a villa so big I needed my passport to get from the bedroom to the bathroom.

Outside, the rising sun dusted the dunes with pale gold light and mist ghosted off the private pool, and after breakfast I found the guide, Claude Abry, outside with a choice of a Heritage Softail or a Road King.

Fascinating character, Claude: from Lyons, he'd moved to Jordan when he got a job as a chef in Beirut then one as the personal chef to King Abdullah of Jordan, whose father Hussein had banned motorcycles from the kingdom after an assassination attempt on him by a biker.

The only people allowed to ride were the King and his entourage, and when Claude said one day in 2010 that it was such a shame that the rest of the country couldn't enjoy the same pleasure, His Motorcycling Majesty thought for a moment, then said: "Claude, you are right. I will change the law!"

He did, and Claude's been riding and living in the Middle East ever since with his wife and children, is fluent in Arabic and has moved on from being a chef to running Jordan's first Harley dealership and now a company which will run bike tours worldwide but specialise in the Middle East to introduce riders to the roads, culture and food of a region that Claude is passionate about and has come to regard as home.

"I love it, and I love the people. We lived in Lyon for years, and gave our baby daughter to our next door neighbours for babysitting, but they never once invited us into their home.

"When we arrived in Beirut, we bought a car and went touring in the mountains. We stopped outside a farm, and the farmer came out and invited us into his house. I told my wife to get back into the car because I thought he wanted to steal everything we had, and we drove off.

"I was ashamed when we got back to Beirut and told people about it, and they said such hospitality and friendship was normal in their country, and in all Arab countries; and they were right."

Indeed, to prove his hospitality, he handed me the key to the Heritage, and after a morning of twisties in the Jebel Al Jais mountains, I'd worn the footboards down to a sliver.

But then, cornering on Harleys is always a graceful waltz rather than the more frantic jive of sports bikes, and the motto of Harley's Discover More touring wing is: "Miles don't matter. Memories and moments do".

Amen to that, I say, and what's not to like about swinging through a sinuous symphony of bends with the burning blue above and the syncopated snore of a V-twin, that most evocative of engine sounds, below?

We wound down through the mountains again, rounded a bend to be greeted by the salt smack of the sea, and rode north to the border between the United Arab Emirates and Oman.

It took an hour in a clean and airy building, a mere bagatelle compared to the three-hour rugby scrum of South and

Central American border crossings I'd once endured riding from Chile to Alaska.

A sign on the wall said: Low jobs will not be allowed in Oman, above a white slotted cube marked Complaining Box.

Beside it, a languid Frenchwoman gazed over through hooded eyes, took in my wedding ring, and glanced away.

Oh well, I thought, there goes my chance of being James Bond for the rest of the day. Or possibly ever.

We filled up at a petrol station just past the border, where the locals were all complaining because petrol had just gone up by 23% to 26p a litre, compared to 17p in Saudi Arabia.

At those prices, I thought as I watched the cost on the pump creep up more slowly than an arthritic tortoise, it would be almost worthwhile driving out from the UK every week to fill up.

Tanks full to the brim, we roared north again on a road of sweeping curves and dips, and surely there can be nothing more perfect than a big bike on a sweeping curve, between the blue of sea and the hot sandstone cliffs.

After the Porsches and Ferraris of Dubai, with its towering buildings and the often ostentatious vulgarity of a place which has gone from camels to Cadillacs in two generations, like an entire city of lottery winners, Oman was a blessed relief.

Fishing boats bobbed in the glittering bay, goats wandered down village streets with that look of baffled malevolence that only they have, and in shady souks the air was rich with the sharp, sweet tang of frankincense, like wandering through pine and lemon groves, and the earthy, liquorice scent of myrrh.

Oman may be almost as prosperous as its neighbour, but it doesn't shout about it, and while Dubai has the gold, Oman not only has the other two of that holy trinity of gifts, but as Claude said, has not forgotten the most important gifts of all: genuine hospitality and friendship from the heart.

By dusk we were at the northern tip of the country, on a kink in the landscape which locals call the Bend. In Victorian times, this was a telegraph repeating station between India and the UK, and soldiers who'd blotted their copybook were sent there as a punishment.

The isolation drove many mad, allegedly giving rise to the expression to go round the bend.

However, we were in for a much worse fate, when we discovered that our hotel, the otherwise splendid and rambling Atana Musandam, didn't have a drinks licence.

Now, as a rough, tough biker, I can go for days without food or a kind word, but no beer is a different matter after a long hot day on the road, and I still have flashbacks to two weeks riding through Iran on the way back from India to the UK and having disturbing visions in the desert of a cold pint with those little beads of condensation on it, only to realise with a sigh that such delights would be denied me until I got to Turkey.

Still, one thing adventures teach you is that no matter how desperate the situation is, there's always a solution, and within five minutes Claude and I were in a taxi to the bar in the nearby Atana Khasab for an aperitif.

The next morning, we discovered that my, er, enthusiastic cornering had worn the footboards on the Softail so thin I could shave with them, which was handy, since I'd forgotten my razor, and Claude generously handed me the key to the Road King, reminding me how much I loved that model.

I'd spent a month riding a red one of these the 2,448 miles of Route 66 from Chicago to Los Angeles in 2000, and loved every minute of it, but I loved this bike even more, with its classical colour scheme of ivory and aquamarine making my heart sing with memories of the 1950s diners, motels and gas stations strung along that iconic route like diamonds on the necklace of dreams.

And the current Road King may maintain the timeless looks of the bike I rode then, but today's version has better brakes, handling, suspension, gearbox and clutch, not to mention a more powerful engine.

The maximum lean angle is better than on the Softail, making it more of a challenge to touch down the boards, but I was doing such a good job of paring them down that I arrived at lunch thinking I was actually getting better at cornering.

Only to have my delusions shattered immediately by Theo Verkamman, a Dutch police motorcycle instructor who's been signed up by Harley to dispel the myth that Harleys don't handle.

After setting up a complex maze of cones in the car park, Theo climbed on the 386kg Electra Glide Ultra Classic and proceeded to weave around them in impossibly tight circles on full steering lock.

First he did at fast, grinding the boards. Then he did it so slowly that at times he was stationary for a second or two. Then he did it with a pillion. And then he did it with one hand.

"Incredible. What's the secret?" I said as he climbed off afterwards.

"Skill," he grinned, which will teach me to ask stupid questions; although he did later reveal that it was what every instructor tells a bike student facing the dreaded U-turn: use the back brake, never the front, and look up to where you want to go rather than down at the front wheel.

Chastened but deeply impressed, I climbed back on the Road King for one last, glorious run through an endless sea of dunes to the Bab Al Shama hotel, a vast and rambling complex in the manner of a desert palace where we would spend a last night before flying home.

And then, a few miles from home, two camels came sauntering down the road.

Cedric was thoughtfully chewing his copy of Camel Monthly, having finished the crossword, and Gertrude was sporting a freshly knitted cobalt blue hat which contrasted exquisitely with the sanguine glory of a lilac and roseate dusk.

So rare, to find camels with such impeccable taste, but then, that's Oman for you.

2018

P is for the Parrot Dating Agency of Puerto Rico

M iriam the rain forest guide had one of those faces which was not particularly beautiful, but was so animated by what went on around her that she was impossible not to like.

She chattered away at the front of the bus as we left San Juan and passed through Puerto Rican countryside strangely like Tyrone in a heatwave, then climbed into the mountains of the rain forest, with the bright parp of the bus horn swallowed up in the tangled shade of bamboo, fern, poison ivy and elephants' ears behind the sandalwood trees.

There was no sign of the rain which gives the forest its name, but every year 180ins of the stuff falls on these trees, compared to 55ins in the lowlands, turning the mountains around us into a vast roofless hothouse.

The first stop was the Yokshu Tower, a circular five-storey structure in faded terracotta which has a long and fascinating history. It was built 20 years ago for the tourists.

After you fight your way through the Sony handycams at the top of the tower and look down towards San Juan or up at the peaks, the forest looks utterly impenetrable, choked with flora like the work of a megalomaniac head gardener, so that you feel a mad desire to borrow a machete and plunge in, living on a diet of orange, lemon, banana, grapefruit and pepper until the job is done.

It might get a bit dull, though. You'd need to hire Miriam to lighten the days. You could live in a tree house with her, watching her face light up with tragic joy as she describes the fate of the Puerto Rican parrot, which numbered a million when Columbus discovered the island in 1493, but of which there are now only 75, flitting somewhere out there in the dappled gloom.

Miriam's tinkling laugh as she described their beautiful downfall would attract them to the tree house, where at first they would peak out from behind the sandalwood trees, then shyly emerge to nuzzle beaks.

We would establish the world's first dating agency for parrots, and be singlehandedly responsible for their resurrection.

There. All that organised, I returned my attention to Miriam, who was leading the way down the road to a waterfall which was supposed to make you look younger if you drank from it.

I got about half a gallon down, but it only made my bladder feel older all the way back to the ship.

Around the waterfall, in the forest dusk, were the bright orange African tulips which the Puerto Rican children fill with water then run around squirting each other from the tiny green phallus at its base. They call it Peepee Three, in their high, dancing voices.

Unfortunately, since I'd spent so much time with Miriam in the forest running the parrot dating agency, I only had time for an hour wandering around old San Juan, its narrow cobbled streets shaded by wrought iron balconies draped with virulent orange-red flowers.

On street corners, serious looking men in Panama hats and unlikely tweed jackets talked business, while exotic women flitted from shadow to shadow like butterflies. There was a wonderful air of imminent danger, like a South American republic just before the cocktail air.

I returned to the ship wishing that I'd been able to spend long enough in the city to see the astonishing fortress of El Morro, started in 1538 and not finished until 1783, which just goes t to prove that builders are the same everywhere.

But then if I'd signed up for the city tour instead of the forest tour, I'd never have met Miriam, and there would be an awful lot of lonely parrots out there, calling down the long reaches of the evening, waiting with their beautiful heads cocked for an answering warble that never came.

Back on board the ship, Ken the cruise director was busy by the pool sorting out the judges for the Best Male Legs on Board competition. There was just no stopping Ken. The night before, he'd started off the sumo wrestling with a bout against his assistant Sean, then got the karaoke underway before nipping down to the lounge to make sure the Country and Western Evening had plenty of both types of music.

It was going to be difficult to wake up every morning at home without Ken's sunny voice over the intercom saying: "Good morning everyone, and welcome to another day in rainy Belfast. This is Ken, your house director, just keeping you up to date with what's happening in your fabulous home this morning. Just to remind you that breakfast is still available in your beautiful fully fitted kitchen at this time, and this morning we're offering the diet special because you did forget to buy your flakes and coffee yesterday.

"Next up is loading your fully automated washing machine with a load of sparkling cotton whites, and then it's an energetic and fulfilling day at work in the company of your friendly colleagues, with a break for a thrifty yet satisfying lunch from the sandwich shop around the comer.

"This evening your washing will be available for collection in the machine, and entertainment options tonight include a trip to the wonderful old pub across the road, with cabaret provided by the drunk at the bar, or for those of you who'd like a quieter evening by the fire, the coal shed is out the back, and there's a bottle of Spanish plonk in the wine rack. Please feel free to get it yourself. Have a wonderful day in your fabulous home, and I'll talk to you again tomorrow morning."

Upstairs I found John and Joanne, a couple from Newcastle who I'd met at the captain's table the night before. He was 5ft 6ins tall and looked like ET with glasses, she was not far behind me in the Whitest Person on Board stakes, and they were great people, like most Geordies.

I asked them if they'd enjoyed San Juan.

"It were grand," said John. "We did tour by taxi. Bugger tried to charge us $76 instead of $40, but I told him we were having nowt to do wi' that."

Also at the captain's table the previous evening had been Joan and Claire from Louisiana, the Cardin sisters.

"As in Pierre, but no relation, unfortunately," they said. They were variously divorced and widowed, in their fifties, elegant and charming, and loved the art of a good flirt.

This evening I found them on the stairs of the atrium, which was the setting for a wonderful tradition which has become established on the ship of the passengers gathering on the curved steps and balconies in all their finery to listen to the string quartet on the podium between the waterfall and the two glass lifts rising and falling among the greenery. Some of the passengers would suddenly waltz without warning, and at the end of every offering of Mozart or Handel everyone would burst into bright applause, bringing to every evening a spectral memory of what the great transatlantic liners of the Twenties and Thirties must have been like.

Indeed, on this particular evening I came down the stairs to find Joan and Claire wearing the shimmering clothes of their own youth.

"Why, ladies, you're, both looking deliciously exotic this evening. And Claire! You've had your hair plaited. Quite gorgeous," I said.

"Heavens, Mr Hill, what a beautiful shirt. Silk, isn't it?" said Claire, flashing me a smile of quixotic southern grace.

"Naturally," I said, pretending to be upset.

It was all wonderful, harmless fun, and much more entertaining than chatting someone up at a disco.

"YOU A NURSE?"

"WHAT?"

We were joined at dinner that night by Henry Eriksen, the first engineer, who insisted on toasting the arrival of each new course by ordering shots of aquavit, the Norwegian potato moonshine

At some stage I staggered to my cabin and fell on my bed, waking at four in the morning to find that I had won the passengers' Aquavit Hangover of the Year contest.

I fell asleep again and woke six hours later to realise to my horror that I'd made an arrangement with Henry to look around the engine room. Even worse, he'd remembered, and was standing beside the purser's desk 10 minutes later looking depressingly sprightly in his dress whites.

The engine room was, in fact, a sprawling complex controlled from a room in which quiet screens glowed with temperatures, pressures and revs per minute in a mute parody of the thunderous reality below, all of it ending in two 16ft propellers thrashing around 173 times a minute. To give you some idea of the scale of the thing, the clutch plate was 6ft across.

I left, loaded down with kilowatts, megatonnes and hyperjoules, to find Romeo Galingen up beside the pool demonstrating how to carve a 6ft high angel fish from a 500lb block of ice. Romeo, from the Philippines, was the ship's full-time ice carver, producing the astonishing creations which graced the midnight buffets, and was looking remarkably cheerful for a man whose treacherous creations vanished the moment he turned his back.

The next morning we arrived at Nassau in the Bahamas, and I boarded the boat for Coral World, an aquarium complex where children were in heaven between feeding the stingrays and pressing their little noses against the windows of the underwater observatory.

"Daddy, look at those lobsters CHASING each other! Look at the colour of all those FISH! Look how far we are below the SEA!"

I was as astonished as they were by the seahorse. It would have been difficult even for Dali to dream up seahorses, with their tails curled around a frond of coral and their eyes, like those of bachelors at a country wedding, shyly watching the bright fish that flirted around them. Occasionally one of them would lean close to another seahorse to nuzzle snouts and compare unknown, innocent confidences.

At the flamingo pool, an American with a beer gut and a cap which showed he had served on the USS Dwight D Eisenhower was circling with a Sony handycam.

"Uh...they're standing on one leg, so I guess...uh...they're preserving energy," he proclaimed into his built-in microphone.

In the trees above his head, tiny armoured spiders the shape of crabs hung in their jewelled kingdoms after the early morning rain.

The flamingos slept on, and the fat American lumbered over to the shark pool and pressed his camera to the underwater window as an 8ft nurse shark slid past, its hard lifeless eye meeting the hard lifeless eye of the American for a meeting with what Anne of Green Gables would have described as a kindred spirit, if she had been a fishmonger.

Another American appeared, this time a woman.

"Look, a baby. It's - kinda cute," she said, pointing to one of the feeder fish which attach themselves to sharks and live off parasites.

Why is that Americans, who are generally intelligent and civilised at home, when they go on holiday turn into educationally subnormal teenagers with a working vocabulary of about 25 words, who cheerily order dry white wine with steak and who seem driven by the worst excesses of adulthood like shopping, gambling and eating until they're broke, bust or burst?

You tell me.

The woman who came to feed the sharks told us that they can go without food for a month. The cruisers, unused to going without food for an hour, gasped.

Below us, the sharks cruised endlessly around the pool, and the tiny fish who shared it with them, knowing that sharks will only eat sick or wounded prey, flitted about, their fins flickering with determined health the way that public relations companies will tell you that all is well even as the removals men are carrying the desks out.

Nassau   itself, once you get past the "Welcome to our beautiful island, mon" guides, "Like a nice girl, mon?" pimps and the "Five T-shirts for $10" shops, is a town of country roads, birdsong and beautiful old wooden homes such as   Dunmore House, formerly the Governor's residence, the officers' quarters of the 22nd West Indies Regiment and a military hospital. Today, part of it is the priory of the adjacent Cathedral of St Francis Xavier, and the rest lies derelict.

A young woman came walking down the road as I sat on the wall in the sun. She was wearing a black hat and a black cardigan over a bright tartan dress. She carried a wicker basket, and there was an elegant swing in her narrow hips as she walked past the house, its windows empty and sad.

She walked on swinging her basket, past a Give Way sign which was exactly the same as at home, since the Bahamas was a British colony until 1973.

Below it, someone had nailed a handwritten sign shakily advertising Royal Novelle Cuisine (opposite the police), Internazinale Chef Vincenzo E. Bess (pizza slice $1.50).

You could still hear, hanging in the dry, hot air, the ghost of the conversation which had gone into the creation of the sign —"Hey mon, how you spell nouvelle?" "Dunno, mon".

Her basket finally disappeared around the corner, and was replaced by a red bag bearing the words Isle of Man Steam Packet Company which I had spotted several times on the ship, coming in the opposite direction.

Its bearer was, it transpired, Dave from Douglas.

We greeted each other, and I asked him after a while if this was his first cruise.

"Er, no, it's my 13th."

"Heavens. What do you like about them so much?"

"Um." He looked at me sideways, then muttered something which I didn't catch.

"Sorry, Dave, missed that."

"Er...romance, I said."

"What, like women?"

He gave me a pained, nervous look.

"No, the ships. I love the Royal Princess best of all. I wanted to join the Navy, but my parents..."

The sentence tailed off into nothing, and he toddled off eventually, leaving a faint whiff of regret and milky tea.

Above us, finches danced in the vaulted blue.

The next night, on the plane home I drank far too much of the right wine with each course, listened to Bach's Jesu, Joy of Man's Desiring on my headphones and fell asleep feeling blissfully, irretrievably European.

1994

Q is for Quebec

As the train hurtled east from Toronto, I held my breath for the moment when we all became *Quebecois*.

The moment when the atmosphere in the carriage suddenly became an ambience.

I looked out at golf courses carved out of the grassy wild, trying to spot the instant that the players started saying: "*Merde!*" instead of: "Heavens — missed again."

I studied back gardens, where men sat reading the Sunday papers by their swimming pools, trying to divine whether they were about to say: "Helen, throw me out a cold one there" or: "*Helene, puis j'ai un martini sec, si'l vous plait?*"

I scanned the sky, waiting for it to darken from true blue to French blue.

But it was no use, especially when I was distracted by Bill, who was sitting next to me. He and his wife Hazel had been to France the year before, and managed to get locked in the gardens at Villandry.

"I tell you, the only way out of there was over a 7ft wall with barbed wire on top. We got over OK, but I ripped my Tilley pants on the way down. Oh, those famous Tilleys."

But somehow none of it rang true, and when Bill got off at Brockville, Hazel was nowhere to be seen.

Perhaps she was waiting in the car park, but it was very sad, the sight of him shuffling in his beige suit and training shoes past a man pushing a pram and a cloud of cigarette smoke before him down the platform, past a cream and red sign saying: "Brockville: City of the 1000 Islands - Relocate to a Quality Community."

Its truth betrayed by its inhabitants, Brockville simmered in the sun as the train pulled out, the potential entrepreneurs in its first class carriage mentally striking the town of the list of possible relocation sites for software plants and Cadillac franchises.

From the well-clipped greens outside town, Brockville's golfers watched the train go by with mournful cyes, as if they knew.

Above our heads, the sky darkened with rain, and soon we crossed the border into Quebec and hissed into Montreal.

I strapped accents to my vowels and went hunting for ambiance in the drying streets.

Although most of the English-speaking minority who once owned 70 per cent of Canada's wealth left Montreal in 1976 after the election of the separatist Parti Quebecois, signs and posters still hung everywhere in perfect Franglais — *Grand Prix Nationale*, Bar *le Rendez-vous, Poulet Frit a la* Kentucky - as if the city was being run by a crazed O-level French student.

Down in the old city by the harbour, painfully elegant people stalked the streets in search of the perfect bistro, couples sought each other in the shadows of horse-drawn *caleches* and moths tangoed to their deaths in the yellow light of ancient lamps.

Above them all, the new moon rose above the steel blue dome of the Bonsecours Market.

I went back to the hotel, and spent five minutes in the bathroom, muttering into the mirror: *"Pas de bidet? Je suis desolee."* (No bidet? I am desolate).

I tried sanity once, but it didn't agree with me.

The next morning, walking through the streets, I realised just what was different about the cities in Quebec to the rest of Canada.

Vancouver had grown up to be a playboy, and Calgary became a cowboy. Edmonton turned into an oilman, and Winnipeg a farmer. Toronto is a banker and Ottawa is a politician.

But Montreal and Quebec, the twin godfathers of them all, still sit in the comfortable armchair of the east looking down on their errant offspring with a faint and weary sneer.

As well they might. When all the rest were forest, swamp and prairie, these two cities were already old.

Montreal, for example, was first settled in 1642 by Paul de Chomedey as a mission.

And even at the advanced ages of 325 and 334, the city was still fit and well enough to organise Expo 67 and the 1976 Olympics respectively.

Both left in their wake several pieces of architectural and financial flotsam which the city has had varying degrees of success in recycling.

Among the ones they don't like to talk about are the Olympic Stadium, originally called the Big 0, then the Big Owe because it cost $700 million and was not finished until 11 years after the event, and now the Big Oh No because the roof is going to have to be replaced for another $50 million.

After an Olympics whose debts gave Quebec's provincial motto, *Je me souviens* — I will never forget — a new twist,

Montreal, to its credit, learned its lesson about using existing facilities for sporting events.

The Canadian Grand Prix track on Ile St-Helene, for example, is open to the public as a scenic drive all year, and in the week before the race is the site of the city's enthusiastic drivers queueing up for a slow motion preplay of the real thing.

And even sites like the futuristic Velodrome, built for the Olympic cycling events and rarely used since, have taken on a new life.

Or, in the Velodrome's case, a lot of new lives, of the assorted beasts which plunge, climb, swim, burrow and snooze in its four artificially created ecosystems — a tropical forest, Canadian woods, the St Lawrence underwater and the north and south poles.

The Biodome, as it's called now, is all very impressive, and 1.25 million visitors have poured through its doors since it opened last June.

But I still suspect that places like this are just designer zoos.

Maybe it does give children a chance to see lynx and otters without getting eaten or holding their breath for 15 minutes.

But when you've stood six inches from an emperor penguin before you've even grown out of short trousers, what are you going to do for the rest of your life?

What's going to happen to your imagination? Or travel companies, for that matter?

I came out of the Biodome feeling a little like the catfish which was unaccountably swimming around in the piranha enclosure — full of admiration, but a little worried.

Perhaps it would have been better if they'd just left it as a velodrome, with a colony of breeding cyclists going round and round watched by groups of visiting penguins.

"Don't worry," one of the penguins would be saying to the other, "they were brought up in the Bronx, so this is like heaven for them."

Penguins like that would also appreciate another of Montreal's new attractions, the International Museum of Humour.

Sadly, when I went there I discovered that it was shut on Mondays — but then, it's rather appropriate that the sociable Montrealers don't feel like a laugh on Mondays.

Any good citizen will tell you that although those stuffy old Calvinist Anglos may have taken all the businesses to Toronto in 1976, when the separatist Parti Quebecois came to power, they left the *joie de vivre* in Montreal.

"In Quebec we say TGIF — Thank God It's Friday — but in Ontario they say TGIM," a woman told me in a bar in the old part of the city down by the docks.

Which, with its warehouse apartments, patio cafés and trendy bistros, is where Montreal goes to play at the weekends when it's not sunbathing in the parklands and forests of Mont Royal above the city.

The old city is still where you'll find most tourists, too — wandering through the cobbled streets, or peering up in admiration at the astonishing carved interior of Notre Dame Cathedral.

Just across the Place d'Armes is the almost as beautiful interior of the Bank of Montreal, although I'll have to take the word of the guidebook on that, since I have an aversion to the inside of banks.

Just down the Rue Saint Jacques, once the rustling heart of Canadian finance, is the Molson Bank building, owned by the Scottish family who started the brewery in 1786.

Theoretically, owning a bank and a brewery seems like a perfect autonomous fiscal system, since your customers take their money out of one and put it in another.

Surprisingly, it didn't work, and the bank was taken over after the Second World War.

But then, Montreal has always had a rather strange relationship between commerce and spiritual matters like drink and religion.

In 1962, when it became apparent that Christchurch Anglican Cathedral was subsiding, a city developer jacked it up then decided to use the space he'd created underneath by building a shopping mall.

Today, that mall is par|, of a complex stretching for 18 miles, and Christchurch is possibly the richest church in the world, taking thousands of dollars in weekly rental from the shops below in a comfortable alliance between God and mammon. Paul Chomedey, who founded Montreal to turn the minds of the Iroquois to God rather than fur profits, would not be pleased, but he would understand. 'After all, what can you expect from Anglicans?' I thought, looking at my watch and realising that it was time to take the train to New Brunswick.

For someone who had just come from well-scrubbed Toronto, Montreal Central Station crackled with the romance of dance hall tunes on an old radio.

It was the flickering lights, the names of the Grande Ligne trains.

And above all, the voice of the French Canadian announcer calling out the destinations like Saint-Hyacinthe in a voice so breathily seductive that you wanted to rush up to the control room and ask her to marry you and move there just so you could ask her to say "Saint- Hyacinthe" to you every night.

Sadly, while I was trying to work out whether this was entirely feasible or not, my train to New Brunswick was called and I was forced to contemplate the more mundane charms of my roomette.

My roomette was a space 5ft by 4ft into which was miraculously fitted a folding bed, an armchair, an ingenious sink which emptied of water when you folded it way, a toilet, a drinking fountain, a luggage compartment, a toilet roll holder complete with soft toilet roll, a set of shelves, several coat hooks, two coat hangers, a pair of electrical sockets and a chrome fan.

There seemed to be only one problem. Since the room was only 5ft long, wouldn't the bed be the same?

But VIA Rail had already thought of that. When the bed folded down, the recess it came out of created an extra foot and a half.

It was astonishing. I was astonished. And what was even more astonishing was the landscape outside, all soggy woods and painfully green fields being devoured by arthritic cows.

It was just like home, except for the train, which was futuristic stainless steel outside and restored art deco inside.

It was like travelling through Monaghan in a spaceship designed by Charles Rennie Mackintosh.

I folded myself into my folding bed, and didn't sleep at all, but somehow managed to wake refreshed.

I pulled up the blind and there was New Brunswick. It appeared to consist entirely of trees.

After some time a clearing came into view, filled almost entirely by a building called Holy Cross House.

Career opportunities in New Brunswick where, it seemed, somewhat limited.

You could either be a lumberjack, or a nun with a temper.

1993

R is for the Rockies, in a Jeep called Arf

By a glacier, we found none other than PY Wong, the intrepid Malaysian motorist, smoking a pipe.

"Tell me, where have you come from?" he said.

"The north."

"Chilly?"

"Quite."

"Ah, in that case I may put up the top," he said, indicating Mrs Wong beaming plumply in the passenger seat of the 1958 MG in which they had completed the 1997 Peking to Paris rally, wrapped in innumerable layers and sporting a pair of navy wool gloves.

They were now driving to Alaska, as one does.

"Tell me," said Mr Wong, simultaneously dousing his pipe and igniting his engine, "but what is the purpose of your expedition?"

"Bears," I said. "We are looking for bears."

Indeed, we had arrived in Vancouver some days previously and signed up for Bears and Beetles, a two-week jaunt through the Rockies in one of the new Volkswagens.

Tragically, when we turned up to collect the car, we found that the travel company had sold all the Beetles, presumably because the bright colours and curvy shape had made the bears think they were sweets ("Mmm, I like these; crunchy on the outside, soft in the middle.")

Instead, we got a bright red Jeep which we christened Arf after its registration in which we spent the next couple of days pottering around Vancouver, a city of so many nooks and crannies that it is like the rambling house of your favourite Aunt Cynthia.

Your favourite Canadian Chinese Punjabi German Italian Aunt Cynthia, that is, who also happens to be a fabulous cook, skier and sailor, and whose husband Rufus was a trapper for the Hudson's Bay Company, the ancient firm whose fur and liquor warehouse still stands on Water Street.

The two of them have a back garden called Stanley Park, a thousand acres of ancient redwoods so untamed that at any minute you expect to walk around a tree and come face to coonskin with Uncle Rufus returning from a fur and liquor expedition, a bear over one shoulder and two bottles of rye clinking in his back pocket.

Here, you sit by a lake and three goslings waddle past. Then a black squirrel sits on your foot. A horsedrawn carriage clops past, and through the trees several chaps are playing cricket on a green by the sea, their West Coast accents mingling quaintly with the click of cork on willow.

If this was the United States, you would start looking behind bushes for Disney engineers, but it is Canada, and real.

The next morning, we climbed into the Jeep and set off for Vancouver Island, looking out carefully for bears.

Or beahs, as Cate would say, being a well brought up gel. Being a ragamuffin from the wilds of Tyrone, I say bears, and if I had to justify it I would say that it must be a bearrr because it says "Grrr", whereas a beah would be more likely to say "Geahhh. Now, are you fwightened?"

Whatever they were, we had seen none by the time we arrived at a lakeside bed and breakfast on Vancouver Island.

In the UK, B&Bs may sport brown Dralon sofas whose finest hour has been and gone, but in north American versions you are more likely to be offered wine, firelight, a hot tub on the patio and a rowing boat. We were offered the lot, although getting the boat into the tub was a bit of a struggle.

"Tell me, my dear," I said as we sat surrounded by rowlocks and rubber ducks, "am I wrong, or is it my birthday?"

"No, you are right," she said, taking me out for an extravagantly fabulous mountaintop meal, as a result of which it was somewhat the worse for wear we returned to the mainland the next day and drove north to Whistler on the Sea and Sky Highway.

Rarely can a road have been better named. On our left were bottomless fiords of a deep so blue it hurt our eyes. On our right, cruel mountains impaled innocent clouds and icy waterfalls dropped hundreds of feet into the dark forest, so close that we could feel the spray on our faces through the open windows. Great hangover cure.

In a landscape so forbidding, it was easy to imagine a Sasquatch pottering about, filing his nails and waiting for a passing fur and liquor trapper for supper.

By nightfall we were in Whistler, a mountain ski resort built in the quaint Hansel and Gretel Gothic Massive style. There were few skiers about this late in the season, but the streets were full of chaps wearing hooded sweatshirts and baggy combat trousers, carrying wide planks and exchanging complex handshakes.

It was, I imagine, a convention of unemployed Masonic carpenters.

The next day we drove east through the mountains and found by chance a gliding club, run by men called Rudi and Attila who wore aviator sunglasses and studied the clouds, reading texts in them that we could not decipher.

We went soaring up the fertile valley with them, curving giddily among the peaks until we found a circular lake so emerald that it seemed like absolute green, compared to all the other greens we had ever seen.

Late that afternoon we found it again in Arf, then crunched on foot through the snowy forest to its edge and took off our clothes. Our skin was a shock against the snow, but not as much of a shock as the temperature of the water. We got as far as our ankles before hypothermia set in.

We returned to Arf, and rose through mountains like a petrified storm, then fell past white churches with wonky crosses to rolling prairies and the ranch where we were spending the night; one of many which in the last century were the homes of remittance men, the daft younger sons of the English gentry, dispatched here with orders not to write often. Among them was Lord Martin Cecil, son of the Marquis of Exeter, who ran his ranch as the base for the Emissaries of Divine Light until his death.

And so to bed, in a rustic cabin. Wildlife count for the day: cows 37, horses six, muskrats two, Japanese tourists one. Bears nil.

All night long we slept the deepest of steeps, in a silence interrupted only by the ranch's two pet emus talking emu business to each other, with a sound like the burping of trumpets.

In the morning we woke to find two horses parked outside, so we climbed aboard and went for a poggle through the woods as the sun burnt off the dawn mist.

Ah, the rhythmic creak of leather, the smell of damp wool, the crack of the whip.

Still, enough about my private life.

We returned the horses to the barn, where they sleep standing up so as not to crumple their pyjamas, and motored on to the most beautiful waterfall in the world, at Helmcken on the way to Jasper. Here, the Murtle River tumbles 450ft into a black abyss, separating as it does into white plumes that look like lost souls plunging to Hades. It is at once thunderous and contemplative, and we could have stayed there watching it all day, had we not had to get on with the business of killing every bug in Canada. For it seemed that no matter how often we cleaned the windscreen, within minutes it had become a bug graveyard.

We drove on, knowing that in bug households all over the land tonight there would be empty chairs by the fire, nervous glances at tiny watches.

And, down at the Bug Bar, tales of narrow escapes by more agile bugs who had caught the airflow and surfed over Arf's roof as deftly as unemployed Masons.

However, at this stage my thoughts on the life and times of bugs were distracted by Cate.

"Oh, look, a beah!" she said.

And it was. A black bear loping beside the road: such a remarkable sight that it was difficult to resist the temptation to leap out of Arf and take a closer look. Many do, and become bear lunch.

There are several ways to avoid being eaten by a bear. One is to live in Clapham. Another is to go to Canada, but stay in your car. However, if you are out for a dander in the woods and you are confronted by a large black furry thing, it is either

a) A mugger in a bear suit.

b) A bear.

If a), hand over your money, credit cards and pizza.

If b), don't run, scream, wear deodorant, climb a tree or make love, because bears are apparently attracted by all these things, which is why you never hear of bears eating fat, smelly monks with vertigo.

What you should do, according to our guidebook, is stand there meekly and mutter to the bear in a comforting voice. The guidebook didn't say exactly what you should mutter, but something like: "Here, I hear they're doing a really good deal on honey down at the Critter Creek general store, which is THAT WAY," might work.

Anyway, where was I?

Ah yes, on the way to Jasper, where we had arrived 58 years too late to witness the building at nearby Patricia Lake of the world's only ever aircraft carrier made of ice.

You see, in 1942 Allied shipping losses were so heavy that when one Geoff Pike came up with the idea, Louis Mountbatten was impressed enough to demonstrate it in Churchill's bath at 10 Downing Street. Whether Churchill was in the bath at the time is not, sadly, recorded.

Pike was ensconced at the time in a London mental hospital, but madness has never bothered Governments, and Churchill sent him to Jasper with a budget of almost £37 million. And that was in the days when £37 million was worth at least six Hungarian ukuleles to the pound.

Sadly, Pike's creation proved less buoyant than Mountbatten's ice cubes, and the project was finally scuppered when the pacifist Doukhober labourers who were building it found out its true purpose, and downed ice picks.

These days, if you want ice, you'll just have to find it on the Icefields Parkway between Jasper and Banff, possibly the finest drive in the world.

If you ever thought you had seen scenery before you drove the Icefields Parkway, you had not. All the rest was God practising, and this is where he got it right.

Even one of these mountains would be mindboggling. But whole families of them, plus the in-laws as well, transcends you to the state of superboggledom in which we arrived at Banff several hours later.

Banff was full of Japanese tourists. When they got home, they would discover that they had no room in their homes for the several million holiday photographs they had taken, so for several years now the Japanese government has been collecting them to sell them to Hong Kong, which used them to build the artificial island for its new airport.

Two nights later we arrived at Revelstoke, where the brochure promised us a sumptuous lodge, to find it not quite built. Still, we opened a bottle of red and spent the evening sitting on the porch of our log cabin in the grounds, looking around at the other brand new cabins and feeling somewhat like pioneers.

On the lake below us, a fat beaver unzipped the dark water, and before us tawny clouds were ruptured by the jagged peaks and fell dying down the mountain towards us, spilling rain.

In the sunshine after its passing, a rainbow curved to the meadow a couple of hundred yards away, in which a familiar furry shape could be seen snuffling through the damp grass.

It could have been Uncle Rufus, but it wasn't.

"Beah," I said to Cate.

"Grrr," she smiled, raising her wine glass to her lips in the golden light of evening.

2000

S is for Spain

A short history

2400 BC
Iberian peninsula inhabited by Beaker People, named after ceramic drinking vessels, and Urn Burial Folk, named after habit of burying folk in urns.

480BC
Celts arrive and attempt to populate peninsula but fail, possibly because habit of cleaning teeth with urine makes getting dates impossible.

20BC
Romans arrive, name country Hispania and bring civic pride, justice, roads, Latin and Christianity.

5th Century
Roman Empire collapses. Visigoths take over, but find the place so well-run they change nothing.

8th Century

Arabs arrive, rename country al-Andalus and bring tolerance, allowing Jews and Christians to retain faith and Frankish kings to potter about in the north.

980
Dictator al-Mansur ruins everything with jihad against Franks which sours relations between Christians and Muslims for centuries. Or possibly ever.

1100-1492
Christians, having warmed up with the Crusades, retake country.

1492
Columbus discovers America, ignoring fact that natives, Vikings and possibly Irish had got there first. Spanish subsequently establish huge empire, kill 20 million natives and ship home mountains of gold and silver which kings such as Carlos I and Philip II spend on succession of wars.

1598
Philip dies, leaving country broke and starting long period of decline into intolerance which reaches its nadir with the Inquisition.

19th Century
Colonial uprisings finally strip Spain of its empire, leaving it bankrupt and backward.

20th Century
Civil war, followed by Franco.

1975

Franco dies. Brits discover Costas. Spanish wonder where it all went wrong, then sigh and open pubs with Watney's Red Barrel on tap, full English breakfast and live Premier League soccer.

Seville

The importance of the hairdryer in the history of the 20th Century is often overlooked.

If young Corporal Hitler had treated himself to a decent blowdry after bathing, for example, the other officers wouldn't have laughed at his wayward cowslick and sowed the seeds of misanthropy which led to the Second World War.

If Stalin had washed, dried and got a nice gentle perm instead of smearing his head with Crimean sump oil, he could well have ended up as a harmless folk singer in a Georgian nightclub penning ditties of unrequited Bolshevik charm.

If Isadora Duncan had been able to dry her famous locks on that September day in Nice in 1927, she wouldn't have rushed out with them wrapped in the scarf which strangled her in the wheel of a Bugatti.

And yet you won't find a single mention of a hairdryer in either Eric Hobsbawm's The Age of Extremes, or the

History of Islamic Spain I was reading as the plane descended towards Seville Airport.

You can imagine, then, my relief when no sooner had I landed than I was rushed straight to the Melia Hotel for a one-hour tour of the bedrooms during which the manager pointed out not once but half a dozen times that every single one of the bathrooms had a hairdryer fixed to the wall.

Not only that, but you could choose between 10 different types of pillow, he said, as we descended to basement conference rooms in which, at a conference on human reproduction, men in grey suits were sitting around tables earnestly discussing oestrogen levels and sperm counts.

Safe in the knowledge that the entire population of Seville would sleep on a satisfying pillow that night before waking the next morning, drying their hair and going forth to propagate the species, I went out to a splendid dinner of giant olives, Serrano ham and Rioja.

Lots of Rioja.

So much Rioja, in fact, that at some stage I wrote in my notebook: "Not many people know that Serrano ham and tomatoes have been officially recognised as a cure for stomach pains by the Middlesex Health Board."

Much, much later, I found myself back in my hotel room watching a TV on which the options seemed to be either Lithuania playing Switzerland at basketball or a Spanish play which seemed to consist entirely of scantily clad women running around a flat roof being soaked by a gardener with a hose.

It was too difficult a choice for any man, so I fell asleep instead and dreamed, not for the first time, that I was just about to do my A-levels and had somehow forgotten to go to any of the classes.

To try and make up, I woke early and read the entire Rough Guide to Seville - the city quaintly described by Byron as being famous for oranges and women - so that when I arrived at the Plaza de España after breakfast, I felt as if I'd been there before. Mind you, it was hardly surprising: when the Plaza was built in 1929, it felt as if it had been there before, too. Planned in 1914, it was scuppered by the little matter of the First World War, and only constructed for the Spanish Americas Fair in 1929, just in time to avoid being scuppered by the Wall Street Crash.

A dazzling mixture of all the architectural styles brought to Seville, it is one of several perfect symbols of this Jerusalem of Europe where Rome, Marrakesh and Constantinople met and married while the rest of western civilisation was still struggling in the darkness.

Spain was an Islamic country from 711 until 1492, when it was finally recaptured by the Christians. But they seem to have been the most relaxed of conquests and reconquests. When the Moors arrived, the Christians were allowed to keep their faith, and responded with a widespread admiration for the luxurious elegance of Arab culture. As the Christians slowly regained power, and in spite of growing tensions, Muslims were allowed the same right.

The result of this benign dialectic was that buildings were generally adapted rather than torn down by invading hordes, a process which is still happily going on. All around the Plaza de España, the 122 national pavilions built for the 1929 fair had been transformed into police stations, lecture theatres and schools. Well, except for Guatemala, which has become a public toilet.

In between the pavilions, white doves fluttered in the love trees, those ephemeral explosions of lilac-pink blossom on what is also known as the Tree of Judas, from which Iscariot is believed to have hanged himself.

The same symbol, of both love and betrayal.

For in Seville, everything is something else. Most of the city's 52 churches, for example, were once mosques; the university, not content with being the building which once housed the country's largest tobacco factory, also doubles as the setting for Bizet's Carmen, and the Alcazar, the great palace of al-Mu'tadid of the Abbadids, was simultaneously a harem of 800 women and a shrine where today you can still trace with your fingertips the verses of the Koran carved into the cool alabaster walls.

Al-Mu'tadid was a keen gardener, but not the sort who would phone up Radio 4 for advice on his hollyhocks, for instead of flowerpots he used the skulls of his slaughtered enemies. After he passed on to the great rose garden in the sky, the Alcazar became the setting for the wedding of Carlos V and his Portuguese bride Isabella, and in the 20th Century the occasional home of Franco, who ordered the kitchens to be expanded so that he could wander through these shady groves of marble with a full belly.

Which reminded me, it was time for lunch - ham and tomatoes, as approved by the Middlesex Health Board, at a little table outside a nearby café, where I had my shoes polished by an old man called Enrique.

"Image is everything in the 20th Century. You need a new pair of brogues," he said, proving that in Seville, not only are the churches mosques, but the shoeshiners are philosophers. And only five minutes' walk away, admiring the nutty gleam of my feet all the way through the tiny streets, I found Seville's most beautiful paradox of all.

The 300ft minaret of the Giralda, one of the most important and beautiful monuments of the Islamic world, was built between 1184 and 1196. After the city was recaptured by the Christian Ferdinand III, the city fathers at first used it as a church, then built the world's largest cathedral onto the side.

Here, within a matter of yards, many worlds meet and history becomes real. In the square where Muslims came to wash their feet and pray to Mecca, you can close your eyes and admire the Moorish art of creating these cool places of marble and tile, orange blossoms and flowing water. Outside, in the brick and mortar join between the Giralda and the cathedral, you can see and touch the physical line where the Islamic and Christian worlds met.

And inside, looking up at the vast, airy archways which were built between 1402 and 1506, you can follow the happy journey between the complexity of Gothic and the simplicity of Renaissance architecture.

The cathedral is the home of two important works of art, the Vision of San Antonio by Murillo and the Statue of the Blind Virgin by Martinez Montanes, so called because she is looking at the floor. Popular mythology has it that she is gazing at the trio of angels at her feet, but the truth is that she has just had her sandals polished by Enrique and is admiring them.

Everywhere, Seville recreates itself. It is still doing so today in the shape of the Isle Magica, an adventure park on the theme of Spain's 16th-17th Century relationship with America, built on the site of a former monastery and surrounded by pavilions from the 1992 World Expo, all designed by architects who wouldn't recognise a right angle if one walked up and introduced itself. And quite right, too -

as any Irishman will tell you, the longest distance between two points is always a straight line.

Nearby, another monastery, built in 1399, became in 1839 the tile factory of English merchant Charles Pickman and in 1986 a local government office and archaeological study centre. The old chapel is still there, for you to sit in the cool and airy shade, and be at peace with yourself, or whatever you call God.

And so, having fed my soul, it was time for my stomach again, and dinner at the quaintly named Hotel Colon, where the bullfighters stay when they win at the nearby Plaza de Toros. When they lose, they stay at the local hospital, and the bulls end up in the kitchen either way, as I found when their tails ended up on my plate at dinner. Still, I'd rather eat the back than face the front, and they were delicious.

Outside the restaurant as we ate, 36 youths were busy struggling to lift what looked like an enormous dining table. They were, in fact, practising carrying one of the hundreds of religious floats which are borne through the streets in the annual Easter parade, a celebration which went on even when it was banned by Franco. When the police challenged the marchers, they simply said: "But we are communists - and this is a communist Virgin on top." In Seville, where mosques become churches and tobacco factories become universities, even the Virgin Mary can become a communist.

And men can become horses - the next morning, driving to the countryside for lunch through fields in which small, dark farmers were out riding their squat, muscular Berber stallions, it was easy to see why, when Hernan Cortes arrived in Mexico with his conquistadors in 1519, the Aztecs thought that his men and their horses were one beast.

Lunch was at Esparragal, a white and sprawling 17th Century farmhouse which takes in paying guests.

We ate on the patio as the sun poured down on us like honey. Bulls slept in the fields around us; horses mated peremptorily in the stables behind us, and storks circled above our heads. On the white linen tablecloth was a chilled glass of the deliciously nutty aperitif Manzanilla.

We broke bread, and drank wine, and gave thanks.

For the bread, for the wine, for the blue sky, and for a city we would return to that evening for dancing and laughter.

A city where many differences meet and which is fascinating because it is the happy dialectic caused by the meeting of differences which creates love and art.

A city which over the centuries has received its invaders, absorbed the best of them, and in an antithesis of the maxim of St Francis that to give is to receive, now has everything to give.

I raised my glass to Seville, to life, and watched the beaded rim rise to greet the sun.

1997

Barcelona

I went out walking with a rusty nose, beneath the bananaless banana trees.

All around, women with eyebrows like angry hedgehogs strode purposefully about, and painfully stylish teenagers on small motorcycles flung themselves suicidally into the traffic, popping up on the other side of the street with surprised expressions on their faces that they were still alive.

But let me explain about the rust.

I had arrived in the Hotel Ambassador and looked in the mirror to discover to my horror that there were hairs growing out of my nose.

And sure enough, when I checked my diary, I was 37.

Unfortunately, the only sharp implement I had on me was a pair of scissors which had been given to me by an ex-girlfriend, presumably with the intention that I should trim myself painfully to death, but which I tossed into the bottom of a damp toilet bag and forgot about.

Hence the rust, which was not helped at all by the drizzle.

You don't really expect drizzle in Barcelona, but then, it is a city which is never sure whether it's a southern city in northern Europe or the other way around.

It's also not sure whether it's rich or poor, ugly or beautiful, serious or humorous, commercial or hedonistic.

In fact, it hasn't even got a clue whether its streets should be big or small.

In the old part of the city, they're so narrow that anyone over six feet tall falling down sideways will get stuck and have to be liberated by the application to their extremities of large quantities of virgin olive oil.

But in the various modern bits which have been built at the drop of any convenient excuse like the Universal Exhibition of 1888, the sequel of 1929 and the Olympics of 1992, the boulevards are as wide as several elephants laid trunk to tail. African elephants, that is.

The most famous of those boulevards is La Rambla, an artery of green which runs for a mile from the Plaça de Catalunya to the sea. Wandering down it is a tradition so enshrined in Barcelona life that it has given the Catalan language the words *ramblejar,* which means to walk down La Rambla, and *ramblista,* which describes a person addicted to the verb. Whoever dreamed up the cliché "All life is here" was, undoubtedly, a *ramblista,* since the boulevard sings with life from dawn to dewy dawn.

From when the chefs of the city's top restaurants gather for the day in the 19th Century covered market of La Boqueria to sniff, squeeze, poke, haggle and finally choose their fresh ingredients for the day. It takes a while —there are 21 types of olives alone.

From that dawn to the next, when the sleepless few finally emerge from the bars and wander home, their bellies full of Rioja and the dying stars reflected in their bleary eyes as they buy the first edition of La Vanguardia from the all-night stalls which sell everything from flowers to caged songbirds, and choose a passing cab. This takes less time than choosing olives, since there are 11,000 taxis in the city.

At the end of La Rambla is a statue of Christopher Columbus, holding what looks like a large cod in his left hand and pointing vaguely out to sea with his right.

He has reason to be vague. Not only did the builders get it wrong and point him in the direction of the Balearic Islands rather than America, but he's now generally reckoned to have found America about 500 years after Bjarni Herfjolfsson, a Viking who got lost on the way to visit his dad in Greenland.

Although you could spend a week's holiday in La Rambla and never be bored, you really should get a guide and see some of the rest of the city.

A guide like Joanne. Joanne was half Swiss and half Catalan, and had an accent that would seduce you at 10 paces.

I could have listened to her all day, even though half the time I hadn't a clue what she was talking about. But then, that's normal for Barcelona. If you ask three different people to tell you the history of the city, you'll get four different versions.

Which brings me to the bananaless banana trees, for the first thing I asked Joanne was what the trees down La Rambla were.

"Banana trees," she said. "But they have no bananas."

I looked out of the taxi window, but it was difficult to tell whether there were any bananas or not, since it had started to rain with such ferocity that I felt as if Joanne and I were extras in Voyage to the Bottom of the Sea.

To say that it was coming down in bucketfuls would have fallen some distance short of addressing the issue. After 10 minutes the streets were a foot deep in water, and it was with a sense of soggy surrealism after another 10 minutes that I looked out of the taxi window and saw the Temple of the Sagrada Familia, or Holy Family, looming out of a gap in the clouds.

I'd seen photographs of it before, but nothing could prepare you for the magnificent irrelevance of the real thing.

The Sagrada Familia is the most famous work of the modernist architect Antoni Gaudi, who gave the English language the word gaudy and whose lunatic creations sit in the middle of otherwise grey façades in Barcelona like clowns at a business meeting.

Gaudi was born in 1826 and became a genius, a recluse, a man who fell under a tram, and dead, in that order. It was three days before. Barcelona realised that the 74-year-old apparent vagrant lying in the mortuary was in fact their most famous architect, which just goes to show you how ungrateful people can be.

The Japanese, by contrast, now love him so much that those who have accidentally booked their Spanish holidays in Madrid regularly take the 2am flight from there to Barcelona, spend two hours touring his buildings, and fly back at dawn.

Gaudi is now buried in the crypt of the Sagrada Familia, which he became so obsessed with that he lived there for the last six years of his life, begging for money to continue building it.

If you can imagine four hock bottles 450ft tall full of holes and with crowns instead of corks, you should see a psychiatrist —but you have some idea of what the Sagrada Familia looks like.

And it's not even finished. Many of the models designed by Gaudi, smashed in the Civil War, have been rebuilt from a mountain of fragments by Jordi Cusso, who admits to frequent nightmares about the complexity of piecing together the third façade and the 650ft central tower.

When, if ever, it will be finished is one of the great topics of conversation in Barcelona, along with when they'll ever get around to fixing the fountain on the mountain.

For in the same way that Irishmen wax lyrical about the best pint of Guinness they ever had and Italians come over all misty eyed about their first Vespa, the good citizens of Barcelona almost hum with bliss when they talk about the fountain on the mountain.

Designed by Carlos Buigas for the 1929 World Exposition, this magical dance of moving water, lights and music comes to life every Saturday and Sunday evening in the Montjuic park high above the city smog.

This is where Barcelonans come on a weekend, to touch the air and breathe the sky, and drape themselves in the rainbow cloak of the fountain up the mountain.

Or came. For a couple of years ago, it went the way of all marriages between metal and water, grinding to a messy divorce in a recrimination of rusty cogs.

The man from the city council came up, had a look, and went away scratching his head. A large sum of money was mentioned. Breath was sharply intaken, and the city council started saving its pesetas.

In the meantime, all is still up the mountain at the fountain, and at the nearby Mies van der Rohe pavilion, a song to simplicity in marble and water, glass and chrome.

The architect Peter Berhens described this German contribution to the 1929 Expo as the most beautiful building of the 20th Century.

The Barcelonans, taking the view that since Berhens was:

a) German

b) Mies van der Rohe's professor

he would say that anyway, dismantled it and only rebuilt it in 1985. Today, like most of Mies van der Rohe's architecture, it looks fresh off the drawing board.

Still, at least you can't accuse the Spanish of chauvinism - they were going to dismantle their own pavilion as well, and it's only recently that they've got around to refitting it properly as the Museum of Catalan Art, containing an astonishing selection of frescoes from 11th and 12th Century Pyrenean churches which were being ruined by renovation, vandalism or theft until a concerted campaign from 1919 onwards to save them. Today, they are brilliantly displayed in replicas of the mountain churches from which they came.

You have to admire the Barcelonans for recycling buildings so effectively, whether it's Expo pavilions or the beautifully cloistered Pedraldes Monastery, formerly the home of the fabulously poor nuns of St Clare and now the home of 72 paintings and eight sculptures from the collection of the fabulously wealthy Baron Hans Heinrich Thyssen-Bornemisza de Kaszon, the only man in the world with an extendable chequebook.

There were once hundreds of Clarissa nuns here, but today there are only 22. The youngest is 35, and the oldest had died three days before.

Upstairs, the dormitory where they slept is the home of the Thyssen Collection, the most famous of which is The Madonna of Humility by Fra Angelico, in which Mary's long-suffering expression can be explained by the fact that the baby Jesus has been tickling her neck with a white lily since 1433.

A little less iconoclastic than the Sagrada Familia, but quite as famous, is the work of Joan Miro, whose simple white museum stands on the Montjuic hill high above the city, near the Olympic stadium and the diving pool where the famous Olympic photographs were taken of tiny Chinese teenagers apparently about to impale themselves on the towers of the Sagrada Familia.

Most of Miro's best work is, unfortunately, on display in New York, but there's still enough in the museum, like an astonishing 50ft high wall hanging and Alexander Calder's fountain of liquid mercury cascading down a series of black metal curves, to make a visit worthwhile.

I bought an expensive poster to try and console myself for the fact that Joanne had somehow forgotten to ask me to marry her when she said goodbye, and got a taxi back into the city for dinner at the Four Cats, the restaurant where Picasso had his first exhibition and didn't sell a thing - rather appropriately, since its name is taken from the Catalan equivalent of one man and his dog, as in 'Nobody turned up, just four cats.'

Like all Spanish meals, it was a dizzy combination of satisfaction and fear. Fear that every time you sat back, patted your full belly and thought what a wonderful meal it had been, another course arrived.

Beneath the huge arched windows at the end of the room, a pianist with a battered face tinkled the minor classics on a baby grand.

Like all the piano players in all the restaurants in the world, he looked as if he had suffered a flat tyre on the motorway of love.

Or was just about to, arriving home to find a note saying:

*Darling, I have left you for someone with a day job. I
cannot bear you arriving home in the middle of the night
with the air of doomed romance which comes from playing
Rachmaninov all evening. The click of the door at three, the
way you climb politely into bed hoping that I am awake, the
way we both know I am pretending to be asleep. I am truly
sorry, but this is your destiny. It is the destiny of all
restaurant pianists.*

Love, regret
Emily

When he left, I held the door open for him. It seemed the
least I could do.

I went for a walk, and at two in the morning found myself
on the seafront. On my left was the giant lobster on top of
the Amerinis restaurant , on my right was the Olympic
village, and behind that were rows of narrow streets in a
state of crumbling, aromatic decay.

In the little squares off La Rambla, a saxophone played,
and teenagers sat at zinc-stopped bars drinking Rioja from
glasses beaded with ice and trying to get each other into bed.

I sat at a table outside in the balmy air, drinking beer and
arguing for the next three hours with a man from Aberdeen
about modernism, which was quite an achievement when
you consider that neither of us knew anything about it.

At five I walked back to the hotel and went for a swim in
the icy rooftop pool as forked lightning flickered across the
city, investigating careless television aerials.

Unelectrocuted in spite of myself, I crept into my warm
bed, only to be awakened at nine by the receptionist on the
telephone.

"I am sorry, but we cannot give you an extra heater in your room," she said wistfully.

"That's all right," I said, since I hadn't asked for one.

I got up and pulled back the curtains. The sun was shining, and all the way down La Rambla the eyes of the caged birds watched the pigeons soaring above the bananaless banana trees until they were lost to sight.

I checked my nose for rust, and went back to sleep.

1994

Almeria:The Good, The Bad and The Tortoise

There was not a minute to lose, for I was on the trail of the Moorish tortoise.

This little-known beast is only to be found near the ancient city of Almeria on the south-east coast of Spain.

And every spring it is the sluggardly hero of an equally ancient but almost unknown festival which was the inspiration for the running of the bulls in Pamplona.

Yes, the running of the tortoises.

Every March, exactly one hundred of the little darlings are released into the narrow streets of this rambling, sunspilt city, which in the 11th Century was the wealthiest of Spain.

And every May, when the tortoises have had enough of a head start, the festival begins with the traditional firing of the noon gun from the battlements of the Alcazaba, the tremendous Moorish citadel which towers over the city to this day.

As the smoke from the discharge clears, there can be seen in the streets below thousands of feckless foreigners, fired up on rough mountain brandy, spring off in search of their goal.

And behind them, more thousands of fearless locals, who have perhaps taken a glass or two of the chilled sherry for which the region is famous, saunter off at a more leisurely pace.

For there is an art to the ancient skill of running with the Moorish tortoise.

Some catch them too soon, and die of boredom waiting for the race to end.

Some never catch them at all, and die of embarrassment.

But others time it perfectly, achieve just the amount of time you would want to spend with a Moorish tortoise, and can be heard in the early hours of the following morning in the tapas bars of the old town, regaling anyone who cares to listen with old tortoise yams.

But that was tomorrow. Today I had a date with Clint Eastwood - boarding a bus which climbed into the high sierra through land which is now the vegetable garden of Spain, but until the Sixties, when sweet water wells were drilled for irrigation, was the country's Siberia, a dirt-poor region to which unfashionably liberal politicians were dispatched by Franco.

Six years after water was found, the area was self-sufficient, and today it has more acres of arable farmland than the Netherlands.

Most of it is now given over to vast plastic greenhouses which, in spite of legislation banning further development, still keep springing up mysteriously on moonlit nights when the government inspectors are in their beds.

Only the almond blossoms are left free to grow in the open air, and every spring they dance on the foothills of the Sierra Nevada, gently mocking the endless sea of plastic below.

And here and there among the almonds can be seen slumped the exhausted remains of the iron mines which were the area's main industry in the 19th Century, and which died out, serendipitously, just as water was discovered.

The minerals buried in the mountains, however, are still put to use high in the mountains, in the San Nicolas spa in Alhama, where rows of rheumatic pensioners sit stiffly outside in the thin, cool air waiting to be carefully plunged into baths of warm mineral water which have been here since Roman times, then decanted onto vibrating benches which have been here since electronic times.

Above their heads as they wobble away, swallows dip and fray in the endless blue, as far from the arthritic suffering below as the almond trees are from the plastic sea.

There are many tiny surprises to be found on mountain walks in these high sierras; the scarlet dusting of poppies in the fields, the deep violet of roadside bindweed and the ripe perfection of oranges swaying against the glossy green of the leaves cradling them.

But most of the life has silted down into the valleys, into a yellow, green and white sediment of lemon groves and cubist villages where the women still gather in the fountainy cool of the squares to do their washing by hand and talk of how much easier life would be, if it were not for men.

We stopped at one, Alboloduy, to drink at the fountain and wander through the white bougainvillea-draped walls while from through the fly curtains at doors peeked young kittens and ancient widows.

It was noon, and so hot that the dogs couldn't be bothered to bark and we had to do it ourselves, chasing each other down the street then stopping for a pee against an olive tree before proceeding inland through a landscape of wild west badlands which look as if they're straight out of a film.

Which is probably because they are. A Fistful of Dollars, The Good, The Bad and The Ugly, The Magnificent Seven, High Noon, El Cid, Back to the Future III and Mad Max were all filmed here because of cheap labour and cheaper light, leaving behind entire towns which have been turned into tourist attractions like Mini Hollywood, the setting for A Fistful of Dollars.

I moseyed into town, spat carefully in the dirt and had me a mess of quiche and Rioja at the eating place. Halfway through the meringue a grizzled priest came in and blessed me comprehensively, which was dead handy, because the next thing I knew I was being hanged in front of the general store.

It was a bit unfair, really. How was I to know it was the sheriff's horse I'd been caught in bed with?

As if that wasn't bad enough, I was just emerging from the saloon half an hour after a very nice glass of 1987 Manzanilla to help overcome the shock of being dead when I was shot down by a bunch of hoodlums robbing the town bank.

Now, getting killed once in an afternoon I can cope with, but twice just isn't acceptable. I returned to the hotel and spent the evening by the pool with a large gin and tonic, killing myself a little more slowly, and a lot more pleasurably, then went to bed convinced that there was something I'd forgotten.

Ah yes, the Moorish tortoise.

But first, the national park north east of Almeria where the Atlantic and the Mediterranean meet and create an environment which is home to 400 indigenous species.

In the middle of the park is an interpretative centre with a witty series of illustrations.

Well, as witty as you can get about flora and fauna. Did you know, for example, that the 120ft long roots of the Ziziphus

Lotus will often spend months wandering around looking for a drink? I didn't, but I know the feeling.

Strangely, there was not a single tortoise in the photographs on the wall, but they couldn't have got too far.

Tortoises never do.

And besides, I wasn't the only one on the trail of elusive species - just down the road I found a couple of baffled looking Norwegians, Arve and Kendt, who were spending two weeks cycling around Almeria on the trail of the elusive marbled duck.

"We saw one this morning," said Arve carefully, with the air of a man who had only a limited amount of excitement and didn't want to use it all up at once.

"Seen any tortoises?" I whispered out of the corner of my mouth.

"Eh?" he said, in that way that Norwegians always have when you ask them about tortoises.

Fortunately, a few yards away was the chief ranger of the park, Jose Manuel Lopez Martos.

"Indeed, we do have tortoises, and they are bilingual," he said. "Some of them are descendants of pet tortoises abandoned by English residents when they got too big."

"English residents always go like that," I said.

"No, the tortoises," said Jose.

Still, this was a new and exciting development. I would not only be able to meet the Moorish tortoise, but be able to ask him for the truth about that story with the hare.

In the meantime, though, the great tortoise hunt was postponed temporarily while Jose took me for a drive through the park in a Seat Ibiza whose arthritic suspension was ill-suited to the task of ferrying five of us over unpaved tracks.

Most men faced with such a situation would react by driving slower, but Jose was, after all, Spanish, and as we accelerated through another boulder-strewn corner, I was filled with astonishment at two things.

One, that the exhaust was still on.

And two, a view outside which around every boulder-strewn corner changed from African savannah to Australian eucalyptus grove to Moroccan desert to a Greek windmill perched on top of a hill so green it had obviously been nicked from Kerry.

Weird. But wonderful. It was so strange that the only answer was to retire to a little fishing village called the Island of the Moors to have lunch on a terrace by the sea, to the accompaniment of waves gently lapping at our feet with the sort of sound you get on those relaxation tapes with whales farting on the other side.

Lunch was bream and salad with a dressing so exquisite that the only thing wrong with it was that I found myself worrying halfway through it that I was reaching the age where dressing excited me more than undressing.

But there were more important things to worry about, quite apart from the continuing lack of tortoises.

Like Walt Disney, for example. For according to local legend, Disney was born in Mojacar, a beautiful village just up the mountain with stunning views of the sea which became so popular as an artists' colony in the Sixties that the artists couldn't get any work done, and left.

The legend has it that Walt was born Waldo, the illegitimate son of the village doctor and a laundrywoman who was forced to flee to Valencia with Waldo and his big brother because of the shame, although why she hadn't fled because of the shame of the big brother is unclear.

Perhaps the Mojacarans take the same view as Wilde, that one birth is a tragedy, but two is careless.

In any case, in Valencia big brother gets a job on an American ship with a captain by the name of Disney, who meets mum, falls in love and ships her and the boys off to California, where the rest is hysteria.

True or false? You decide.

In the meantime, I was off to a little taverna for dinner, and then bed, convinced that there was something I'd forgotten.

Ah yes, the tortoises.

But first, the Sunday morning market, at which one intriguing stall was selling only beds and garlic. Single beds, naturally.

Afterwards we ate sardines and paella down by the harbour in the old town of Almeria. The afternoon curved around, perfect and true, and along the edge of it from time to time appeared diminutive sailors and brides - local six-year-olds dressed up for their first communion, when according to the fondly nurtured mythology of their parents, they become Christians by choice rather than birth.

As the sun tilted into the west, a symbol of an older mythology, we walked through the town in the cool of the day, stopping to drink at the fountain. They say that if you drink the water here, you will return, as opposed to London, where they say that if you drink the water you will never leave.

And on, up the hill to the Alcazada, the Moorish citadel which in the 11th Century was home to vast gardens, fantastic inner palaces and 20,000 inhabitants.

At the entrance to this once fabulous fortress, under the lilac shade of a jacaranda tree, was once the hall of mirrors, a terrace from which the darkly bearded denizens of the

Alcazada would send elliptical heliographs to their curved ships prowling the dangerous seas beyond.

But there are no mirrors any more, and as a scimitar moon rose over Almeria this night, its light danced only on the thousand gins of the yacht owners who flock south at this time of this year to escape a northern winter.

And above them, on terraced gardens, harems and groves empty of Moors, concubines and tortoises.

I went to bed knowing what it was I had forgotten, and left for the airport at dawn the next morning, tortoiseless.

It was no use. I would never speak French properly, dance the tango, learn to fly, buy an old motorbike* or run with the famous tortoises of Almeria.

But patience. After all, if dreams lived next door, we would never visit them.

* The good news is that the year after this, my mate Paddy Minne and I bought two Royal Enfields in India and rode them back to the UK; and three years later, I learnt to fly. So never give up on your dreams. I still haven't run with the tortoises of Almeria, mind you.

1997

T is for Tunisia

"The last two times I was here," said Moncef Battikh as we pulled up outside the hotel in Tunis, "was with Ursula Andress and Sean Connery."

"She was lovely, but he was a bit of a problem. He fell in love with the belly dancer, and she already had two husbands."

We unloaded our bags, donned ties and went to dinner in a little Moroccan restaurant nearby.

As the resident belly dancer worked herself into such a frenzy that her navel was later found several blocks away, we tucked into a spread of, by my estimation, 610 courses. Which was, by a remarkable coincidence, exactly the year that Mohammed sat down under a tree and started writing down the Koran as God dictated it to him, occasionally interjecting as the day wore on with a tetchy:

"Slow down, slow down, for, well, Your sake, really. Now, what were those directions to Mecca again?"

Fortunately, God took his advice, the Koran was published, and unlike most first books, made a significant prophet.

Anyway, where was I?

Ah yes, in the bar listening to two Tunisians telling an old joke about a Tunisian who comes across a Libyan in the desert whose Mercedes has broken down.

"Ah, my brother, a car is like a balloon. You can fix it by blowing into the exhaust," he says.

Several hours later, as the exhausted Libyan is still blowing into the exhaust, another Tunisian comes by and receives a stream of abuse for the foolish advice of his countryman.

"Ah, my brother, he was right, and it is you who are the fool. You have forgotten to wind the windows up," says the Tunisian.

As I said to Moncef the next morning over breakfast on the patio, I was sure I'd heard the some joke last year about a Kerryman.

"Ah, we have a lot in common with the Irish," he said, "We both drink like fish and adapt our religion to our needs rather than the other way around. Even our national poet. Abou Nawas, says: 'Wine today, decisions tomorrow'."

At our table, sunlight danced between the glasses. Beyond, it filtered down through the plain trees which shaded the graceful French colonial boulevards, and beyond that, daisy meadows sloped down to the sea.

A butterfly rested briefly on the tablecloth, then fluttered on.

Coming from the long curse of a British winter, I felt suddenly blessed by heat and light. And then blessed again, later in the morning, by the colours at the Bardo Museum, the former royal palace which now houses the finest collection of Roman mosaics in the world.

Inside, over every wall and vaulted ceiling, are a million postcards from the edge of an empire's imagination.

All of them are remarkable, from the remarkable everyday - a herd of ostriches being prepared for the hunt - to the remarkable mythical - a group of Cyclops wielding mighty hammers as they forge thunderbolts for Jupiter. Even two millennia on, you still step back from the heat of their massive endeavours.

There was a time, of course, before the blazing glory of Rome came to Africa. It was the time of Carthage, and we shall never know whether it was dark or light, because the Romans laid waste to that city so utterly, even ploughing salt into the ruins so that nothing would ever grow there again.

Today, as a result, we know little of it. We know of Dido and Aeneas, we know that its noblest citizens sacrificed their favourite children to Baal, and we know that Hannibal left it with his elephants to cross the Alps.

But all that remains of it in the Bardo Museum is a little collection of self-effacing statues in a comer room, and the site of Carthage itself, just up the coast from Tunis, is even more poignant.

The city, as you may remember, was founded by Dido, Queen of the Phoenicians, in 814BC. According to Virgil's Aeneid, she came home from hard days on the building site, threw off her hard hat and jumped into bed with Aeneas, sole survivor of the Greek destruction of Troy.

This is usually taken as myth nowadays, since Troy fell five centuries before Carthage rose, although it could just have been typical builders: "Listen, Mrs Dido, I know we said three weeks, but those architraves are a bloody nightmare."

Of the city itself, there is nothing . In a way, because Carthage died so young, it has become the James Dean of cities, its mythical glories forged almost entirely in the crucibles of our imagination.

If we imagine it at all, we imagine it walking down a wet New York street, its collar up and a cigarette clamped between its teeth, or driving its Porsche down a sunlit road, blithely unaware that

the Romans are hurtling towards the junction in a truck.

"Anyway, enough culture," said Moncef, interrupting my thoughts. "Time for dinner."

Dinner was so much cous cous that I looked around in vain for someone else to eat the other cous.

At midnight, just as I was looking forward to bed, Moncef announced that we were going to a wedding. We got into a taxi and drove 10 miles to another hotel, in which a vast room was filled with women like Sophia Loren and men like Lee van Cleef. Everyone was drinking Fanta.

At one in the morning, the bride and groom arrived and sat on matching white thrones onstage beside the band. He looked like the cat who had got the cream, and she looked suitably virginal, for although Tunisia is the most secular and liberal of Arab states, men are still expected to sow entire fields of oats before marriage, and women to remain pure

How this is supposed to happen simultaneously is a subject that is not discussed in polite Tunisian society, but at least it's a change from the days when the bride's mother observed the consummation; a practice whose psychological effects must have done more to reduce national population growth than any government family planning scheme,

The next morning, my eyes prickly with sleep, we drove south to El Jem, accompanied by Moncef's sister. On all sides stretched the descendants of the olive trees planted by the Romans which had first made this country rich 2,000 years ago.

We stopped once, to buy warm bread. Outside the butcher's next door hung a cow's head, looking rightly pissed off that it wasn't still attached to the rest of the cow hanging next to it.

We drove on, through fields of lavender from which rose at last the great colosseum of El Jem, only slightly smaller than the one in Rome and the single most impressive Roman monument in Africa.

Its isolation has left it almost intact, down to the tunnel where the gladiators awaited their fate, its walls lined with graffiti saying "Maximus is a big girl's blouse" and "Well, Decimus did say he likes a lion on Saturday mornings".

Even today, standing in the sandy oval arena and looking up at the rows of seats, you can almost smell the fear and sweat, almost hear the roar of the mob.

Better to climb to the highest point of the expensive seats, look down and thank the gods that rather than dying that day in the sand, you are going home to a glass of wine and a warm concubine.

The next morning, breakfast with the Minister for Tourism was cancelled: praise Allah, for it gave me the morning off to have bread and honey on the lawn as bees hummed and an ancient retainer trimmed the hedges.

It was like being in Kent, and that afternoon I found myself in Tunisia's Tuscany, the fertile western region of verdant hills and olive groves which cosset Dougga, the country's best-preserved Roman site.

With an almost complete amphitheatre and capitol, it is all the more remarkable for its rural setting, with a couple of

Algerian picnickers and a baffled goat adding to its surrealism.

"Tell me, Moncef," I said the next morning as we drove to the airport, "what did you do before you joined the tourist board?"

"Well, my first job was feeding the lions at Regent Park Zoo, if you can believe it."

I did. In fact, I checked with one of the lions.

Who, funnily enough, was a direct descendant of the one who had eaten Decimus at El Jem all those years ago.

2003

U is for Upgrades

One of the great joys of travel is getting an upgrade. There are several ways of doing this. The first is paying for it, but since an average business class fare across the Atlantic is about £2,500, it would be cheaper to buy a secondhand microlight and fly yourself over.

Furthermore, since actually paying for something is against the strict code of journalistic ethics, I always try to use one of the other three methods:

1) Wear a smart suit and look as if only a tragic gambling debt or the loss of the family rubber plantations in Malaya have prevented you from claiming your natural place at the front of the aircraft.

2) Be at least 6ft 7ins tall, and drag your left leg up to the check-in desk as if you are in the early stages of DVT.

3) Be with the boss of the airline you are flying with.

As a result of an assiduous combination of these three fundamental principles, I have on occasion been admitted to the holy of holies. Of the most memorable occasions, one was by design, and the other by chance.

The first time, I had been in Japan for several weeks, and had run out of money after, oh, 48 hours. Having lived on noodles from street stalls since then, I crawled up to the British Airways check-in desk at Tokyo Airport weighing less than my ticket.

"We have a request here for an upgrade for you. Would you like to move up?" said the girl behind the desk sweetly.

"Lovely," I croaked faintly.

Ten minutes later, I was sitting in an armchair being served champagne by a man in a white jacket, and over the next 12 hours I proceed to drink all the drink, eat all the food, listen to all the music and watch all the movies on the plane.

The second time, I was checking in at Mexico City with a group which included a fat, pompous woman from the Daily Mail. We had been promised a chance to try out BA's new first class sleeper seats, but it turned out there was no space in either first or business class.

"This is preposterous!" spluttered Daily Mail woman. "I am a travel writer for a national newspaper, and I always get an upgrade. I am a personal friend of Lord King, and I'll have your job, young man."

The young man, who politely declined the offer to tell her that she could have his job anytime if it meant dealing with people like her, replied that he would be only too happy to give us seats, if there were some, but there were not.

In any case, we got on, and found there was plenty of room to stretch out in economy. I was just opening a book to read when the stewardess tapped me on the shoulder.

"Here, you don't have much legroom there," she said.

"No worries. I've got three seats here, so I've loads of room," I said.

Two minutes later, she returned.

"Come with me," she whispered. "There's one seat left in business."

I looked across to where Daily Mail woman was glaring the other way, and tiptoed up to the front.

However, I had never dared to try all of these techniques at the same time until a couple of weeks ago, when I found myself in Abu Dhabi queuing for a flight to Bangkok with Ahmed Hussain Aljanahi, the marketing manager of Gulf Air.

The airline had been started in 1940 by Freddie Bosworth, a Scottish ex-RAF pilot who arrived in Bahrain with a seven-seater Anson and a dream to make a living offering sightseeing trips around the islands. Freddie, who was killed on a test flight in 1964, would hardly have recognised the vast silver beasts which made up his airline today.

"Let's see if we can get into First," Ahmed said suddenly, interrupting my thoughts.

"But Ahmed, we've already had dinner, and it's midnight. It'd be a complete waste of time," I wailed.

But it was too late. He had already gone off to talk to persons of influence, and 15 minutes later I found myself being carried up the aircraft steps by carefully oiled Nubian slaves while several Balinese dancing girls wafted my fevered brow with ostrich feathers.

Upstairs, they laid me down gently in an adjustable armchair which ran the gamut of positions from Languid but Alert to Comatose but Happy

From a bottomless fountain up the front, a Thai stewardess brought me champagne which according to the wine list was "a sober wine, with a touch of natureal and a hint of local specific taste".

It went on: 'In the mouth, it surprises by its liveliness. It lines the palate, frank and mature. Its moderate evolution shows its happiness with ease."

Heavens. That was a lot to ask for, in just one glass. It was a Heidsieck Heritage, in case you ever want your palate lined frankly and maturely.

A personal chef asked me what I would like for dinner, then cooked it for me, and the rest of the night passed in a happy welter of fine wines, fine food and fine music.

Well, almost fine music: no matter what audio channel I turned to, I always seemed to end up back at the Arabic one featuring those old desert favourites Stop the Camel, I Want to Get Off, and I'd Love Her if I Knew What She Looked Like Under Her Burqa.

I finally found a classical channel, and fell asleep at three in the morning listening to the strains of Grieg's Piano Concerto.

Thanks to a man from Bahrain, I was on an airline started by a Scot, full to the brim with wine and food from a Thai stewardess and French chef, falling asleep listening to one of the finest creations of a Norwegian composer and on my way to the exotic and mysterious Orient.

It was, to be frank and mature with you, a first class experience.

2003

V is for Vietnam: the Ho Chi Minh Trail in a US Army Jeep

I 've finally realised why the USA pulled out of Vietnam. They got fed up waiting to cross the street.

So constant is the relentless flow of scooters in cities like Hanoi that in the end I gave up, got into a Jeep and drove to Ho Chi Minh.

Now, you'd think driving a former US Army Jeep down the Ho Chi Minh Trail would be, to paraphrase the late Kenny Everett, not in the best possible taste.

The truth, remarkably, is the opposite: the Vietnamese say that since they won the war, these are highly prized war trophies and cult vehicles.

The company behind the jaunt was Great Road Journeys, run by Englishman Steve McCullagh, who back in 2006 had it all: the top job as MD of a car leasing company, the company Porsche and the jet set lifestyle.

But he didn't have a life, particularly involving his twin loves of travel and classic cars – which is why he jacked it all in after taking 60 friends on a driving tour of southern India in Hindustani Ambassadors, the Indian equivalent of 1950s Morris Oxfords.

He's still doing that, as well as tours around southern India and the Himalayas, and added the Vietnam tours in 2012, making his the only company doing self-drive tours in that country.

It was my first time in Vietnam, and my immediate impression as we drove through Hanoi to meet Steve's fixer Cu'o'ng Phung, Vietnam's top mechanic and the man who sorted out the Top Gear team and Charley Boorman with transport for their jaunts through the country, was that the city had a shambolic post-colonial charm, and that the people managed to look simultaneously serious and optimistic.

The former, presumably, was because of centuries of suffering under the French and the Americans, and the latter because they hoped all that was behind them for good.

Although not quite yet: every man in Cu'o'ng's village came home from the war missing eyes, arms or legs, and his father, a worker in a steel processing plant bombed by the US Air Force, later died of his injuries when Cu'o'ng was 13.

"His three brothers were killed in the war as well, leaving my aunt with no children," said Cu'o'ng. "She cried for two weeks, then forgot it."

You see, while Vietnamese will tell you they are Buddhists, they aren't really: they'll eat meat and drink beer, but they have retained two more important Buddhist characteristics; being nice to people who aren't trying to kill them, and acceptance.

Even when the poverty caused by the war's legacy is such that when Steve's road manager Thuan Le Minh's mother was giving birth, the baby was in the wrong position. By the

.

time the family came up with the cash an hour and a half later for a Caesarean, she had died.

When we arrived at Cu'o'ng's garage to pick up the Jeep, we found him slightly downcast because he'd just bought five unexploded wartime bombs for $1,200 and the police had confiscated them before he could sell them on for a profit.

"Still, never mind. In return they sold me those 70 ex-police Minsks for $150 each," he said, indicating a pile of 125cc bikes stacked along a wall.

"But Cu'o'ng, they've got no front wheels," said Steve.

"I know, I know. But even if I can't find any, I'll use them as decorations in this biker café I'm opening," said Cu'o'ng.

It's a wonderful irony that although the communists won the war, one of the things the Americans left behind, apart from Agent Orange, napalm, unexploded bombs and Jeeps was capitalism, and the Vietnamese are black belts at the art of the fast buck, although in the most charming way possible.

The US left behind thousands of these Jeeps when their troops pulled out in 1973, and although no one could use them until petrol became freely available in the late Eighties, the canny Vietnamese stored them away, and they're now worth up to £15,000 each, with an endless supply of spare parts also left behind by the Yanks available from a vast warehouse in Ho Chi Minh City.

Mind you, that's a bargain compared to a stinging import tax on luxury cars which makes a new Range Rover there £150,000.

Which reminded me: I needed some fuel and beer money for the trip. I walked around the corner to an ATM and got out £100, or about three million dong, which makes Vietnam the home of the world's worst insult: "Darling, you look like a million dong".

Not that you'd need it, since the women are stunning, in a seriously optimistic sort of way.

We had lunch of pho, the spicy beef noodle soup, in the old quarter, a rambling maze of narrow streets, each devoted to a particular traditional craft: the street of bamboo, the street of copper, the street of candles, the street of smartphones, and so on.

Our penultimate call before hitting the road was Hỏa Lò Prison, where the guillotine used by the French to execute political prisoners still stands stark and chilling, and where the North Vietnamese later kept the US prisoners of war who nicknamed it the Hanoi Hilton.

And after that the vast mausoleum where the Vietnamese still file respectfully past the body of Ho Chi Minh, the father of the nation, in their hundreds every day.

Uncle Ho, as they call him, looked surprisingly well for someone who's been dead since 1969, but then he had just been to Moscow for his annual spruce-up.

Before we left Hanoi, we drove past Huu Tiep Lake, now in a built-up area but on December 27, 1972 in open countryside when a B-52 crashed into it.

Today, its remains and two wheels still rise from the placid green surface like the skeleton of a long-dead war.

And since the route we were following was the Ho Chi Minh Trail, it seemed appropriate to call in to the museum celebrating the 12,000-mile north to south route which kept the Viet Cong supplied for almost a decade.

The US Air Force bombed it 70,000 times with seven million tons of bombs, more than twice the payload of bombs dropped in the Second World War, but still the

Vietnamese kept coming, carrying food, guns and ammunition; on their backs, across rivers and swaying rope bridges, on bicycles, horses and elephants.

It was a timeless tenacity which eventually won against a wealthy and technologically superior superpower, but in spite of all the statistics of bombs dropped, and of the human cost: 58,183 US and an estimated 1.2 million Vietnamese dead, one of the most appalling images of just what it cost on an individual human level is an American soldier holding up what at first looks like shredded scraps of uniform.

Except there is a head hanging off the bottom of the scraps, and a hand sticking out the side; all that is left of a Vietnamese soldier hit by a shell, the expression on his face in the moment before he died one of calmness and hope for the future.

Compared to that, all we had to worry about as we drove south through the cool and misty morning were the traffic policeman in their caramel uniforms and red cap bands, like butterscotch Angel Delight with cherries on top.

When they're not handing out parking tickets, their other job is stopping anyone riding a scooter solo and ticking them off for not being a proper Vietnamese person and cramming at least another four people and the weekly shop on board.

Beneath us, the trail which in the war was dirt track is now mostly tarmac, and around us, limestone columns punching skywards from paddy fields, but we were too busy getting to grips with the charming idiosyncrasies of 1960s Jeeps to notice.

Since we'd drawn the keys out of a hat, it was pot luck whether you got a flawless one or not, but Cu'o'ng's mechanics were always on hand for everything from roadside repairs to overnight gearbox rebuilds or driveshaft replacements.

Some sounded like asthmatic chain smokers starting first thing in the morning, although mine always burst into life with a lusty roar.

Anyone who's driven an old Morris Minor will be right at home with the light, slightly vague steering, the brakes needed to be told what to do with a firm foot, and the four-speed gearboxes required either double declutching, once into neutral and once into the gear of your choice, or just a gentle touch to let the revs settle before you shifted.

Once you finally got into top gear, it was so tall that overtaking in top had to be planned with the aid of a calendar in which you could write careful copperplate entries saying: "Wednesday: began overtaking. Saturday: completed manoeuvre."

Having said that, it was so torquey that you could leave it in top all day as you bimbled along admiring the view.

And anyway, what was the rush? All 40 of us in 20 Jeeps were here to potter, and all were enjoying it from the off, whether the 30 who had been one of Steve's trips before and come back for more, or the 10 newbies.

We were a strange and wonderful social mix, too, from ordinary blokes and blokesses who had been saving up for a while for this trip of a lifetime to captains of industry like the erudite, urbane Stephen Davidson, a serial director of a handful of major companies, and top music agent Garry Blackburn, who handled Madness, Fat Boy Slim and Idris Elba, among many others.

Not to mention their wives; fragrant English roses like Kate Siggers, who out of a tiny suitcase somehow managed to produce a new outfit every day for two weeks.

Or Pippa Kirkbride, who with husband Nick had been on Steve's India trip and loved it, and who on even the hottest and most humid days looked like she was on her way to have afternoon tea with the Queen.

And if that wasn't enough, Nick may have been wearing shorts, but his shirts still had cufflinks in them.

Not that there was anything faintly snobbish about any of them: they all had that most agreeable of English qualities: effortless charm laced with a taste for adventure.

Nick, for example, while still a 17-year-old schoolboy at Oundle, had driven an ex-Army Bedford truck from Afghanistan back to the UK with a classmate in the summer holidays, and while on a university expedition to the Himalayas, bought 40 horses in Leh to carry supplies when the scheduled transport failed to turn up.

Another, Tony Colston, after two many glasses of wine one night with a biker in January 2003, had somehow agreed to ride from Los Angeles to Milwaukee for Harley's 100th anniversary celebrations that summer – in spite of the fact that he had neither a bike nor a licence.

He did an express riding course in five days, bought a Fat Boy, rode it to Barcelona two days later, and that July was proudly riding out of LA, next stop Milwaukee.

"The thing I love about these trips is the permanent feeling of excitement; getting up in the morning and not having a clue what the day will bring. It's brilliant," said Pippa as we set off – not in convoy, but each at their own pace using Steve's rally-style road books.

They are, in fact, group trips for people who don't like group trips, and you could see why Dave and Natalie Crosland had been on 12 trips with Steve, and why 85% of Steve's customers have been on previous trips with him: the flawless organisation, the adventures without the hassle of organising them, Steve's daily erudite and witty briefings, the tireless work of Cu'o'ng and his mechanics, and the perpetual presence of Thuan, who was like a hilarious combination of Jeeves, John Inman and the Duracell bunny. You'd stop in the middle of the jungle, and five seconds later he'd be at your side with a tray of cold drinks.

As for Pippa, she was certainly right about not knowing what the road would bring that day, as it turned from tarmac to mud and gravel. Just as the rain started.

Splashing and sliding, we twisted up the mountain roads into the clouds, past terraced rice fields and through hamlets of wooden stilt houses, from beneath which hordes of children would rush to wave and cry: "Hello, hello!" as we drove past.

"*Xin chào!*" we cried back, using up most of our Vietnamese in one fell swoop.

From time to time, beautiful women would emerge from the clouds on bicycles, wearing black pyjamas and conical straw hats, and with the pearls of moisture on their skin as elegant as the heirlooms of any society hostess.

At last we fell to the plains again, leaving behind the clouds and the beautiful women as we drove on, steaming gently, to Vinh. Most Vietnamese are secular or Buddhist Lite, but this area is Catholic, with impressive churches rising from the fields; an appropriately Irish scene, since the fields are of an iridescent green rarely seen outside Kerry in the Irish wet season. Which now that I think of it is all of them.

As the sun sank like a blood orange in a violet sky, we came at last to Vinh, of which there is little to say. Bombed so comprehensively by the US for eight years that its population in 1972 was officially listed as zero, it was

373

rebuilt after the war by East German architects. Draw your own conclusions.

The next morning we stopped at Dong Loc, where in 1968, 10 young girls keeping the trail clear were killed during a bombing raid.

Surrounded by fields still cratered today by that bombardment, each of their simple white graves bears their photograph, each with that familiar national look of earnest optimism.

The end of the day could not have been more different to the remembered rage and thunder of that time; being paddled through Phong Nha, one of the world's largest caves.

In the vast, sepulchral and beautifully lit space, the only sounds were the suck and gloop of the boatgirl's single oar and the plink of drips falling into the dark water from the stalactites high above.

In that moment, they sounded like the still, small sound of peace.

And then, if we'd thought the first part of the trip had taken us into the heart of rural Vietnam, on the road the next day through Ke Bang national park, until recently closed to foreigners, the only signs of humanity we saw were children playing in the road and their grandmothers sitting on the porches of wooden stilt huts smoking pipes and chewing the betel nuts which stain their teeth as black as the water of Phong Na cave.

In the cool of late afternoon we rolled into Khe Sanh. Today it is a peaceful valley of coffee farms ringed by hills, with chicken pecking among the daisies beneath an abandoned Huey helicopter and Hercules troop carrier, but in 1968 it was hell on earth: the base for 6,000 American troops trying in vain to stop supplies getting down the Ho Chi Minh Trail.

They were surrounded by North Vietnamese troops, and in spite of the USAF blasting the surrounding hills with 100,000 tons of high explosive, the equivalent of five Hiroshimas, 75 days later the US admitted defeat and pulled out.

That, and the Tet Offensive the same year, was when Americans watching it on TV every night back home started to question what their boys were doing dying in a country on the other side of the world they couldn't care less about.

Of course, the 58,183 US fatalities pale in comparison to an estimated 1.2 million dead Vietnamese, and 10,000 of those killed on the Ho Chi Minh Trail lie down the road in the Truong Son National Cemetery; row upon row of white marble headstones, every single one decorated with a spray of flowers.

In both scale and serenity, the emotional impact is the same as the vast military cemeteries at Flanders, as is the message: war kills people.

As I emerged, a group of ancient Vietnamese war veterans arrived, their chests bright with medals.

One of them spotted Andrew Fryer in our group, with a silver crewcut and wearing an olive green T-shirt with Old Navy on the front, and mistaking him for a former adversary, came over, bowed and shook his hand. It was as humbling an example of forgiveness as you could wish for.

And so from death to life, and the Vinh Moc tunnels nearby in which hundreds of Vietnamese lived night and day sheltering from the pounding of American bombs.

The two slogans repeated several times in the wonderfully jingoistic documentary in the on-site museum are "To be or not to be" and "Blood, sweat and tears". No wonder the

Vietnamese won. With Shakespeare and Churchill behind them, how could they not?

On we rumbled, past another four billion waving children, through a landscape of poor houses with rich neoclassical facades, and even more ornate tombs in the fields behind, reflecting the Oriental obsession with face, which is another word for bankrupting yourself making a good show of things.

Mind you, we were glad of it when we arrived at our hotel for the night in Hue. Whereas last night's had been the most basic of the trip, the Saigon Morin was a paradigm of luxury.

Built in 1901 and the centre of French social life in the city, it saw hand to hand fighting in the corridors during the Tet Offensive, and after the war hung its head in shame as a $2 a night backpackers' hostel before the tourist board, realising it was causing them serious loss of face, spent a fortune restoring it to its former glory.

Which is pretty much what's happening to the rest of the city, particularly the Citadel, the vast palace complex of Emperor Gia Long from 1802 to 1885, when the French stormed it, burned the imperial library and looted every single thing of value down to the toothpicks.

After the North Vietnamese stormed the city in the Tet Offensive and killed 6,000 intellectuals, civil servants, businessmen, monks and suspected collaborators, the US retaliated by blasting the Citadel with bombs and napalm, leaving only 20 of its 148 fabulous buildings standing.

It will be astonishing when it's finally restored, although I suspect it's even more impressive to stand before the emperor's throne in the ironwood and gold leaf inner sanctum, gaze at the gilt and rubble ruins all around, and imagine what once was.

However, that wasn't my final memory of Hue. No, that was being beaten lovingly to death by a tiny Vietnamese masseuse, then sipping a martini while watching the sun go down over the Perfume River from the 16th floor rooftop bar of the nearby Imperial Hotel.

For a moment, I felt like James Bond, only older.

The streets of Hoi An, our next stop, once echoed with the cries of merchants from a dozen countries who came sailing up the Thu Bon river from the sea to trade in silk, porcelain, tea, sugar, molasses, elephant tusks, beeswax, mother of pearl and lacquer.

These days, though, the river has been silted up for over a century and a half, and they ring instead with cries of: "Sir, sir, lovely silk shirt for you by this afternoon!" for it's the home of an estimated 500 tailors who for £10 will rustle you up a handmade shirt in a couple of hours, or for £60 a suit overnight.

It's also the culinary capital of Vietnam, and although virtually all of the meals on the trip were included, this was one of the three free nights, and a few of us took a taxi to the Brother's Café recommended by Thuan, walking over a little Japanese bridge to a leafy riverside terrace to eat exquisite food to the chorus of the frog in the lily pond beside our table.

Even better, the town survived the war unscathed, with 800 of its buildings now preserved by Unesco, and as you wander through narrow streets past lovely old ochre houses and shops unchanged for centuries, you expect to round a corner at any minute and come chest to face with a Japanese merchant on his way to seal a lucrative lacquer deal.

Instead, of course, you meet one of his descendants taking a selfie with her iPhone. Oh well. Same same but different, as they say in this part of the world.

And so, a tearful farewell to our Jeeps, and hello to Ho Chi Minh City, or Saigon, as most older Vietnamese still call it.

Dinner was a cornucopia of the best street food in the planet at Ben Thanh, in a vast marquee surrounded by a block of stalls selling genuine fake everything.

The whole complex is built then torn down every night, as we found next morning wandering down the same street and wondering if we'd imagined it as we made our way to Reunification Palace, where at noon on 30 April 1975, tanks of the North Vietnamese Army under the command of Colonel Bùi Tín burst through the main gates to find South Vietnamese leader General Duong Van Minh and 30 of his advisors waiting for them on the palace steps.

"I have been waiting since early this morning to transfer power to you," said Minh.

"There is no question of your transferring power. You cannot give up what you do not have," was Tín's curt reply.

Not far from that is the city's holy trinity of French belle époque colonialism: the 1897 Opera House, Gustave Eiffel's glorious 1891 post office and the 1883 Notre Dame Cathedral, in front of which stands a statue of the Virgin Mary which caused a riot in 2005 when it apparently shed a tear.

Scientists later claimed that it was the stone leaching moisture, but locals insist she was crying because she was the only virgin in Saigon.

A short walk away is the Rex Hotel, where war correspondents gathered every day for what they sarcastically called the Five o'clock Follies; the absurdly optimistic US briefings about how well the war was going.

Instead, the truth about how bad it was going is to be found in the War Remnants Museum, where I accidentally went backwards around the halls, undoing decades of death and suffering as I went.

But what I could not undo were the images of the babies deformed by Agent Orange, which haunt me still.

We emerged blinking into the light, glad to be alive, and as we climbed the aircraft steps for the flight home, took a last look at the long road north and wished that we were back on it in our Jeeps, driving down a trail which had once been a symbol of war, but which over the past two weeks had become a beacon of life and hope in every waving child we passed.

2016

…and Vermont

"Have you ever been convicted," the US immigration form asked, "of moral turpitude, drug trafficking, espionage, sabotage or war crimes?"

"Funny you should mention it," I wrote carefully, "but I did strangle my granny because she sold my SS uniform to buy heroin while I was away on that Iraqi intelligence job. Mind you, I think the old bat was just annoyed because I was sleeping with my sister."

Several months later, I emerged from jail to find Cate waiting patiently for me.

"Hello dear," she said pleasantly, "our motorcycle's here."

We climbed on, zipped up our leather jackets and adjusted our shades. As we left the bike hire depot in Boston, we had a full tank of gas, the open road and a week in Vermont in front of us.

It was a state I knew practically nothing about. I had a vague childhood memory of an autumn postcard from a distant aunt which looked like a riot in a forest, with angry leaves of every description demanding their territorial rights on a spectrum from acid yellow to vermilion. There was also, although I may have made this bit up, a white church steeple sticking up somewhere.

It made me wonder quite what we were doing, in black leathers and on a big motorbike, booked into some of the most genteel inns in New England.

Still, no point letting reality change anything. I gunned the throttle and we turned west for Vermont.

If you are unfamiliar with the state, it is the shape of Arnold Schwarzenegger's torso, with his head in Quebec and his naughty bits in Massachusetts. Thankfully, we entered at the waist, crossing the river bridge from New Hampshire and realising immediately that there was something heartstoppingly special about Vermont.

Perhaps it was the fact that we were on a motorcycle. As Robert M Pirsig pointed out

in *Zen and the Art of Motorcycle Maintenance*, in a car you are completely cocooned, but on a bike everything is real: the road rushing a few inches below our feet, the cool wind on our arms, the sweetness of pine and maple in our nostrils, the flicker of sunlight through the passing trees.

No, I know what it was. It wasn't the flicker of sunlight through the trees, it was the fact that we could see the trees: in Vermont, roadside billboards are banned and chain stores frowned upon.

As a result, in 800 miles of travelling over the next week, we were to see one mail and two McDonald's, and in every village, with its green, its two-pump gas station, its general store and its white wooden church, which I had not imagined after all, we found an America that I thought had vanished in the 1950s.

For heaven's sake, they even leave their cars running when they go to the post office in the morning. Mind you, at a quid a gallon, they can afford to.

"I asked one of them about that," Jack Bums, an innkeeper who moved there from New Jersey, told me. "He said: 'Well, everyone knows it's my car. If it wasn't me driving it, they'd know something was wrong'."

And when Jack and his wife bought their inn in Chester two years ago and asked the lawyer for the door keys, he scratched his head. It's not that they don't have house keys in Vermont. It's just that no one can remember where they've put them.

"The first time I went to the grocery store," said Jack, "there was only one woman in the queue, so I thought I'd be out of there in a minute. It took half an hour. The next time I gave up and joined in."

People come here to slow down, and we did too: our bike could do well over a ton, but at times we found ourselves going so slowly we were in danger of falling over. Once we joined a queue of cars that had pulled over for a jaywalking duck.

All this Arcadian bliss, however, doesn't mean that you're bereft of the pleasures of urban sophistication; they may stop to let a duck cross the road, but that evening you'll find it on your plate with a very nice cranberry glaze. I polished off the little darling, who had not died in vain, and went to bed. In the night it rained, and the next morning, steam ghosted off the road in the summer sun.

That's another thing about Vermont: they have proper seasons. In winter, snow piles to the eaves. In spring, the forest bursts with iridescence, in the summer the heat hangs heavy in the glades and in autumn the trees are ablaze in a riot of colour.

But nature is only half Vermont's story. The people are the other half. Night after night we arrived at elegant inns dusty, sweaty and with the sort of wild hair you get from a day under a helmet, only to be greeted like long-lost cousins.

And it wasn't just have-a-nice-day friendliness: arriving at an inn in Stowe, we got talking to a woman climbing into a convertible. We were still there after half an hour. Two days later, as we were leaving a shop on the other side of town, she crossed the road to say hello and see if we were enjoying ourselves. We were, believe me.

The best thing is that all of it's entirely genuine, and not invented yesterday by a public relations company: down the road from Chester, for example, we found the extraordinary Kim Kendall, sole proprietor of an eponymous barn packed to the rafters with treasured junk. He had been there forever, and the junk for even longer.

And a few miles away from his bargain basement of retail therapy was the Vermont Country Store in Weston, selling everything from traditional canoes to tins of fiddlehead ferns. (You eat them, since you ask).

Only in rural America could you find, sold without irony, a publication entitled The Good Citizen's Book, a compendium of government manuals since the 1920s, which starts: "Only by pursuing proper dental hygiene, cheerfully paying your taxes and obeying even minor laws can you ensure the prosperity of your family, community and country."
Other sections include The Importance of a Meat Diet and Why it is Never Right to Poison your Neighbor's Dog.

Old canoes and fiddlehead ferns notwithstanding, Vermont is most famous for the brave new world of independence, socialism and eco-capitalism. Ice cream, in other words, which is why later that day we found ourselves near Stowe having the Ben and Jerry experience.

It all began, as you may know, at a Long Island high school in 1963, when the chucklesome duo discovered a mutual dislike of exercise and love of food. In 1977, with the help of a $5 correspondence course in How to

Make Ice Cream, they started a corner shop that is now a $235 million international business. There are 700 staff in the Stowe factory alone, most of them fighting to work in the tasting section. "Not much turnover in that team. but a lot of growth," said Phil the guide.

Forthcoming flavours, and you read it here first, include The Full Vermonty – presumably you strip off and rub it all over – while outside is a little graveyard for the flavours that didn't make the grade, like Fred and Ginger, Tennessee Mud, Oh Pear! And Sugar Plum.

Tragically, the merry duo have sold the business to another little family business run by a Mr and Mrs Unilever, but their spirit lives on in the expanding waistlines of the nation at large.

Talking of which, it was time for lunch. We found it at Pickwick's in Stowe, an English pub run by a former Royal Navy man, Chris Francis, and his wife Lyn.

"We came out here for a holiday and fell in love with it. The people are genuine, caring and endlessly helpful. They've got zero crime, good steaks, four seasons and beautiful surroundings," he said over fish and chips on the porch.

"And the food's better too," said Cate, tucking into ploughman's lunch. "It's not fluffed up, blow-dried and pre-digested like most other places in the States."

Indeed, something was happening to me. I was being seduced by Vermont. I wanted to live here and bring up little Vermonsters who would live on free-range chicken and ice cream, hike in the summer, ski in the winter, let old ladies cross the street and grows up to be the world's first caring lawyers.

To celebrate my decision I had a beer in a nearby sports bar, in which several fat blokes were watching large black millionaires put a ball through a hoop.

When that finished, the news came on, read by Marselis Parsons and Sera Congi, whose parents had obviously picked their names from a Scrabble set.

That night we found ourselves at The Inn at Mountain View Farm, originally a gentleman's farm built by Elmer A Darling to supply the Fifth Avenue Hotel in New York founded by his grandfather Ebenezer in 1859. When young Elmer graduated from college, according to the clipping on the wall from the St Johnsbury Republican of May 2, 1906, he was employed to do all the marketing for the hotel.

Heavens, I thought, how very prescient to have a head of marketing in 1906. But then I read on.

Elmer's job, in fact, was to go to the market at four every morning and buy fresh food for the hotel.

How very Vermont, I thought, to have a head of marketing who gets up at dawn and goes to buy carrots rather than dressing up in a suit and selling everyone a hill of beans.

2002

...and Venice

We normally have pizza delivered on a Friday evening, but a few weeks ago we thought we'd eat out for a change.

Lovely little place. If you go around the back of Belfast City Hall, you just keep going along Bedford Street and the Dublin Road until you get to St Mark's Square in Venice, and it's on the corner of the second street on the right.

Rome may have the size and Florence the art, yet it is Venice, beautiful yet dying, romantic yet sad, that has always attracted lovers drawn to its aching *tristesse*.

Once the most powerful city state in Europe, it has, in fact, been dying since 1499, when Vasco da Gama discovered a new route to the Orient and began the long, slow drain of wealth away from Venice towards northern Europe.

It seemed appropriate, then, that as we stepped off the plane and onto a *vaporetto* to take us across the lagoon to our hotel, a funereal bell was tolling.

Since this was Italy, I had taken care that my socks matched not only my shirt, but each other. For you can never be too overdressed in Italy: although it was the depths of winter, the entire crew of the boat was wearing sunglasses, the woman sitting in front of us was wearing a fur coat, and her husband sported a pearl-grey fedora at the rakish angle prescribed by the meeting of the Italian Style Council in January 1826.

 Unlike the slightly more stuffy French, though, the Italians dress with the happy artlessness of children going to a never-ending party

 Anyway, where was I? Ah yes, on a water bus across the lagoon, with the silhouette of Venice rising out of the mist in shades of opalescent grey

 It felt infinitely evocative, as if we were the main characters in a flickering black and white film, arriving to fulfil our tragic destiny in matching socks.

 There was only one problem: since I was also sporting a £5 suede jacket from a charity shop in Stockholm and neither of us was wearing our shades, our tragic destiny was likely to be being left out to die in the snow, like Eskimo grannies.

 Until then, though, arriving by boat in Venice was everything you would imagine: the winter sun had burnt off the mist and awakened the buildings, which were fighting each other for architectural supremacy; the stallholders had rolled out their awnings and were selling sardines, carnival masks and silk capes; and the merry gondola pushers of old Venice town, in striped shirts and ribboned boaters, were languidly rowing tourists up and down the canals for about £4,000 a minute,

 Unlike most cities, though, there was not a stray cat in sight, presumably because of the quaint city tradition at Candlemas of shaving your head and battering a plump white cat to death with it. Although the custom has lapsed, the cats of Venice upped and left in furry outrage, leaving behind bald men with time on their hands and tiny women in red macs who leap out and stab you to death for not wearing matching socks, as they did to Donald Sutherland. Still, at least he got to ravish Julie Christie first.

Thankfully, we made it alive to the Bridge of Sighs, across which Casanova fled to freedom from a jail sentence, and over which passed the less fortunate prisoners who gave the bridge its name, on their way to a damp incarceration.

These days, it's even damper: the fragile city is crumbling, and the lagoon is rising to meet it, like two doomed lovers destined for a soggy consummation.

Aiding and abetting this Romeo and Juliet of time and tide are the moon, global warming, depopulation and economic decay while trying to keep them apart is a series of movable dykes, currently halted by controversy. As dykes tend to be: look at kd lang.

Until then, enjoy it while it's there. Take your *passagieta* along the ancient buildings of the Grand Canal, listen to the songs of the gondoliers and the slip-slap of water on the hulls of the *vaporetti*, and watch the sun sink in a hymn of flame reflected on the statue on the Custom House roof, of a golden boy holding what looks like a giant haddock, but is in fact an angel's wing which swings to and fro on the winds of fortune.

Inside St Mark's Basilica, the same early evening light falls like a blessing on the glorious mosaics, engages each and every detail of them at length, then slides exhausted to a floor made of an infinite number of tiny shards of marble, all collapsing into curves and swells which mirror the lagoon outside.

In winter floods, the lagoon often comes m to join the floor, lapping at the foot of the pews.

Outside, the square which Napoleon called the drawing room of Europe is in winter often waist-deep in water, and in summer often waist-deep in Japanese tourists.

Rather appropriately for a square which floods annually and whose bell tower collapsed in a thunder of baffled bricks in 1902, the lofty buildings around the square were once occupied by insurance companies.

Today, the square was packed with the tourists who all come at this time of year to escape the crowds. However, walk 100 yards down any of the side streets, and you find another kind of beauty A real Venice, if you like, where you emerge from a narrow alley, cross a little bridge as a gondola slides by underneath, and come out into a square. On your left is a fabulous church, and on your right a terracotta town house, its windows ablaze with geraniums.

We wandered in a daze for hours, until darkness fell and a fat moon rose. And, since we could hardly come to Venice without taking a gondola, we took one the only way we could afford: across the canal rather than along it. It was only a minute of magic by moonlight, but it was magic all the same.

By now we were starving, since we had only eaten two grapes since breakfast. Raw ones at that. Two of our guidebooks recommended a restaurant called Da Aciugheta as being cheap and excellent, but in fact it was a charmless cafeteria which shovelled tourists in and out with brisk efficiency. A cooking pot hung from the ceiling in an attempt at rustic charm, and the waiters overcharged you in three languages.

Even worse, Italian pizzas aren't as good as the ones you get in Belfast, which are all made by Iranians.

"Maybe that's the answer to world peace," said Cate as we wandered away, mildly disgruntled. "Point out to the Americans that Iranians make the best pizzas on the planet."

I didn't answer, since I had just spotted the last cat in Venice: a fat ginger torn keeping a careful look out for skinheads.

We followed him for a couple of streets to a little grappa bar, then got utterly lost on our way back to the hotel: in the next half hour we passed the same courting couple so often that I thought they would ask us to join in.

We fell at last into the downy billows of our vast bed at the Danieli and slept the sleep of the blessed, waking only just in time for breakfast. This, taken on a rooftop terrace overlooking the islands of the city, must be one of the great pleasures of life, apart from being ravished senseless after a day wearing matching socks.

Below us on the Grand Canal, *vaporetti*, *gondoli* and elegant wooden tenders pottered
about, and in the sunlight beside our table, two sparrows were waving their wings about
eloquently as they discussed the best way to land.

And, lest you think I jest, last year Canadian scientists researching the way bees communicate with each other by waggling their wings and dancing found that Italian bees used three times more waggling than was strictly necessary.

We walked out of the hotel and were immediately mugged by a charming and elegant chap offering us a free water taxi to the island of Murano, where the eponymous glass is made.

There, the master glassblower produced a vase out of thin air and magic, then blew a glass bubble so thin that it crumbled and vanished in our disbelieving fingers.

"The maestro is only here in the mornings," said Paolo, our bow-tied guide. "He will make two pieces, then go home. But he creates more beauty than someone who works 12 hours a day, making the same thing over and over again.

"It is a better way of living. You see, everyone worships the god of money, but there is a more important god, of feeling."

Unfortunately, the only people who can afford the maestro's icons of beauty are those who have been worshipping the god of money all their lives, so we left empty-handed and took the *vaporetto* home.

As we puttered back across the lagoon, I realised just what it was that made Venice so different. Water; that's what, which combined with the madly eclectic architecture makes it like a sort of underwater Prague.

But it means no cars, no fumes, and little traffic noise. Everyone: commuters, policemen, bin men, ambulance drivers and white van men, go about in boats.

That's the answer to Belfast's problems. Flood the streets and we'll all go to work in a *vaporetto*. Heavens, it might even make London livable, apart from the couriers on jet-skis.

But enough philosophy: it was time for the Doge's Palace. This, on the edge of St Mark's Square, was the home of the elected aristocrats who ruled an empire that lasted for a thousand years until the end of the 18th Century.

Inside, every stair and corridor and room leads to the Grand Council Chamber, an emporium of gold and frescoes so vast that 2,000 nobles would meet here at a time.

Imagine, if you will, arriving in the 16th Century from the frozen courts of northern Europe and stepping into this room, like a vision of heaven to which you could never aspire.

We emerged, suitably boggled, only to realise that the sun was already setting on Golden Haddock Boy, and we had not even begun our planned walk through undiscovered Venice.

Tragically, my sense of time and place is so misguided that we never even arrived at the start of the walk, never mind the end. So we never did get to see Piazzale Roma, or the Angelo Raffaele, or the oldest gondola makers of old Venice town.

Even worse, no one complimented me on my socks, which were matching for the second day running. Still, at least we hadn't seen a single Venetian blind the whole weekend, which was a blessing.

And we did find a little taverna with bench seats, fabulous pasta and cheap wine. Then, as we wandered back through the dark streets, a guitarist playing in a moonlit square.

Enchanted, we bought a CD from him.

Since he was Polish, and it was called Sound of Florence, when we listen to it we will always have Venice.

2003

W is for Western Australia

I had bought the floppy hat, and almost killed myself drinking the dozen bottles of wine for the corks to hang from it.

And, although I believe a criminal record is no longer necessary, I had brought with me a copy of Rolf Harris' Stairway to Heaven just to be on the safe side.

It was, as you may have guessed, my first visit to Australia. I arrived in Perth, bought a pair of sunglasses and walked out of the shop straight into a downpour.

As a result, my first impression of the city was that it was dark and wet. It also seemed to be filled with people strangling cockatoos then running away. However, when I took the sunglasses off, this turned out to be the rather strange sound of Perth pedestrian crossings: a muffled squawk followed by a receding pitter-patter.

Perth was part British Colonial and part Oriental, both high-rise and low-key, like Vancouver on valium.

The glittering steel and glass towers of the city centre are the legacy of the Eighties economic boom, fuelled by men like Alan Bond and Kerry Stokes, whose mansions line the lapping shores of the Swan River to the south-west of the city.

Those of you who believe that wealth is no measure of style will be pleased to know that many of these overblown homes look as if they were designed by two blind architects who were not on speaking terms.

The river flows into the Indian Ocean at the sleepy little town of Fremantle, which in 1987 woke up, rubbed its eyes and realised with a mixture of excitement and panic that the Aga Khan and thousands of sailing aficionados were arriving in town for Australia's defence of the Americas Cup.

"Great time, mate. Non-stop bonking," said one Fremantle taxi driver about that summer. In Australia, taxi drivers do exactly what they say on the tin, and then some. Within five minutes of getting into a cab, you will know their opinion on everything from women: "I knew this Pom Sheila once..." - to Aborigines - "I'm not a racist, but..." - to sport - "Aussie Rules, that's the stuff, mate. Soccer's for pansies. Except quokka soccer on Rotto, and that's been banned."

Rotto, or Rottnest Island, is where Perth escapes for the weekend. A miniature version of Australia, it has little hills, little beaches, little lakes and trees, and a little church, pub, library, cinema, police station and restaurant, all frozen in the amber of the Fifties.

It even has little kangaroos called quokkas which the local lads used to celebrate the end of the high school year by playing football with. Hence quokka soccer.

Looking at quokkas, it is hard to believe how anyone would want to harm them. As I cycled around the island, one hopped out in front of me. I got off the bike, bent down and stroked the soft fur behind its ears. It looked up at me with glossy, innocent eyes, and wet itself.

In the taxi from the Fremantle ferry terminal back to Perth, the taxi driver had an opinion on Rottnest Island too.

"Nothing to do there but drink. Bloody perfect, mate."

Not that all Australians are beer-swilling boors: most cringe at the thought that Sir Les Patterson or Paul Hogan are their countrymen. But even when liberals are recalling a particularly fine Shiraz or a bloody marvellous night at the opera, their opinions are always presented as an instantly open book.

In Australia, a spade is always a spade. No wonder they have such a distrust of Japan, where every truth is hidden beneath a thousand layers of ritual.

"They're taking over everything, mate. Bloody organised bunch, though," said the taxi driver on the way to the airport for the flight north to Paraburdoo.

I climbed into the plane and rose into the uncanny light, then fell at last through white clouds and a vermilion sunset to the black earth. And woke the next morning to the red heart of western Australia.

At a hearty breakfast of toast and Vegemite - the indigenous yeast extract which tastes of salted tar with a hint of anchovies - I met my guides for the day. Richard was an ex-accountant from British Columbia. Tim was a former sheep shearer from just up the road, and their vehicle of choice was an Oka, which looked like a civilian troop carrier.

"Is this in case we get attacked by rabid crocodiles?" I said.

"No, it's so we can get more beer in," said Richard.

The Karajini area, where we were heading, is big mining country. Long ago, before the Queen Mother was born, unimaginable pressures crushed the earth here into the diamonds and gold, opals and sapphires which, along with pearls from the coast, are borne south to Perth then out into the turning world, where the necks and wrists of gracious society await them.

But it is iron ore which has made this land so rich and so red, and from which it is hauled in vast quantities. The trains carrying the ore south on the world's largest private railway are up to four miles long, hauling 540 cars and weighing 57,000 tonnes each. Oh, and the workers laying the track drank 400 gallons of beer for every mile laid.

From the coast it goes to Japan, where it is turned into Toyota Land Cruisers, which are shipped back to Australia, where they eventually rust back, with a wonderful circularity, to exactly the same colour as iron ore.

Anyway, where was I? Ah yes, driving through the Outback with Richard and Tim. This used to be big sheep as well as mining country, but today wool is a fifth of the price it used to be.

"Synthetics. Everyone's buying them," said Tim, and laughed. "What we need is a good war. In a cold place."

Out here the land is vast, and part from the rich red earth, the colours are tiny even after rain: purple and yellow flowers, or little flames of periwinkle blue dancing in the breeze. The sounds are tiny, too; just the fluting curves of a butcher bird's love song.

Strangely, it is only when you descent into the cool of a gorge that colours hit you in the face again: the receding blue of the sky as you climb ever deeper, the oxide earth inches from your nose, the white of tree bark clinging perilously to a crack, the white of your knuckles clinging to the same crack, the dusty green of the water far below.

We climbed deeper into the gorge, swimming through icy pools then inching along nervous ledges. If I had fallen I would have died, but I dared not ask if this was all a bit dangerous, or I would have been pointed out forever as the whinging Pom who was afraid of a little death.

In the last pool, as cold as ether, tiny fish investigated our toes and a waterfall rainbowed off our brows.

Late that afternoon, we finally climbed back into the sunlight, and Richard reached into the Oka and handed me a tinny from the Esky. Or a beer from the coolbox, for those of you who are hard of Strine.

"Here, this beer's warm," I said.

"No, it's ice cold. You're just colder than it is," he said.

I liked it so much that I had several more that night at the only pub in Tom Price, a mining town so basic that Richard's tour of it had taken 28 seconds.

Beside the pool table and jukebox, an entire wall was filled with greyhound racing schedules.

"Looks like the whole country's gone to the dogs," I said to a bearded man who was trying to find the bar so he could lean on it.

"Yeah, we like a good gamble, we do," he said blearily.

"No, I mean the country's gone to the dogs," I said, tilting my head meaningfully towards the wall.

He looked at the wall, then at me, with amiable bafflement.

"Fancy a pint, mate?" he said. He was, it later transpired, the local JP.

This is not to say that Australians have no sense of humour. It's just that, like Americans, when they emigrated to the New World, they left irony behind as unnecessary baggage.

I staggered home from the pub and went to bed after saying my prayers. Of course God, like the seasons, the night sky and the water going down the plughole, is different in Australia.

"G'day God, and forgive me, for I have sinned," I said. "I said a bad word when I saw two kangaroos, three emus and a 6ft lizard, and when my foot slipped on that ledge. Also this morning I accidentally boiled a cockroach in the shower, and this afternoon I stood on three ants."

"No worries, mate. The little buggers deserved it. Take three tinnies and a meat pie," said God.

However, my penance was to be somewhat more dramatic. The next day I went snorkelling off Ningaloo Reef with Eddie Izydorski, a man who had perfected the didgeridoo player's art of circular breathing so that he could talk all day without pausing. Fortunately, he was so interesting I could listen to him all day as well. Looking for whale sharks, which in theory only eat small fish and are perfectly safe to swim with, we headed out past the reef and over the edge of the continental shelf.

Down below, careless crabs out for a Sunday stroll plummeted into deep space with expressions of baffled regret, and all around us, the swell was like a turquoise rollercoaster. Overhead, a spotter plane radioed down. Eddie listened.

"Shark! Eighteen-footer!" he shouted suddenly. "Get in the water!"

Now, I have had some breathtaking experiences in my life: Cate's apple crumble and my last bank statement spring to mind.

But plunging into the water and seeing a shark 10 feet away coming straight for me was right up there. I did what anyone would have done in the circumstances: discovered that you can't swear into a snorkel, and turned right.

There were other moments: the extravagant sinuosity of a manta ray, and a swarm of tropical fish, as if someone had torn up a rainbow and scattered the fragments, but the memory of the shark was still with me the next day as Richard dropped me at the little local airport, a song of aluminium curves and primary colours soaring from the silent desert.

The staff numbered two, and on the wall was a sign saying Fish may not be carried on as hand baggage.

Half an hour later, the plane carried less than a dozen passengers as it rose above a region which is still the great undiscovered secret of Australian tourism.

So go there. But don't tell a soul.

2002

...Wolves

In an ideal world, a chap would prepare for an expedition such as this by sitting in front of the fire in his study with a smoking jacket and pipe, reading My Life with Wolves by Freddie Fortescue-ffrench.

However, there were two problems. Freddie did not exist, and I had employed for the renovation of our house a team of builders who, unfortunately, did.

As a result, the study resembled a building site, possibly because it was, and I spent the evening before leaving in it, covered in plaster dust and looking out with wistful irony at the wooded hill where the last wolf in Ireland was allegedly killed early in the 18th Century.

The next morning, I rose at dawn, put on a fur hat and left for Sweden, my sole knowledge of wolves, gleaned from boyhood books on Canada, that they stood on stark peaks howling at the moon, weighed as much as a man, hunted in packs of 50 and ate trappers called Black Jacques or Sven the Swede for lunch, and sometimes afternoon tea as well.

None of which, it transpired, was true. Wolves, for example, have rarely attacked humans, and humans have just as rarely returned the favour. Demonised as symbols of the devil and the dark by everyone from Descartes to Little

Red Riding Hood, European wolves were driven to the edge of extinction. In Sweden in the Fifties, there were six left. Today there are about 100, but sightings are rare. Which is why I needed a man like Anders Stahl: wildlife painter, ex-soldier, Arctic ranger, fireman, guide and wolf tracker. He was standing on the platform at Leksand as I stepped off the early train north from Stockholm into flurries of snow. We climbed into his Toyota, called at the grocers to pick up provisions - unaccountably, I bought three bananas – and set off for the wilderness. It was not too far away, since Leksand is exactly between nowhere and nowhere else.

After an hour we abandoned the car, shouldered our rucksacks and took to the forest on foot. Wearing borrowed Dutch paratrooper's trousers, a Russian fur hat and Anders' old Swedish army winter smock, I looked like a reject from a Nato charity shop as we set of on the trail of a pack once led by a great wolf who had died three years before.

Since then his partner had led the pack alone, but then found a new mate, presumably after an ad in the lonely hearts section of Wildlife Weekly saying: Partner wanted for friendship and possible romance. Must have own fur coat and like long walks, cold nights out and raw elk. Non-smoker preferred. Must be a wolf.

There were, it had to be said, plenty of elk to eat: the population numbers a quarter of a million, and 90,000 are culled every year by jolly Swedish hunters. The older, wiser elk, who know something is up, escape by donning sunglasses, leaning against a tree and saying: "Me? No, I'm not an elk. He is, though."

At least I think that's what Anders said. I was busy trying to keep up with him through a landscape of silver birch and

lakes so cold that the air above them dared not move in case it cracked. There was no sound except the crunch of our feet in the snow and the occasional muffled thwack as I walked into a tree.

Suddenly, Anders held up his hand and looked down at a row of tracks in the snow. But they were too tiny to be the might pawprints we were looking for.

"Fox," said Anders. That's the way men talk when they're outdoors.

"Or a wolf wearing stilettos?" I suggested.

"In this weather?" he said, and proceeded.

Then, a hundred yards later, the real thing, each one six inches long and five across. There was, I have to say, something spookily primeval about looking at tracks in the snow and saying: "Wolves were here."

We moved on, up hill and down dale of increasingly deep drifts. After another hour, the snow was, oh, about up to our necks. Ahead of me, Anders stopped, unshouldered his rucksack and produced two aluminium and leather tennis rackets.

"I think," he said with Nordic stolidity, "it is time for snowshoes."

He was right. The going went from impossible to almost impossible. I looked up to thank him when I realised he had vanished. I hunted around in vain for five minutes, vaguely aware of the stupidity of not being able to find prints the size of tennis rackets, then spotted a large pile of elk poo. And another.

Finally, by following the droppings, I found Anders standing in a clearing with the elk responsible. It hadn't run away as he walked up to it, probably because half of it was missing. As someone from the Sainsbury's school of

Buddhism, who loves animals but refuses to see any connection between them and the contents of the meat shelves, it was both troubling and humbling to be confronted with the fact that I was so obviously wrong.

Nearby was a smattering of wolf droppings, black with blood. "Smell it," said Anders. I did. I wish I hadn't.

"Right," he said, "have you ever used cross-country skis?"

After a mile we came across fresh wolf tracks. Darkness fell in a silent storm of lilac, but we plunged on regardless, keeping our track by the North Star. Oh, and by following the path. After a while, though, even that ran out, and after another hour of colliding with trees and stepping into icy streams all exactly an inch higher than the tops of my boots, I saw to my complete astonishment that Anders had found the log cabin which was to be our billet for the night.

He produced an axe from his bottomless rucksack, and I set to chopping firewood while he rustled up sausage and pasta. Then we had some howling to do.

Anders stepped on to the porch, cleared his throat, and produced a sound that was not quite of this earth. The hairs on the back of my neck stood briskly to attention.

"Anders," I said, "how do you do that?"

"Practice."

But from the forest there was no reply. The pack were all down at the wolf bar, telling tall elk tales. We curled up in our sleeping bags, and slept the exhausted sleep of men who have been out not finding wolves all day.

2002

...and the Wiener Kreis

In the Twenties and Thirties, Austria was the home of the Wiener Kreis, a group of logical positivists who, having nothing else to do in the long winter evenings, invented the verifiability principle which stated that things were only meaningful if you could prove they existed.

They suffered a serious blow when the Nazis arrived in 1938, since although you can't prove a stormtrooper exists, having one on your doorstep is still deeply meaningful.

However, they suffered an even more serious blow when they realised that they couldn't even prove that the verifiability principle itself existed.

At this point the heads of several members exploded, and most of the rest went to America to become taxi drivers, leaving only Ludwig Wittgenstein, who spent the rest of his life analysing language before realising that he couldn't really use language to analyse itself.

Faced with such a national predilection for imploding paradoxes, you can see why Julie Andrews thought it was far simpler to fling on a habit and skip down a mountain singing The Hills are Alive.

And yet, within an hour of arriving in the country I hadn't seen her once. Nor had I seen anyone slapping their lederhosen, playing the alpenhorn in an oompah band or wearing one of those little felt yodelling hats with a feather up the side.

Even worse, in spite of the fact that it was midsummer's day, it was pouring with rain.

Still, since I couldn't prove it, there was no point analysing it, so I got on a bus to Söll, the village where in 1945 the Germans surrendered to the Yanks at a round table in the Postwirt restaurant, then ordered pudding.

I found a nice little hotel and had a beer. It was so good I had several more, gazing out of the window at the twilight and the mist embracing each other around the mountains.

After a while the waitress seemed to be bringing more beers than she was taking away glasses, and at first I thought this was due to the effect named after the Salzburg scientist Christian Johann Doppler, who discovered that the frequency of a note changes as it approaches then leaves an observer.

But then I realised it was because Austrian beer was stronger than I had thought, and had reduced me to that absurdly happy state known as illogical positivism.

Since by now I was incapable of proving the existence of anything, or analysing it using language, I went to bed, and dreamt of marmots.

The regional mascot of the Tirol, these look like gerbils on steroids, and last year became an endangered species because summer tourists fed them so much chocolate that by the time winter came, half of them were too fat to get back into their burrows, and froze to death.

The rain was still hurtling down when I woke the next morning, so I took a bus to a spa in Holzkirchen and spent the morning lying in a large wooden bath full of hot, oily water, while across a screen on the wall flickered time-lapse clouds and falling leaves.

As content as a stuffed marmot, I strolled through the village and found a steam train just about to leave for the journey down the mountain and along the lake to Jenbach. During the war, this little train bad been used to transport parts to the Messerschmitt factories in the bomb-proof caves up the mountain.

I climbed aboard and we set off behind a tiny locomotive which seemed like a distillation of the day as it huffed and puffed its way through the dripping undergrowth, the clouds of steam issuing from its funnel mingling imperceptibly with those already resident in the treetops.

In the afternoon, the rain stopped enough to take a cable car up to the rather appropriate spot of Hexenwasser, or Witches' Water, a series of ponds and waterfalls which in the 16th Century was the site of the home of two sisters.

When bad weather ruined the crops in the valley below once too often, the farmers came to the inevitable conclusion that the sisters were witches, stormed up the mountain and burnt them at the stake. This is known as illogical negativism.

These days, Hexenwasser is a children's playground of wood, water and stone overlooked by a restaurant. I ordered a bowl of cheesy noodles and sat at a table outside, waiting for Anita to take me barefoot forest walking.

Anita, when she arrived right on time, was the sort of hearty outdoor type who looked as if she was happiest splashing around naked in mountain tarns, and indeed, five minutes later we had whipped off our shoes and socks and were off into the woods, tramping across grass, mud, pine cones, fir branches and river beds while singing selected hits from The Sound of Music.

Honestly, you wouldn't believe how difficult it is yodelling My Favourite Things.

It was all delightfully squelchy and organic, like being a couple of giant hobbits, and we emerged blinking into the sunlight to find Alex standing in a mountain glade.

Alex was an instructor in Nordic walking, a sort of permanent lunging which looks like cross-country skiing for people who've forgotten their skis: hardly surprising, since it was dreamed up by Finnish skiers who wanted to practise in the summer.

It feels as silly as it sounds, but after an hour of lunging heartily across mountain pastures, sending cows stampeding in a symphony of bovine campanology, I felt as if I had gone three rounds with a demented marmot.

Inspired, I went back to the hotel and invented the sport of Nordic drinking. Here are the instructions.

Place pint on bar. Stand well back. Lunge towards pint, sip and hold position. Return to start. Repeat with other leg and arm.

Advanced Nordic drinkers can set up two pints and use continuous alternate lunging, although do be careful not to break your nose on the bar by lunging forward with both legs at the same time.

Tragically, the next morning I discovered that Nordic drinking gave me the same hangover as normal drinking.

What I needed was some gentle activity, like edelweiss arranging, to ease me gently into the day, I thought as I emerged from breakfast to find Anita standing in the lobby.

"Ah, good morning," she said in a hearty fashion which suggested that she had spent the night sleeping deeply in a moon-dappled meadow, covered in a warm blanket of organic hay, "are you ready to go paragliding?"

Half an hour later, I found myself in a field 4,000ft above the valley, being strapped into a harness by a grizzled veteran called Reiner, then sprinting down the grass and rising gently into the air.

It was the most dream-like of experiences, drifting high over cow pastures and pine forests, and for a man suspended several thousand feet above the earth by only a few lengths of nylon, I felt illogically positive.

Which, as any member of the Wiener Kreis would tell you, is a great feeling, even if they can't prove it.

2004

X is for Dr Xavier Furtwangler's School of Getting to the Point

This was a newspaper column about a conversation with Joris Minne, brother of Paddy, the world-famous Franco-Belgian motorcycle mechanic, on the subject of sponsorship for riding two Royal Enfields from Delhi to Belfast.

It later became part of the original manuscript of the book Way to Go, but was cruelly cast aside by the editor for missing the point, even though I pointed out that missing the point was the whole point.

After crying for a few days, I swore I would get it published somewhere, somehow, some sunny day, and here it is. If you see the publishers, for heaven's sake don't tell them.

Heavens, schmeavens, and buckets of pink socks with little yellow bobbly bits on, but I've been overwhelmed by a deluge of criticism over the fact that the account of my conversation with M. Minne the Slightly Elder which I published in my column last week ended without getting to the point.

Colleagues have stopped me in the office and poured warm chocolate over me, friends have phoned me up in a state of bafflement and one elderly reader is suing me for hastening her decline into terminal bewilderment, in spite of me pointing out to her that you don't need to be elderly to be terminally bewildered, since I've been that way since I was born.

The problem is, I told them all, that they had fallen into the trap of assuming that all dramatic constructions have to conform to Aristotle's definition of having a beginning, a middle and an end, and that because they had this expectation, they were, naturally, disappointed.

It would have been much better, I said to them, if they had adopted the principle of the Buddha when he said that when you expect nothing, then everything is a gift.

In that way they would have appreciated last week's column for exactly what it was - an exercise in the stillness of perfection.

But it was no use: they were all members of Continuity Zen, who believe that if you don't find perfection just the way you want it, you insist that someone changes it immediately, or else you'll be around with a bunch of indolent youths armed with a wet lettuce.

Finally, a decision was reached - I would have to sign up immediately for a course at Herr Doktor Xavier Furtwangler's School of Getting to the Point, high in the Austrian Alps.

A whip-round was organised for my travelling expenses, reaching the princely sum of £1.27, five Spanish pesetas, an old teabag and a piece of fluff of dubious origin, and I was off, wobbling my way towards the Belfast docks on the company unicycle, which the editor had been kind enough to lend me. Mind you, he could have put a tyre on it, but I suppose I shouldn't be ungrateful.

Anyhow, after several weeks of cycling, during which time the solitary wheel had collapsed, reducing me to pogoing along the verges while huge transcontinental lorries thundered past, covering me either in a miasma of fine dust or a sprinkling of fresh rain, depending on the weather, I arrived outside the town hall of the little Austrian burgh of Feldkirch, where I had arranged to meet Gretchen, Dr Furtwangler's assistant.

As I dismounted from the unicycle - not a difficult task, since by now there was nothing left but a saddle - a large, black, very old Hispano Suiza limousine swept into the cobbled square and drew to a halt beside me.

A tinted rear window slid down to reveal Gretchen, even at first sight a charming girl with hair like sunlight which had fallen to earth and been woven by the trolls who live beneath the mountains, eyes the colour of rainwashed meadows in spring, and skin which spoke silent volumes of a life far from the cares of the grey city which I had left many weeks before.

"Mr Hill, I presume," she said in a delicately ironic voice which was the most beautiful thing I had heard since I dreamed one night that I had arrived at Verdi's funeral at the very moment that the thousands of people who had turned up to pay their last respects began spontaneously to sing the song of the Hebrew slaves from his opera Nabucco.

Gretchen pressed a hidden lever, the door of the limousine swung open, and I found myself sitting beside her clutching the saddle of the office unicycle as we left the village and began to climb into the mountains.

I closed my eyes and drank in all the sensations that the interior of the vehicle offered me: the occasional touch of the freshly laundered cotton of Gretchen's blouse against my arm as we rounded corners, the dark and nutty aroma of leather seats which have been worn and cared for over many decades, the staccato play of light on my eyelids as we drove past a stand of firs. I even imagined I could smell the walnut of the dashboard, an aroma quaintly reminiscent of Manzanilla, the fine aperitif which the Andalucians are fond of drinking before lunch.

At last we rounded a final bend and I opened my eyes to behold the remarkable sight of an entirely white building so close to the top of the mountain that its spires seemed to be only just short of reaching heaven, and yet so close to the edge that the building looked to be at risk of plunging in its entirety to the other place.

And yet I knew this to be an illusion, for this was none other than the famous Feldkirch Sanatorium, built so that the tens of thousands who suffered from the tuberculosis which was endemic between the great world wars could escape from a life of blood-spotted sheets and unendurable inactivity to recover in its pristine air.

The limousine ground to a halt in front of a side door, and Gretchen gently took my hand and led me into a spartan room in which the furnishings, though few, were evidently of the highest quality.

And there, behind a massive desk, sat the great man himself, his grey eyes unblinking behind a pair of polished steel-rimmed spectacles.

"Ah, Mr Hill," he said in perfect English as Gretchen closed the door behind us. "And what can we do for you?"

"Dr Furtwangler, it seems impossible," I replied. ``For two weeks now I have been trying to say in my newspaper column that Nambarrie the tea company have sponsored my attempt to ride back from Delhi on two Royal Enfield

Bullets with Patrick Minne, the world-famous Franco-Belgian motorcycle mechanic, and have been completely unable to get to the point."

Dr Furtwangler smiled, in a stern yet kindly fashion.

"Mr Hill, you have cured yourself," he said. "Gretchen, fetch us three glasses and a bottle of the 1957 Gevrey-Chambertin."

"Ah, the wine of which Victor Hugo said: 'I cannot remember the town, and the name of the girl escapes me, but the wine was Chambertin'?" I said.

"Precisely. And while Gretchen is fetching the wine, can I offer you a cup of tea?"

"Nambarrie?"

"Naturally," said Dr Furtwangler, as a merry tinkle heralded the return of Gretchen.

1998

Y is for Yachting

There are many ropes on a boat, but none of them are ropes.

Some of them, for example, are halyards. They are the ones which make the sails go up.

Lazy jacks occasionally lift a hand in spite of themselves to help when the sails are coming down.

Sheets, on the other hand, make the sails go in and out, and painters are the ones you hold when you are standing on shore to stop the boat drifting off in the general direction of America.

Unless you decide to go off to the pub and tie them to a bollard, a tree or a passing

pensioner, in which case they become warps.

Except when they are stopping the boat drifting forwards or backwards, in which case they are springers. Or if they are attached to a dinghy, in which case they are painters.

Lazy jacks, finally, are not to be confused with lazy lines, which are ropes lying in the water that you tie the bow of the boat to when you moor, holding it in a delicately tender opposition to the gently swaying warps on the stem.

There. I hope that's all clear. Now, if you'll excuse me, I'm going to lie down in a darkened room for a while.

Except there are no rooms on a yacht. They are called cabins, the kitchen is called a galley and the bathroom is called a head.

I looked at my watch.

"What's six o'clock on a boat?" I said to Paul, who was busy tying a double clove overhead slipdonglehitch to a cleat.

"About four bells."

"And what's a gin and tonic called?"

"A gin and tonic."

"Thank God for that. I think I'll have one."

Ah, that was better, and just in time for our briefing by Simon, the flotilla skipper for our week in Croatia.

Simon, who was a lawyer until he realised there was more to life than getting rich by pushing paper around a desk, was one of those impossibly healthy, blue-eyed young Englishmen who had been doing outdoorsy things for so long that, although he knew he must have a suit and a pair of shoes somewhere, he couldn't quite remember where just at this minute.

He briefed us for a good three-quarters of an hour on the workings of the boat, and the only word I understood completely was fridge.

I was becoming aware of two things: that Cate and I were glad that Paul and his wife Sharon, both experienced sailors, were with us.

And that boats were designed by midgets who never went to bed, probably because they were up all night designing the perfect windlass. If I had designed a boat costing £130,000, for example, I would have included big, spacious, airy bedrooms with the sun streaming through French windows and dancing playfully on the pure white Hungarian goose down duvets, filled with fluff picked from the virgin breasts of 10-day-old Kecskemét goslings.

Not a slightly widened coffin whose already claustrophobic ceiling had been further lowered by the addition of several bumps, comers and edges all perfectly placed to fracture heads, elbows, toes and any other innocently passing extremity.

Oh well, there was nothing else for it than to make supper.

As the sun went down in a blaze of glory across the bay and a fat yellow moon rose over the mountain, we ate pasta and sausage, drank wine with indecipherable labels, and felt deliciously, exotically abroad.

We put everything away for the night and, after several hours, Cate and I had managed to laboriously fold ourselves into bed for the night. I plumped up my pillow and, with a deep sigh, prepared to sink into a deep and dreamless sleep.

Then realised that I had to go to the toilet.

I sighed, even more deeply, and began the whole process in reverse.

The next morning, there was Simon again, bright-eyed and bushy-tailed, with the sailing briefing for the day. He talked for half-an-hour this time, and I understood the words island and beer.

So I went and bought some beer, and we set off for the island, motoring out to sea then switching off the engine and hauling up the sails using various halyards, sheets, gizmos and bonglesprockets.

Tragically, no-one had told the Croatian weather that it was supposed to be late summer, and as we left the shelter of the mainland it was to a hefty swell and dark clouds. Still, apart from the giant waves, torrential rain, sub-zero temperatures and the fact that Cate whacked her spine painfully on the edge of the oven and Sharon threw up over the side, it was a splendid day, and it was in a state of only mild hypothermia that I was prised from the helm at teatime.

We had docked in a little wooded cove lined with ancient red-tiled houses, a mist-shrouded church in which several locals were praying for sunshine, and a solitary restaurant which must have been, oh, a good 10 yards away. It was too small a place to have been blessed by the presence of guidebook writers, and was none the worse for that.

We sipped beer at the back of the boat as rain dripped slowly off the awning. It was like childhood holidays in Rossnowlagh in Donegal, when we sat for two months every year listening to the rain on the caravan roof, playing Spot the Earwig and Guess What's for Supper (Clue: it was always Fray Bentos steak and kidney pie; the one with the crust a quarter of a micron thick).

Still, one of the pleasures of adulthood is that you can always have another beer, so I had another beer.

After that, I looked at the dank, dripping forests rising all around, and felt as if I was in the South American jungle and was, rather than a little boy growing up in Tyrone who went to Donegal for his holidays, the son of the Swedish ambassador to Bolivia, a country to which, as Martin Stephenson has pointed out in a song which deserves to be better known, you cannot catch a boat.

A son who would grow up to be, not a diplomat like his father, but an SAS airline pilot who married a stewardess from Uppsala and realised, almost too late in life, that he was a better writer than a pilot, subsequently penning a short but beautiful novel which made grown men sigh with vicarious happiness for the insight it gave them into a more noble and heroic life, and which made grown women cry for the insight it gave them into what they had previously dismissed as the closed or, at best, indifferent hearts of men.

"What are you thinking, love?" came the voice of Cate, interrupting my reverie.

"Several things at once, dear, which cannot be good for me," I said, and went off to get another beer.

The next morning, things looked up. The sun came out, and we slid painlessly through the little islands, stopping at little coves which were completely deserted except for other yachts which were using the same Guide to Croatia's Deserted Coves as we were.

We swam, and sunbathed, and thought, and paddled, keeping a careful lookout for the agonising spines of sea urchins. These are easy enough to spot, since they are usually lined up on the seabed singing selected hits from *Oliver*.

In the afternoon, as the boat plunged through heavy swells, I spent several happy hours keeping the handrail on the horizon by moving my head up and down. You wouldn't believe how entertaining this is. You can do the same thing on trains with an imaginary radio-controlled plane, making it dip and swoop over passing houses, hedgerows and cows, who will never know how close they came to being rammed by an aeroplane that wasn't there.

In the balmy evening, we docked beside a little restaurant, under a sign announcing that night's special - lobsters at £50 a kilo.

Fifty quid? I knew fish were scarce in the Adriatic, but fifty quid? I went over to the lobster tank, to see if they were Gucci lobsters or something. There there were, scuttling about waving their antennae, and every so often turning around to exclaim: "Here, where's Jim gone? And how come we're so expensive, if there are so many of us? And has anyone seen Larry?"

Faced with guilt and penury, I had the squid.

At midnight, the rain came again, and then the lightning, leaving the freshly washed night smelling of iodine and singed photons.

The next day turned out lovely, thanks for asking. Well, apart from the lashing rain and 40mph gusts which signalled the arrival of the bora, the big wind which normally arrives in October, but which had obviously got led up sitting in the wind waiting room chatting up mistrals, scirrocos and meltimis, and decided to bugger off and create havoc a month early.

But apart from that, and the fact that one of the gusts blew away Paul's favourite shorts, and a large bee, seeking shelter from the storm, crawled up my own shorts and stung me on the bum, all was well.

We found ourselves a haven in a little harbour and, pausing briefly to foul the propeller with a mooring line as a finale to a short but disastrous day, finally tied up for the day. As the torrential rain, impossibly, got even more torrential, and was joined in the heavenly cacophony by lightning and thunder, we battened down the hatches, changed into what dry clothes we had; and opened a bottle of 1998 Fonseca.

It was not their finest year, but any port in a storm, I always say. And besides, there was someone worse off than we were: Simon the flotilla skipper, who according to the radio, was out there in the howling gale under one of the boats, trying to unblock the septic tank.

All in all, the scene beneath the frazzled sky and the turbulent waves must have been much calmer, as several dolphins took turns trying on Paul's shorts, saying: "Here, Cynthia, does my bum look big in this?" then collapsing into fits of hysterical laughter in the way that only dolphins, of all the creatures in the otherwise humourless sea, do.

However, the Croatian weather is as fickle as Zsa Zsa Gabor, and by evening the sky had transformed itself into a palette of slate grey, rose and duck egg blue that could have been painted by Turner after a bottle of Maraska gin.

It was a harbinger of the day to come, which dawned as still as a canvas. We hoisted all the sails we had, and set off into the blue at a rate so languid that several sea snails hurtled past us with looks off unaccustomed mockery.

Still, at least we now knew what we were doing enough so that, when Paul called out: "Sheet in the main" or: "Unlock the jib halyard", we no longer looked around with the expressions of rabbits caught in headlights.

And, since Simon now trusted us not to get lost or sink the boat, we were set free from the flotilla for a couple of days to potter across the high seas, practising tacking, gybing and reaching, whatever they were, for several happy hours before berthing in the harbour of the striking medieval town of Korcula with such professional aplomb that three local fisherman paused from repairing their nets and leaped up bearing placards saying 5.9, 5.8, 5.9.

Tragically, the gloomy harbourmaster then came over and told us rather snottily that we couldn't park there, and must either go around the comer to be battered into oblivion by the onshore wind, or moor in the sophisticated marina, which would cost us £30, not including lobster.

Naturally, we cut his throat with a breadknife, machine-gunned all the inhabitants of the town except the three fishermen, and burnt to the ground the lovely old town which had stood since the 15th Century, given rise to some of the most exquisite synergies of Gothic and Renaissance architecture in the Balkans and been the birthplace of Marco Polo, author of the world's first great travel book and founder of a very fetching range of Swedish leisurewear.

Oh, all right, only joking. We just sailed around the corner, and after wrapping the dinghy rope around the propeller in a playful riposte to our earlier hubris, anchored in a little bay where we swam, drank, cooked pasta and fell asleep at last under the gently rocking stars.

2003

Z is for Zagreb

The rich harvest of human diversity has rarely been expressed more comprehensively than in Croatia, where over the centuries, a wide variety of ethnic groups have met, mingled, explored their differences then killed each other.

To read the history of this part of the world is to wade through pages of assorted Croats, Serbs, Ottomans, Slovenes, Dalmatians, Venetians, Albanians, Austro-Hungarians, Christians, Socialists, Communists, Cetniks, Partisans, Liberals and Gay Whales Against the Bomb activists all slaughtering each other with such tireless gusto that at the end of it you are surprised to arrive in the country and find anyone still alive.

Things got so bad that when a Serb park warden up in the mountains was eaten by a bear in 1988, his colleagues immediately claimed that the bear must have been a Croat.

And these days, when someone in Croatia tells you that something happened during the war, your immediate response is to languidly reply: "Oh? Which one?"

Thankfully, all this finally stopped in 1995, and the shiny new, peaceful Croatia was a baby as beautiful as its birth was painful, with that cultural diversity which in war had led to bloodshed, in peace leading to a wonderfully European synergy between the Catholic West and the

Muslim East, and between the hard working north and the fun-loving south.

In other words, a people who work hard at making great pizza, then feel guilty because they're not praying five times a day.

More importantly, though, from a tourist point of view, Croatia has more stunning coastline, Roman ruins, medieval walled villages and fairytale castles than you could shake a guidebook at.

Lucky, then, that I had the man who wrote the guidebook with me: Piers Letcher, a lofty and entertaining intellectual who had been a scriptwriter for the UN until he got fed up hearing Kofi Annan and Nelson Mandela spouting theories he'd made up the day before.

We drove into Zagreb in a thunderstorm. Thunder rattled the rooftops and lightning split the sky, illuminating a series of surreal vignettes: posters of women advertising lingerie they were almost wearing, trams rattling through the streets with a palpable air of yearning for the lost days of the Austro-Hungarian empire, and on all sides the stolidly romantic buildings of the Hapsburg Neoclassical Romantic Revival Giant

Wedding Cake style, with which I am sure you are familiar.

In the foyer of the Hotel Opera, a man in a dark suit stood holding a small but menacing laptop. Hearing my accent as I checked in, he sidled over.

"Where are you from, then?" he said.

"I'm the Swedish ambassador," I said, "here to export a brace of Istrian trufflehounds who have been bred to withstand the cold northern air, and who will be used to start a new Swedish pre-frozen truffle industry. Naturally, I will now have to kill you because you know too much."

"You can't fool me," he said. "I'm from Coalisland, and that's an Omagh accent if ever I heard one,"

In the bar, Piers was busy unfolding his limbs.

"Well, Piers," I said, "what are we doing tomorrow?"

"Museums," he said, with the sort of wicked grin only a former public schoolboy can muster. "Lots of them."

On the TV in the corner of the bar, Scotland was playing Frankfurt at American football. I sighed, and went to get us a couple of beers.

The next morning, I found myself in a room full of naked women: the sensuous, elemental figures of illiterate peasant turned national sculptor Ivan Mestrovic, now displayed in the cool, airy spaces of his former home.

It was a gentle start to the day, girding our loins for the Museum of Zagreb, an entertaining rattle through the history of the city, from the bones and pots of a pre-Christian Celtic settlement to gracious Austro-Hungarian drawing rooms festooned with the empire's standard, a double-headed eagle which looks more like a schizophrenic swan.

There are also several bits which fell off the cathedral in the 1880 earthquake, including a gargoyle of a splendidly baffled gecko.

Your historical dander through the city's past ends in the shattered living room of the President, which was hit by a rocket minutes after he left it in 1991.

The attack was later claimed by the Croat-Serb Bear Unification front as revenge for the false accusations over the 1988 warden incident.

However, the most fascinating museum in Zagreb is the Mimara: the lifelong collection of Ante Topic Mimara, a Dalmatian as fascinating as his priceless hoard of paintings, sculptures, carpets, icons and archaeological artifacts.

No one knows how he afforded the collection, or how he paid for the houses in Tangiers and Casablanca, or the castle near Salzburg. Legends abounded that much of his collection was Nazi loot which he picked up in a tank boot sale at the end of the war, or that many of the assorted Rembrandts and Rubens are fakes. Other legends abounded that even the man himself was a fake, and stole the documents identifying him as Mimara from a fallen comrade in the chaos of a First World War battlefield.

However, all that pales into insignificance compared to the greatest mystery |of all: one which I have never solved, and which returns to haunt me every time I look at Renaissance religious art: why was there such an obsession in the 15th Century for painting the baby Jesus with curly ginger hair?

I was still thinking about it when I found myself in yet another museum, |this time the arts and crafts one. However, after several rooms of clocks which did not tick, bells which did not ring, plates with no food on them and chairs | which would never see a bottom again, I had had enough museums for the day.

"Right, Piers," I announced. "All museum'd out. Need some fresh air and real life."

Outside in the square, the statue of poet Peter Preradovic looked down at a man selling popcorn from a stall emblazoned with a lunatic clown.

Languid intellectuals sat outside cafés drinking coffee, their hair long and their glasses fashionable for about half a second, and two nuns rolled silently across the square on the castors that nuns have instead of feet.

We took the tiny funicular up through the former red light district to the ancient city walls, where every day for centuries the noon gun has been fired.

At about noon, since you ask: and the same man has been firing it every day since 1975, so don't ever complain again that your job is boring.

Inside the large baroque church of St Catherine's, all was quiet except the walls, and outside the presidential palace nearby, a solitary policeman passed the time of day with a man in a straw hat, near a Teutonic entanglement of black Audis waiting in the sun for the President and his entourage to emerge and rush off on some Presidential errand or other.

We walked off down the cobbled streets, between buildings leaning drunkenly in, and passed through a dark arch in which an ancient woman and a spiky teenager were praying in front of an icon of the Virgin which was miraculously preserved from a fire in 1731.

A stall was selling votive candles to light: on the other side of the arch, since it would be a splendidly bitter irony if one of them were to set the icon on fire.

Piers looked at his watch. "Time for tea," he said.

We retired to the Paviljon, a neoclassical pile built as a part of the World Fair in Budapest in 1898, then dismantled, brought back to Zagreb and rebuilt in a park opposite the railway station.

I had steak and truffles, for less than a tenner. There was clarinet music in the air, a little aeroplane pottered overhead, and as dusk fell, the old man came by lighting the city's gas lamps, as he has for even longer than the man who fires the noon gun.

The wine flowed, the moon rose and the clarinet played on.

I was beginning to like Zagreb, museums or no museums.

2003

...and Zebedee

Zebedee was the husband of Salome, the uncle of Jesus and the father of James, who arrived in northern Spain in the year 44.

Unfortunately, the apostle did not enjoy his visit, since he had just been beheaded by Herod.

His body, the legend goes, was taken by two disciples from Jerusalem to Jaffa, where a stone boat without crew or sails carried them to the Spanish coast in seven days at a speed barely equalled by the cocaine smugglers who arrive on that same coast today in black speedboats from Colombia.

The body was then rather carelessly lost for 750 years until a shepherd called Pelayo saw a star in a vision and dug up the saint's bones in a field. The local bishop, Theodimir, immediately pronounced the bones authentic and Santiago de Compostela, which means St James of the Field of the Star, became the destination for a pilgrimage which would soon overtake the great routes to Jerusalem and Rome.

James, inspired by a fame in death he had never known in life, promptly started popping up all over the place to help the Spanish in their holy war against the Arabs. At the battle of Clavijo in 844 alone, his ghost personally dispatched 60,000 uncircumcised unfortunates, and over the next seven centuries he was spotted helping out at 40 battles, even lending a hand with the massacre of American Indians in the

New World - all of which, since he was originally a fisherman, must rank as the most successful late career change ever.

Today, thousands of pilgrims every year still make their way from all over Europe to Santiago de Compostela, knowing that by doing so they halve the time they will spend in Purgatory.

This year, since St James' Day falls on a Sunday, a pilgrimage to Santiago means that on the Monopoly board of Catholicism, 1999 is a Go straight to Heaven, do not enter Purgatory year. In terms of salvation, it's like getting all your hotels on Mayfair, which means that the city is expecting up to half a million faithful to make the long trek this year by foot, by foot, by bicycle, by horse and by bright yellow sports car.

Ah yes. This is, I should say, the traditional lazy Protestant's method. It is, in fact, a very new tradition, but that's because I've only just thought of it.

Even worse, before I picked up the car in Dover, I had spent the night dancing at a jazz club in the crypt of a church in Camberwell. It could only be a matter of time before God got me in the back of the neck with a well-aimed thunderbolt.

I had, in fairness, tried to get a couple of proper Catholics to come with me, partly in mitigation and partly in the hope that God, whose eyesight can't be what it was when he was a younger God, would hit them instead.

But fate had taken a hand, and it was alone that I sat on the boat to Calais, realising with a sinking feeling that my entire preparation for the trip had consisted of reading a book on rural Japan and a copy of Biggles Hits the Trail (the one with the giant Tibetan caterpillars, if you remember).

Still, at least I had brought with me A Journey to the West, the diary of a 17th Century Italian pilgrim called Domenico Laffi.

I arrived in France to find everyone speaking French, which never ceases to amaze me. If you ask an American where he's from, for example, he'll invariably tell you his family are Irish, Polish or Italian.

Nobody in London is from London, and if you approach someone on a main street in Yorkshire, you will invariably find that their grandfather forsook the aromatic slopes of Darjeeling for a two-up, two-down in Bradford.

But everyone in France is from France, which is why they speak French so well. Even little children can speak it, although it's a foreign language.

I was still trying to work it out that evening as I drove through the ancient gates of the village of Montreuil-sur-mer. Montreuil has not actually been sur mer since its harbour silted up five centuries ago, but before that it was a major stopping point for pilgrims from northern Europe.

As a result it was once coming down with churches, although many were destroyed in the 16th Century when the village was sacked rather unluckily by the English and the Spanish in quick succession, and one became a pub, a brewery and a garage in that order.

I hurried past, sure that if God caught me near any more examples of religious buildings turned secular he wouldn't miss and hit the wall, never mind his dodgy eyesight, and found myself in the relative sanctuary of the pilgrims' hospital chapel.

Above the altar in a tiny glass phial was a piece of the true cross, one of only, oh, 15 trillion which exist in the world, and dotted around the walls were scallop shells, the traditional symbol of the Santiago pilgrim, beautifully carved by members of the Companions of St Jacques, a bunch of tradesman who did the pilgrimage as a sort of medieval NVQ during which they picked up new skills and styles in cathedrals en route.

Well, that was quite enough culture for one day, and it was well nigh dinnertime, so the next thing I knew I was sitting in the dining room of the hotel tucking into snails and frog's legs.

To be honest, I can't think what came over me: any time I order snails I imagine them trying to escape across the kitchen floor at 0.00001mph while a crazed sous-chef pursues them with a meat cleaver, and with frog's legs I always think of that cartoon where the man is just about to tuck in when the kitchen doors swing open and a sad little convoy of frogs in wheelchairs emerges.

I can only think that I was attempting to plunge into French life at the deep end, a suspicion confirmed when I proceeded to a bar near the pavée St. Firmin, where Victor Hugo set much of Les Miserables, got remarkably drunk on marc, the stuff they distil from the skins of grapes, and had a lengthy conversation about postmodernism with Claire, an architect from Paris.

This was a remarkable conversation for two reasons: first, my French is so bad that even I don't know what I'm saying, and second, I don't even know what postmodernism is in English.

Tragically, at this point Claire's boyfriend arrived and took her home, so I was unable to pursue the matter any further in either language.

However, they say that the sin is in the thought, and the next day I paid the price for sliding off the pilgrim's path by driving the long road south to Poitiers listening to French radio, which was a choice between pop music so inane that the government had to pass a law forcing stations to play it, monumentally dreary chamber music and heavy metal so dire that not even a Norwegian Hell's Angel would give it the time of day.

Thankfully, halfway through the afternoon the classical channel presenter died of depression and was replaced by a woman whose tastes veered between Wagner and Debussy, so that for the rest of the day I alternated between tearing along Teutonically and waltzing lyrically down the centre of the road.

Still, at least the car, an Ibiza Cupra Sport lent to me by Seat, turned out to be entirely splendid: whenever you pressed the thing on the floor, it overtook everything else on the road while a very satisfying noise came out of the back.

Not only that, but a readout on the dashboard told me how long I had been driving, how many miles I had done, my average mph, mpg, engine oil temperature and outside temperature.

I imagine if I had known the right buttons to press it would have told me the time of high tide in Shanghai, the capital of Outer Mongolia and the last time I changed my underwear.

Those of who like Wagner, meanwhile, should be aware that he reduces your average fuel consumption by 34.7 per cent.

Indeed, he was entirely to blame for the fact that I overshot the Loire Valley and ended up in Poitiers, whose most surreal attraction must be Futuroscope, the theme park where for about 14 quid you can engage in a series of experiences such as *Le Tapis Magique*, in which you fly to Mexico on the back of a giant butterfly.

Tragically, by the time I got there it was closed, so my alternatives were to drive the 400 miles north to Amsterdam, where for about a fiver I could have a similar experience in a coffee shop, or drive the seven miles south to Poitiers, where for about the same price I had a pizza in an Irish pub while watching the Australian skydiving championships on television.

On the wall in front of me as I watched Brad plummet to victory was a graffito saying: "An Irishman is never drunk so long as he has a blade of grass to cling to."

Next morning, I had my first every power breakfast: a meeting with Mme Sarazin and Martine Brissoneau from the tourist board, who presented me with 15,000 brochures and a list of the five million essential sites I had to see on the road south before I stopped in Blaye that night.

As a result, here is the potted history of the late 20th Century pilgrim's essential guide to the road between Poitiers and Blaye:

Poitiers: home of the world's longest job interview, in which for three weeks Joan of Arc had her ideology and virginity extensively verified by the local bishops and matrons respectively. Also home of France's weirdest church, Notre Dame de la Grande, the western façade of which is covered in a riot of carvings detailing the early life of Jesus.

In one scene he lies snoozing in his crib, being admired by a baffled sheep and a daft pig, and in another he sits in his bath with a bemused expression while apparently being interfered with by a couple of dodgy looking handmaidens.

Poitiers also home of university where Descartes wandered around gloomily wondering whether he existed or not. He eventually proved he did, then went to Sweden and died of pneumonia, after which he didn't.

Lusignan: village built by a fairy called Melusine, who married a mortal called Raymondin on condition he never saw her on Saturday, when she did all her building. When he did, she turned into a dragon. Motto: if your wife goes out on Saturdays with a magic wand and a hod, give her the benefit of the doubt.

Melle: without the help of Melusine, the locals went mad in the 11th and 12th Centuries and built three churches. Best is St Hilaire, where below the simple nave a local woman had placed a little display of sand, rocks and wild flowers in memory of her dead son. Christian church, atheist pilgrim, Zen moment.

Aulnay: Romanesque church, façade of which depicts diminutive breed of Poiton donkey, resembling shaved teddy bear, and eternal battle between wise and foolish virgins.

Question: if they were so foolish, how come they were still virgins? Discuss. Write on one side of the paper, but both sides of the virgins.

St. Jean-d'Angély: twinned with New Iberia, USA. Home of twin-towered abbey on hill which must have been astonishing sight to pilgrims. Also home of museum containing first caterpillar car to cross Sahara, and souvenirs of classic Citroëns, the cars of which weary mechanics say: "Ah, if God had meant life to be simple, he would never have invented hydropneumatic suspension".

Sainte: 11th Century abbey run by nuns, stunning remains of 20,000-seat Roman amphitheatre, rare double-decker church, St Eutrope, in which monks worshipped above and pilgrims below, in the same way that pilgrims were asked to use side entrances of churches rather than front. Theological reason: they were unclean. Practical reason: they were unclean.

Pons: a brief history: built Middle Ages, destroyed by English, rebuilt by French, regained by English, regained by French, besieged, all dead, destroyed except tower. Now wet, closed except tower. Sole contents of tower tourist office. Other features: pleasant hotel with view of winding river. Winding river with view of pleasant hotel.

Pons, a briefer history: best visited before 1178.

Phew. Late that night I arrived in Blaye, which is notable for having a citadel bigger than itself, and spurned my hotel to dine in a café which in England would have been naff, but in French was quaint.

What a splendid creation, though, is the French provincial waitress, and indeed, waiter: they give you enough time after they deliver the menu and wine list to allow for suitable dithering, they ignore all your choices and suggest much better ones, they leave you plenty of time between courses to digest their choice, they don't ruin your meal by constantly asking if you're enjoying it and, best of all, they don't tell you that their name is Crystal and they're really an actress.

As a result I went to bed entirely content. Tragically, the next morning I walked up to the citadel to find inside an entire town much nicer than Blaye.

Even more tragically, although last night I had completely failed to find a mention of Blaye in my guidebook, this morning an entire page had magically reinserted itself which would have told me this. Hindsight is, in retrospect, the most exact science there is.

Still, it was fine to walk through the beetling arch to the citadel walls and wander around its grassy slopes and little houses amid a welter of birdsong.

And to sit on a stone bench at the highest place and imagine what joy a pilgrim must have felt, hundreds of years ago, to sit on this very spot looking down at the Gironde estuary on one side and the pilgrims' hostel on the other, knowing that he was now over halfway on the greatest journey of his life.

I made it back to the car just as the rain started, and drove south to the rhythm of the wipers, with little to amuse myself with except playing with the car's computer - I think it shows you've got to a certain age when you're more interested in the mpg than the mph – and spotting Norbert Dentressangle trucks.

In all the time I've travelled on European roads, I've wondered about Norbert. In an age of global homogeneity in which everything is owned by vast, impersonal corporations, even his name is a beacon of iconoclastic idiosyncrasy. I imagine him sitting at a scrubbed wooden table by the fireside of an evening, a cat on his lap and a pipe in his mouth as he works out the accounts while Mrs Dentressangle makes a nice *carbonnade flamande.*

By dusk, by which time I would have been completely drenched had I not been surrounded by a car, I was in St Jean Pied-de-Port at the foot of the Pyrenees.

Which is where Domenico Laffi comes in, for although I had come from the north and he from his native Italy, St Jean was where all the pilgrims met before they struggled across the mountains and on to Spain.

It was a shame that Domenico had been dead for three centuries, for I would have enjoyed a good natter with him: curious and erudite, he found the joy of travelling in practically everything, and even when he didn't was funny about it:

"We came upon a peasant in the company of a miller, who were having a meal. After we had pleaded with them for a long time, they gave us a little bread and cheese (which must have been made in the age of Romulus and Remus) and a little wine which, from being near the water, had become its sworn companion. "

I read his journal for a while, then used my Swiss Army knife to cut a length of hair which had been hanging in my eyes all day. By not charging myself for this, I saved £15, which I spent on supper in a bar in which everyone, including the staff, was 16 trying to act 40. Just wait until they try to do it the other way around.

Still, if I thought I was sad, the man at the next table was wearing Wellingtons and reading Paul Theroux.

In the morning I walked out of town on the main road and came back by the pilgrims' path, through the gate below the citadel and down the cobbled street past the half-timbered houses, one a pilgrims' hostel.

At the end of the street, the Pyrenees were shrouded in snow. Domenico would have wrapped his cloak about him and set off. I got into the car and switched on the heater.

At Roncesvalles, high above the snowline, the retreating Roland, hero of the medieval Chanson de Roland, sounded his horn in vain for reinforcements until it cracked, then was massacred with all his knights by the Basques.

I gave the car horn a little toot of empathy, but the only effect it had was to send a griffon vulture wheeling into the frozen sky and bring a hum of resonance from the bell of the little chapel of Ibañeta, where Domenico and his fellow pilgrims had taken refuge for the night.

And then, suddenly, I was in Spain, where I had planned to pay a surprise visit to my old mate Carmen, one of the most vivacious people I knew, who had suddenly and mysteriously quit her job as head of the Spanish Tourist Office in London to become a nun in Vitoria.

I was quite looking forward to seeing her, since I'd never hugged a nun before, but when I phoned the nunnery they told me she'd just started a six-week vow of silence, which in this rain would have reduced the conversation to Marcel Marceau goes scuba diving.

I put down the phone and tried hard to imagine Carmen being silent for even six seconds. It was impossible.

So instead I had lunch in Pamplona, where every year bulls from all over Spain turn up to run with the people, and set off for Hondaribbia, in whose central square stands a splendid palace turned luxury hotel, started in the 10th Century by Sancho the Strong, who was 7ft 4in, continued in the 14th by Carlos V, who was much smaller, and stayed in during the 20th by me, who was somewhere in between.

Pausing for a moment to free several locals who had become trapped in the hotel's revolving door by putting all their Basques in one exit, I checked in then went for a wander down Calle Mayor, the street up which Steve McQueen wandered at the start of Papillon, then wandered around the block, or whatever they have in medieval towns, by which time I was soaked.

It was no use. It was never going to stop raining. I retired to the hotel bar, sank into a deep sofa with the sort of gin and tonic they only make in Spain - one gallon gin, one gallon tonic, one whole lemon, one iceberg – and read about Domenico Laffi getting soaked instead.

Then I went out to a little restaurant in the old quarter and ordered a meal in Spanish so bad that both the waiter and I were surprised when the food arrived.

At the next table but one, a Dutch family slapped vowels around each other.

And when I went out, it was still raining.

As it was in the morning when I threw back the curtains. In fact, the more I thought about it, I could not remember a time when it had not been raining. I got into the car, turned on the wipers and drove west to Guernica. Since I only knew it through the eponymous painting by Picasso, I half expected it to be full of three-legged women with eyes on top of their heads, but it was normal to the point of dullness. That Picasso. What a lad.

Question: If Picasso painted a fish caught off Sellafield, would it look normal? Discuss.

It was probably as a result of making fun of Picasso that two hours later I got completely lost in Santander, with hailstones bouncing off the windscreen. Still, they made a nice change from the rain, and it could have been worse: I'd originally planned to do the trip on a motorbike.

After a while the hailstones turned into rain again, and the rain got worse. I wound up the windows and floated west past Bilbao, where the Guggenheim museum sat glittering on the rusting scrapheap of Spain's industrial past, while around the city the glass and steel subway shelters of Normal Foster picked up its light and gave it back, like architectural apostles paying homage to the only art museum in the world more artistic than its contents.

At length I found myself in Santillana del Mar. Even Jean-Paul Sartre, the second gloomiest writer in the world after Paul Theroux, described Santillana as the most beautiful village in Spain, and it is. It is the sort of place where you imagine absurdly happy families live. The sort who hug their cows.

Absurdly happy, I wandered around in the rain looking for a cow to hug, but finding none, bought an absurdly happy flowerpot instead.

Above the village in a hill are the famous Altamira caves, covered with a series of paintings which made it the Sistine chapel of 12000BC. They were discovered 100 years ago by a little girl called Maria with the immortal words: "Look, papa - cows!" Tragically, she went on to marry a banker.

I floated on, to Comillas, home of a monolithic Jesuit seminary high on a hill which sent forth from its thousands of bare cells those stormtroopers of Christ to wreak havoc among the untouched souls of the world.

Around its walls hang painting of hundreds of former inmates, and only one of them is smiling. Step forward Sr Dr Segundo Garcia Mendes, 1929-31. The rest of them put the fear of God in me. If those were the good guys, I hope I never meet a bad one.

I got back into the car and floated on through the Picos de Europa mountains. Darkness fell, the rain fell, my spirits fell, the moon rose, I found on the radio an old bossa nova channel, my spirits rose.

I turned the heater up and drifted west in a Latin American micro-climate, while far above, the reflection of the almost full moon tinkled off the snowy peaks with a sound that men cannot hear.

Finally, many hours into the night, I was washed up on the steps of the Hotel de la Reconquista in Oviedo, a former 17th Century children's hospital and pilgrims' hostel.

They tied up the car to stop it drifting away, led me to a suite the size of a planet and poured me a very cold gin and tonic and a very hot bath. I poured the first into myself, poured myself into the second and felt very much better, thank you for asking.

Several miles south and three centuries earlier, Domenico was having a similar end to his day:

"At the end of it we came to a hospice, which for its size seemed like a city in itself. I don't think there is another like it in Spain. They give much charity to pilgrims and treat them very well as regards eating and sleeping."

The next morning, it was still raining. It was raining all along the Calle de la Magdalena, where the pilgrims used to trek up the street past the old fish market - presumably the fish were always fresh, since they could swim up the street - past the erotic magazine shop and up to the cathedral, where the front door contains a carving of Eulalia, patron saint of Oviedo, tossing a pitcher of water over the city.

You wouldn't think she needed to bother, but when Laffi passed through here in 1670, the area was in drought and he was knee-deep in locusts which the locals ran around whacking with wooden bats.

Well, Eulalia, I've got news for you: you've succeeded too well. Get back here with a miraculous mop, you over-achiever you.

Pilgrims, of course, entered by the side door into a little chapel, which was blown up by disgruntled miners in 1934, and then into the cathedral itself, where today I could see the Bishop of Oviedo showing a papal nuncio a statue of St Anthony with a rather fetching small pig.

Beyond was the mindboggling baroque altarpiece detailing the life of Christ, and the even more mindboggling baroque sidepieces. What on earth can baroque architects have been thinking of?

"Hey, Luigi. I've just had a great idea - let's make everything as vulgar and overblown as possible, and see if we can fool people into liking it!"

They were, I suppose, the Gianni Versaces of the 17th and 18th Centuries.

But onwards, through the green and rainwashed mountains, their peaks wraithed in mist and their valleys filled with industrious farmers, burbling rivers, little fat trains pottering to and fro, and me in my bright yellow motor car.

It was all impossibly idyllic, and even the rain was of an unusually soft quality: the sort that makes you feel gentle all the way through to your soul, like some sort of existentialist fabric conditioner, so that you feel you could sidle innocently up to a farmer's daughter, make harmlessly illicit suggestions in a spirit of universal love and harmony, and not get a boot in the bollocks.

Absurdly happy again - at this rate they'd be melting me down to turn me into Prozac -I had lunch of an apple and a pear by the harbour of the beautiful little fishing village of Cudillero - and set out on the last leg to Santiago de Compostela.

Remarkably, during the afternoon the rain finally stopped, and it was in dazzling sunshine that I finally crested the mountain called Montjoie after the pilgrims' cry when they climbed it and finally saw their destination.

Here I was, 1,286 miles and six days from Calais (at an average speed of 39mph and average fuel consumption of 37.6mph, since you ask). And here beside me, on this very spot three centuries earlier, Domenico had crested this rise and looked down on this same city.

Strangely, on his last stage he, too, had been drenched by the rain and then dried
by the sun. And when he finally saw the twin towers of the cathedral from this mountain,
he wrote:

"On seeing the city we fell to our knees and, with tears of great joy falling from our eyes, we began to sing the Te Deum.

"But we had sung no more than two or three verses when we found ourselves unable to utter the words because of the copious tears which streamed from our eyes, so intense were our feelings.

"Our hearts were full and our unceasing tears made us give up singing, until finally, having unburdened ourselves and spent our tears, we resumed singing the Te Deum.

Singing as we walked, we carried on down... and came to the gate of the town."

I went down myself, and took a bed for the night in one of the most beautiful hotels in the world, the Hostal de Los Reyes Católicos, built in 1592 as a hospital for the pilgrims, many of whom had set out to Santiago for their last journey on earth after being told they were dying.

I had lunch in the former mortuary, now the hotel restaurant, and set out to buy a scallop shell, the traditional pilgrims' symbol. But everyone was at Mass, so I filled the car up at a Shell station instead and joined the queues waiting at the cathedral door under the joyous façade, in the centre of which a smiling St James welcomes his faithful as they kneel and press their fingers into the worn indentations below his feet, and make their wish.

Communion was just ending, and eight men in burgundy robes were preparing the *botafumeiro*, the world's largest incense burner, 58kgs of brass and smoke which they hauled back and forth until it was sailing up to the rafters then whistling inches above the heads of the congregations.

It was such pure theatre that when it ended you had to put your hands in your pockets to stop you applauding and holding up a scorecard of perfect sixes.

Then I ticked off the pilgrim's final duties - tapping my head three times at the feet of Master Mateo, viewing the casket containing the bones of James the Apostle and hugging his statue, and then finally standing on the shell engraved in the centre of the square outside.

And that night, the ghost of Domenico Laffi and I went out and found a little tapas bar, and got very drunk. The rain had started again, unfolding upon the bar roof with a sound as if someone was wrapping cellophane from a gift.

Sometime after three, we staggered back through the winding, hilly streets. The rain had stopped, and above our heads people were opening the arched windows of the 18th Century galleries on the top floor, flooding the damp air with laughter and light, music and the delicate spin of Rioja.

Above that, a full moon edged through straits edged with gargoyles, then sailed into the wide open sea of the cathedral square.

I arrived just behind it, feeling as if my soul had just been scrubbed clean.

For a fake pilgrim, it was an appropriately secular, but surprisingly real epiphany.

I turned to speak to Domenico, but he had gone, like the ghost of imagined memory.

1999

Acknowledgments

Thanks to Geoff Martin, the former editor of the News Letter, for having the vision to see that readers are interested in the world beyond the parish pump, and to Nigel Wareing, his successor, for continuing that vision. Several of the stories within were originally published in the News Letter, and are reprinted here with their permission.

Thanks also to Michael Kerr, Richard Madden and Adrian Bridge of the Daily Telegraph, the late Jeremy Atiyah of the Independent on Sunday, and Paddy Tyson of Overland magazine, who also commissioned several of the pieces.

Printed in Great Britain
by Amazon